CONTENTS

KU-710-663

Page

Introduction: the 1980 Assembly
J L M Trim and J M C Davidson   1

Resolutions of the 1980 Assembly   6

SECTION I: FOREIGN LANGUAGE TEACHING
EXAMINATIONS

Report of Working Party A   9

What place should modern language learning have in
the curriculum if it is to contribute to a soundly
based general secondary education?
J L M Trim   14

P H Hoy   19

D G Smith   32

F Weiss   46

On the justification of curriculum content: a case
for modern languages and European studies
D N Aspin   51

SECTION II: LANGUAGE POLICIES IN SCHOOLS

Report of Working Party B

The relationship between teachers of English and
teachers of modern languages during the last seventy
to eighty years
G E Perren   69

The concept of a school language policy
W H Mittins   79

Language teachers speak with forked tongue
B C King   91

The relationship betwen the study of language and
the teaching of languages
A J Tinkel   106

iii

Language policies in schools: a critical examination
D Sharp   124

Bibliography
H N Lunt and J Price   138

SECTION III: METHODOLOGIES AND MATERIALS FOR
LANGUAGE TEACHING

Report of Working Party C   142

Teaching English as a foreign language
J McDonough   159

Foreign language testing
B Mason   164

Teaching English as a second language in England
E Reid   169

English mother tongue teaching
G Taylor   175

ISSUES IN LANGUAGE EDUCATION

Papers arising from the Second Assembly of the

National Congress on Languages in Education, 1978-80.

Edited by J M C Davidson

Centre for Information on Languages Teaching and Research

First published 1981

Copyright © 1981 Centre for Information on Language Teaching and Research
ISBN 0 903466 34 1

Printed in Great Britain by Staples Printing Group

Published by Centre for Information on Language Teaching and research, 20 Carlton House terrace, London SW1Y 5AP

INTRODUCTION: THE 1980 ASSEMBLY

J L M Trim & J M C Davidson

The first assembly of the National Congress on Languages in Education took place in Durham in July 1978 and brought together representatives of a wide range of associations connected with the fields of foreign language and mother tongue teaching. The work of that assembly and in particular that of the working parties which led up to it, is described in NCLE Papers and Reports Nos. 1 and 2.

Following that assembly, three Working Parties were set up to investigate further areas identified as important:

WORKING PARTY A

A study of the relationship between what should be taught in the modern language classroom and what should be examined through public examinations, taking account of present practice in both these fields.

WORKING PARTY B

Language policies in schools with special reference to co-operation between teachers of foreign languages and teachers of English.

WORKING PARTY C

A comparison of the various methodologies and materials involved in the teaching of English as a foreign language, modern languages and the mother tongue, and an examination of their relevance to each other.

In each case, members of the working parties contributed papers for discussion and these papers constitute the bulk of this document.

The discussion papers, together with conclusions and recommendations from the working parties, were circulated to constituent associations of NCLE in the Spring of 1980 and discussed in depth at the second assembly of the Congress, again held in Durham, in July 1980. The Standing Committee of the NCLE is guided by these discussions in establishing a programme of activities which will culminate in the third assembly.

As in 1978, the assembly passed a series of resolutions which are intended to serve as a platform for action by constituent associations and by the Standing Committee of NCLE which is elected by each assembly. Most of the 1978 resolutions concerned the teaching of foreign languages, and they were for the most part re-adopted by the 1980 assembly. They are reproduced as an appendix, together with a bibliography of policy statements, reports and discussion documents since the 1978 assembly and affecting the teaching of language and languages.

A study of these documents reveals the extent to which the views of the Congress as expressed in the resolutions are reflected in thinking elsewhere. Notable are the now generally voiced acceptance of the need for diversification in foreign language provision and the recognition of the place of a foreign language within any common core curriculum in secondary schools.

As a result of approaches made by the Standing Committee of NCLE following the 1978 Assembly, the Schools Council has conducted an investigation into the teaching of first foreign languages other than French, and a report of this survey, published by the Schools Council, is available from the Centre for Information on Language Teaching and Research.

The first assembly of NCLE brought together representatives of associations concerned with the teaching both of foreign languages and of the mother tongue. Teachers of foreign languages greatly out-numbered their mother tongue colleagues and in debates the issues of foreign language teaching tended to dominate. Even when common ground was found, communication between the two groups was limited - but a beginning was made. Significantly, two of the working parties set up following the 1978 Assembly addressed themselves to topics - namely school language policies and teaching methodology - which spanned the great divide.

The width of that divide is well known to those who have stopped to contemplate it: not all have bothered to stop. Foreign language teachers found galling the absence of reference to their subject in the Bullock Report. Teachers of Humanities subjects, seeking blocked timetables for their mixed ability charges, have been amongst those most hostile to foreign language teachers seeking daily single periods for their selected pupils. However, comprehensive reorganisation is providing teachers with opportunities - indeed is presenting them with the obligation - to consider the contribution of their discipline to the whole curriculum, and to the education of all pupils. It remains a sad truth nevertheless that, for example, teachers of foreign languages and teachers of English have few professional contacts with each other.

Thus, while it may be true that recent government statements suggest that the place of foreign languages in the core curriculum is secure, the omission of reference to foreign languages in the Schools Council's planning document Principles & Programmes (Schools Council, July,

2

1979), should perhaps be seen not as a slight but a challenge to foreign language teachers to lay out their wares and indicate in what way they see themselves contributing to the curriculum of all children on an equal footing with teachers of other subjects.

Attitudes, then, have changed since Bullock. How much has practice changed? Eric Hawkins in his papers to the 1978 Assembly (The Linguistic Needs of Pupils, NCLE Papers and Reports No. 1, and Language as a Curriculum Study, NCLE Papers and Reports No. 2) develops ideas which he himself was putting forward at the Joint Council of Language Associations conference in York in 1970. Yet examples of syllabuses based on these ideas are still rare. Furthermore, as Derrick Sharp points out in his paper reproduced in this volume, examples are hard to find of co-operation between teachers of English and modern linguists in the development of language policies in schools.

It would therefore seem appropriate to quote here the principal recommendations of Working Party B which was chaired by Derrick Sharp:

'Teachers of English and teachers of foreign languages should clarify and co-ordinate their views about the nature of language and about children's acquisition and development of language skills.
'At present pupils receive conflicting and confusing messages about the nature, function and use of language from teachers of English and teachers of foreign languages. To avoid this, specific areas of school work where co-operation and co-ordination between the two is necessary should be agreed and defined.
'Old-established differences, often arising from historic subject allegiances, exist between the two groups of teachers. In encouraging co-operation, these should be understood rather than ignored.'

Whilst the working party members arrived at no agreed view of 'language' as a separate curriculum study, they considered that carefully monitored experiments in its teaching would be justified and offered a number of questions for further consideration.

Participants at the Assembly addressed themselves to these questions with some commitment, but with the recognition that a common strategy would be hard to find. While the appeal of general curriculum policies implemented by whole staffs of sensitive teachers was strong, the way ahead seemed to lie in limited initiatives involving like-minded colleagues, whether within schools or in initial and in-service training programmes.

An important bridging role between foreign language teaching and mother tongue teaching is played by English as a Foreign Language (EFL). Not only is it a thriving practical activity, a large and profitable British export industry, but it is also closely linked at university level with general and applied linguistics. Encouraged and stimulated by the British Council, with its world-wide contacts and responsibilities, EFL has made great strides in the methodology of teaching and learning language for communication in this country and abroad. It is of necessity based on an explicit knowledge of English as a communication system and its use in a wide range of social situations. Clearly, then, EFL is ideally placed to mediate between modern languages and English and it was no accident that a particularly satisfactory, coherent and fruitful report was produced for NCLE by the working party set up under the chairmanship of Professor J Sinclair of Birmingham University to look into the methodological relations between the teaching of English as mother tongue, English as a foreign or a second language, and modern languages.

A third NCLE working party, under the chairmanship of Mr M R Wigram, was asked to study 'the relationship between what should be taught in the modern languages classroom and what should be examined through public examinations at 16+, taking account of existing practice in both these fields.' This working party arrived at much the same conclusions as the editors of the recent CILT publication on Modern languages examinations at 16+: a critical analysis. They agreed 'that there should be a constant emphasis on language for the purposes of communication in circumstances as authentic as possible'. Judged by that criterion, they found present practice in teaching and examining inadequate. A NALA survey indicated that, certainly by the fourth year, teaching was concentrated on the 'activities which closely mirror those to be found in public examinations at 16+ and later.' Since the examinations 'are characterised by a limited range of test-types' in which 'forms of language appropriate to written usage predominate', and the passages 'narrative/literary in type' with 'the subject content frequently trivial', it is not surprising that the working party came to the conclusion that 'significantly few of these activities are likely to be required in a real life context by the majority of language learners'. They also found that too much classroom time was taken up with teachers talking English, 'with consequent lack of opportunity or encouragement for pupils to become competent in oral/aural skills'. They recommended examining boards to 'give urgent attention to the consideration of syllabuses which would encourage pupils to achieve higher levels of performance in everyday communication within a more limited linguistic range in respect of both lexical content and grammatical coverage'. In view of the success of the Graded Objectives movement with pupils in early language learning, it is to be hoped that this advice will be borne in mind as the criteria for the new 16+ examinations are considered.

While continuing to act as a forum for discussion on matters affecting language and languages in education, the Congress appeared more ready in 1980 than it did in 1978 to recognise its role in formulating recommendations for policy and action by central government and local authorities. Certainly as far as foreign language teaching is concerned increasing pressure is being felt both within NCLE and outside it for a 'national policy' of some sort. Educational change is a slow process. Classroom realities cannot be changed overnight, and while administrative structures and examinations can be reformed 'at a stroke', the men and women who control them are far too conscious of their responsibilities towards parents, teachers and above all children to do so lightly. But given sustained pressure at all levels, policies which are convincing and have the active backing of the teaching profession as a whole can permeate the attitudes, thoughts and actions of the many partners to the learning process until their implementation seems natural and relatively uncontentious.

NCLE is important in this process in that it brings together all modern language teachers, whatsoever their language speciality, in schools, colleges, polytechnics and universities and enables them to hammer out a common policy, coming to terms with the differences of concern and even conflicts of interest which have led them to assert their separate identities in the past.

The elaboration of such a policy will no doubt involve foreign language teachers in the main. Its successful implementation will require that it be understood and accepted by teachers of other subjects, and not least by those of the mother tongue. The 1980 Assembly may be remembered as the point at which a breakthrough in communication was made.

RESOLUTIONS OF THE 1980 ASSEMBLY

NCLE seeks to contribute to the movement towards a national language policy by expressing the consensus view of its constituent organisations on major issues. The following is a list of resolutions adopted by Standing Committee on the recommendations of the 1980 Assembly.

On the basis of the resolutions passed by its Assemblies, the Congress urges its Constituent organisations, and all competent authorities, to take appropriate action to implement the following recommendations as steps towards the evolution of an agreed national policy on languages in education:

(1) LANGUAGE IN THE CURRICULUM

Within the framework of the development of an overall curricular policy, we recommend that:

1.1 A policy of diversification of foreign language provision should be pursued at all levels with the aim of increasing the proportion of students studying languages other than French, especially as first foreign language.

1.2 The experience of learning one foreign language should form part of the core curriculum for pupils 11-14 (12-14 in Scotland); any pupil who can benefit from the study of a foreign language to the age of 16 should be encouraged to do so; the opportunity to study a second foreign language should be made generally available in secondary schools.

1.3 In view of the success which can be achieved in teaching a foreign language to pupils below 11 years, opportunities should be provided for schools to continue to gain experience of an early start; it is stressed that this requires well-qualified teachers, suitable materials and effective arrangements for continuity.

1.4 Opportunities for the continuation of modern language study beyond 16+ in school or college should not be limited to A-level courses, but should include languages as ancillary or subsidiary subjects. The same principle should apply to full-time courses beyond 18+ in higher and further education.

1.5   Options should be provided for in syllabuses at GCE A-level or its equivalent. Such A-levels should be accepted for the purposes of admission to university language departments.

1.6   The further development of combined degree courses in which a foreign language is a major component throughout should be encouraged.

1.7   All schools should be encouraged to pursue an overall policy for language development, embracing the use of English (or any other language) used as a medium throughout the curriculum as well as the study of foreign languages (where applicable).

1.8   The expansion of foreign language teaching should not prejudice the teaching of Welsh or Gaelic as a first or second language where this is appropriate.

1.9   Since linguistic variety is a resource to be valued by a multicultural society, steps should be taken to maintain, develop and build upon languages and varieties in use by all ethnic groups resident in the United Kingdom.

(2) EXAMINATIONS AT 16+

Accepting that public examinations exert a powerful influence on what is taught, we support the efforts of those boards which are seeking to provide more explicit information on syllabuses, criteria and assessment, and which are endeavouring to identify and test the skills and knowledge most appropriate to the majority of candidates at 16+; and urge that where good practice exists in these areas, it should be generalized at the time of the re-organisation of the 16+ examination.

In particular we recommend that:

2.1   Examinations boards should seek to provide examinations which will foster a practical command of language, an understanding of how the language works, and some insight into the target culture.

2.2   The structure of the examination system should be sufficiently flexible, and its coverage in the case of modern languages sufficiently broad, to give recognition to attainments differentiated according to the varying abilities and needs of the pupils.

(3) TEACHER EDUCATION AND TRAINING

We consider that improvement of certain aspects of initial and in-service training must have high priority and recommend that:

3.1   Steps should be taken to ensure an adequate supply of teachers of foreign languages, and in particular of languages other than French.

3.2   Within a teacher's job description, in-service education should figure both as a right and as a regular commitment, at times outside as well as within the pupil's or student's normal day or academic year; such commitment should be used by both employing authorities and teachers to ensure that regular periods of residence abroad form an integral and essential part of in-service education.

3.3   The job description of Heads of Departments in schools should specify their responsibility for providing in-service training within their own departments; this implies that they themselves may require in-service training and a modified normal teaching load to enable them to fulfil the task.

(4) LANGUAGES IN EMPLOYMENT

The place of modern languages in the curriculum should be firmly based on their contribution to a balanced education, but we urge that their value in future employment be more widely recognised. We therefore recommend that:

4.1   Employers should recognise and publicise the value of the specific language skills required for a growing range of occupations at craft and technician as well as executive and managerial levels.

4.2   Careers advisers should be fully informed of the advantages of possessing foreign language skills when associated with other qualifications and be reminded of the continuing demand for language teachers.

4.3   Education authorities and institutions should encourage and support employers in providing opportunities for employees to learn languages.

SECTION I: FOREIGN LANGUAGE TEACHING AND EXAMINATIONS

Report of Working Part A

A study of the relationship between what should be taught in the modern languages classroom and what should be examined through public examinations, taking account of present practice in both these fields.

REPORT OF A WORKING PARTY COMPRISING:

M R Wigram (formerly HM Staff Inspector, Modern Languages), Chairman
A I Leng (Malvern College)
J A Partington (University of Nottingham School of Education)
Dr A Harding (University College of Cardiff)
A Moys (Centre for Information on Language Teaching and Research),
    Secretary

BRIEF

The origin of the brief was a recommendation from the 1978 Assembly that a Working Party should study 'the assessment of performance in modern languages in a context of aims, objectives and motivation in secondary and tertiary education. Special attention could be given to the 16-19 age group'.

As a result of recommendations for the Working Party, Standing Committee agreed that the brief should be reduced in order to provide a more manageable task. Rather than attempt an impossibly difficult survey of the secondary and tertiary scene within one 2-year cycle, the Working Party should focus its attention on secondary education in the two years preceding the 16+ examination, in the hope that further cycles of NCLE work could continue the study with a focus successively on 18+ examinations, and tertiary examinations.

Accordingly the following brief was agreed: 'A study of the relationship between what should be taught in the modern languages classroom and what should be examined through public examinations at 16+, taking account of existing practice in both these fields'.

PROGRAMME OF WORK UNDERTAKEN

The Working Party sought to answer two questions: What is the present relationship between examinations and classroom practice? What should the relationship ideally be? The first question involved factual evidence; the second involved the eliciting of informed opinion.

To obtain the current picture on a national scale would have been beyond the resources of the Working Party. Within the constraints imposed, the Working Party was, however, able to undertake a number of small scale studies. It conducted or commissioned the following investigations into existing classroom practice in 1979:

(a) The observation of 100 fourth year modern language classes to seek to establish what teaching and learning activities take place in later stages of preparation for the 16+ examinations.

(b) A survey of teaching exercises used in the fourth-year, based on information obtained from a questionnaire returned by 97 teachers of modern languages from several parts of the country.

(c) A survey of teachers' reasons for using Mode 3 examinations in foreign languages.

(d) The Working Party also studied views on the value of a modern language qualification at 16+ for pupils entering employment.

The Working Party took into consideration documentation and evidence from the following independent activities:

(a) Data assembled by CILT for a book: 'Modern Language Examinations at 16+: a critical analysis' published early in 1980. The book gives detailed information about all currently available GCE O-level and CSE examinations in modern languages.

(b) A report of the current situation in the field of graded objectives and tests. This report is not included with these papers, since it does not at present relate principally to 16+ examinations.

(c) Regular reports on the work of the Assessment of Performance Unit (APU) working group in establishing a rationale and devising a test model for monitoring performance nationally at 13+ in the first foreign language.

To canvass a wide range of views on the place of one or more foreign languages in the curriculum, the Working Party commissioned the views of a number of eminent contributors. They were posed twelve questions which the Working Party felt must be borne in mind when considering the place of modern languages in the curriculum.

FINDINGS AND THEIR MAIN IMPLICATIONS

In considering its findings, the Working Party was drawn progressively by both the commissioned articles and by its members' knowledge of current practice in the early stages of the foreign language course to adopt the view that there should be a constant emphasis on language for the purpose of communication in circumstances as authentic as possible.

This aim is not intended to limit language activities to oral and aural skills but necessarily includes reading and writing and, if communication is to be flexible (and not restricted to a phrase-book approach) a study of the structure of the language appropriate to the needs of the pupil at this age. This view is based upon the personal experience of the Working Party members and their assessment of the likely needs of the majority of language learners at this stage. It is reinforced by the recurring statements of language associations, conferences of modern linguists, the EFL world and the work of the Council of Europe.

What is taught?

1. The evidence is that, for whatever reason, many teachers concentrate their energies at fourth and fifth year level on a limited range of activities which closely mirror those to be found in the public examinations at 16+ and later. The most common of these are reading comprehension with written answers, reading aloud, oral question and answer, translation into English, and guided (narrative) composition. Significantly few of these activities are likely to be required in a real life context by the majority of language learners. Purposeful communication as a principal objective is all too often abandoned.

2. Pupils spend most of their time on work centred upon or arising from the forms of the written language, and relatively little on listening to or speaking the foreign language. Teachers are likely to need help in providing a far wider range of linguistic activities than are currently to be witnessed in modern language classes at this level.

3. Insufficient account appears to be taken of the differences between the written and the spoken language.

4. Foreign language teaching, as observed, was highly teacher-centred and lessons were often characterised by a high proportion of teacher-talk and a relatively small proportion of pupil-talk.

5. English is most widely used as the medium of instruction at this level, with consequent lack of opportunity or encouragement for pupils to become competent in oral/aural skills.

6. There is nothing in the surveys conducted by the Working Party to suggest that 'background' or 'civilisation' is allocated a significant place in modern language teaching at this level. The opportunity to cultivate informed attitudes to foreign countries is thus frequently lost.

What is examined?

The aims and syllabus content of examinations are often not defined, or are defined in insufficient detail.

Examinations are characterised by a limited range of test-types which have generally changed little in the last 25 years. For the sake of achieving the necessary economy, reliability and discrimination the less easily measured criterion of validity is often sacrificed.

Marking schemes in many instances tend to emphasise negative rather than positive aspects of performance, often ignoring other valid criteria such as the effectiveness of the communication. This preoccupation with avoidance of error as opposed to positive aspects of pupil performance becomes a teacher preoccupation also.

The balance of skills is uneven across the range of examinations available. Generally, forms of language appropriate to written usage predominate. Furthermore, the language forms presented for listening comprehension, and even to some extent the forms expected in oral examinations, are often those more appropriate to written than to spoken usage.

The language of examination passages tends to be narrative/literary in type, to the exclusion of other forms of the written language. The language is often adapted to facilitate the testing of specific points. The subject content is frequently trivial, and the topics are not always relevant to the interests/maturity of the candidates.

At CSE level, most teachers are using Mode 1. A substantial number of teachers choosing Mode 3 do so out of dislike for aspects of the Mode 1 examination.

What ought to be emphasised in teaching modern languages?

1. Although none of the contributors commissioned by the Working Party formulated comprehensive criteria to be applied in the modern language classroom, there was a high measure of agreement that first priority should be given to the cultivation of communicative skills. While there is evidence that at present employers are unable to make use of the language skills of school leavers at 16+, a course in communicative skills extending to the age of 18 would be more likely to command their interest and respect.

2. If pupils are to learn to communicate effectively in the foreign language, the use of English in the foreign language classroom should be the exception rather than the rule.

3. Tasks should be related to real life, and their content should be related to the candidate's likely level of maturity.

4. One of the highest priorities for the language learner in school is to learn how to learn a language efficiently. The successful learning of at least one foreign language represents a major step towards this goal.

5. For many English speakers it may be more valuable to acquire a usable level of competence in two or three languages than a higher level of competence in only one.

What ought to be emphasised in examining modern languages?

1. The examination at 16+ should be more generally supportive of the aims and emphasis of modern language teaching programmes as presented to pupils in the early stages in many schools. The present system, often involving a fundamental change of direction by year 3, is hard to justify and tends to discourage curriculum innovation.

2. The Working Party's view that there should be an emphasis on communicative skills implies the need for a different range of examination activities, with different methods of assessment.

3. Examining Boards should give urgent attention to the consideration of syllabuses which would encourage pupils to achieve higher levels of performance in everyday communication within a more limited linguistic range in respect of both lexical content and grammatical coverage.

4. A clear specification of syllabus content is required together with a clear understanding that specific and identified levels of candidate performance will achieve predictable grades. This inevitably implies a move progressively towards criterion referencing. The current system of norm-referencing, with its need to discriminate finely between candidates, often leads to definitions of language error which, while not universally valid are arbitrarily applied, and which may distort the assessment of what candidates say and write.

WHAT PLACE SHOULD MODERN LANGUAGE LEARNING HAVE IN
THE CURRICULUM IF IT IS TO CONTRIBUTE TO A SOUNDLY
BASED GENERAL SECONDARY EDUCATION?

J L M Trim   Paper I

The most difficult of the questions posed by the Working Party is
the first. To be asked 'what considerations govern your view of the
secondary school curriculum in England in the 1970's and '80's?' is to be
invited to confront basic issues of educational philosophy and to
enunciate principles which will enable one to interpret events of the
recent past and predict future events in the short and middle term. Hier
stock' ich schon!

A general view of the curriculum cannot be taken in isolation from a
general view of society and the role of the formal educational system
within it. Some principles have been set down in NCLE's memorandum
to the Schools Council: 'A balanced curriculum is presumably one in
which studies that increase the young person's knowledge and
understanding of himself and his environment are combined with others
which enable him to develop the physical and mental equipment with
which to face the problems of adult life'. This view of the function of
education is essentially enabling, with its emphasis on understanding and
equipment. The body of knowledge and skills which is acquired by the
individual learner as he progresses through the educational system are
seen not as ends in themselves (though the activities and goals which
dominate so long a period of a person's life, perhaps one of the most
intensely experienced, must of necessity have a considerable intrinsic
value) but rather as providing a base of intellectual and attitudinal
presuppositions upon which a stable adult life can be based. This is not,
of course, to imply some once-for-all investment. If we speak of 'a
thirst for knowledge that will last a lifetime', it is the thirst rather than
the knowledge that we expect to endure. The changing conditions of
adult life in our time, individually and socially, render much of the
knowledge and skill painfully acquired in early life obsolete long before
its end. Successful adjustment to new conditions means new learning on
various theoretical and practical levels. We inhabit a world characterised by rapid technological changes, of which the microprocessor is the
latest agent, possibly most far-reaching in its effects. These changes
make increasing intellectual demands upon the work force and leave
those who can supply only unskilled muscle-power and thoughtless
routines increasingly vulnerable. In a variety of forms and contexts,
continuing education and training are becoming part of the normal
expectations of everyday life. There is every reason to expect that this
trend will continue, at an accelerating pace, throughout the forseeable
future, and that the broad masses of the population will be involved.

14

These developments are clearly opposed to those concepts inherited from the ancient world in which the helot is distinguished from the free, and human activities hierarchically ranged in peira, empireia and episteme (Robbins). Manual work, skills and techniques, and understanding are no longer so clearly associated with different major social classes for whom radically different educational provision is appropriate. Much educational thinking (see Lord Annan's biography of Roxburgh) has been built on this distinction up to the present day. But, as stated above, sheer bulk muscle-power is now at a discount, whilst the microprocessor is widely expected to oust human routine semi-skilled operations in the factory and office within the next decade or so. Notoriously, craft skills (eg printing) are being displaced by computer technology. As a result, many kinds of work, perhaps most, require workers who are adaptable, capable rapidly of understanding the principle underlying new techniques and dealing with non-routine tasks (eg tracing and repairing faults in complex machinery). The young person who enters the labour market with nothing to offer but strength and willingness to work hard and do what he is told is now perhaps in a weaker position than ever before. On the other hand, we do not seem to be in sight of creating adequate alternative employment for those displaced. An increased amount of 'enforced leisure' seems at present to lie ahead of us.

The implications for the school system seem to be that:

(a) Educational sights have to be raised for the whole working population. We cannot afford a nineteenth century style proletariat. Basics are a necessary but not sufficient basis for adult life in the years ahead.
(b) Initial full-time institutional education lays the basis for continuing education and training, rather than provides knowledge and skills, once and for all.
(c) Accordingly the development of study skills and enabling skills predominates, with the aim of producing an adaptable autonomous learner rather than a person highly trained in a narrow specialism.
(d) Education for leisure becomes a necessity, not a luxury.

This is not the place to explore the manifold implications of these changing conditions of life for the organisation of schools and the curriculum in general. What are the implications for modern languages?

First, adaptability includes the ability to adjust rapidly to a different pattern of life, and a new environment. Mobility transcends national and linguistic frontiers (24 million migrant workers and dependents in North West Europe). There is an increasing impact of international contact on work and leisure. This increased contact will on the one hand greatly increase the size of the group of professional intermediaries (interpreters, translators, tourist industry, etc) but also the direct usefulness of some knowledge of one or more foreign languages. However, while intensified contact will lead to the interpenetration of languages and an increased proportion of 'international words' (loan words, loan translations, neoclassical vocabulary, etc), no one language is likely to emerge as a <u>lingua franca</u> in the sense that the mass of non-native speakers wil command it as a means of expression equivalent to the mother tongue. English, being predominantly the first foreign language where it is not the mother tongue, will however be widely understood, and used for transactional purposes in stereotyped contract situations. Beyond this, the actual language needed by an adult in the international contact which punctuate adult life is unpredictable. Accordingly, we have no need to look under stones or behind curtains to find the justification for modern languages in the curriculum. They are increasingly and directly useful in adult living, but are unlikely to be acquired by most children out of school, since children naturally live more enclosed lives. Much of education is an introduction to a wider environment; language learning is part of that process. The peculiar position of English, however, may mean that it is more important for an Englishman to be able to respond to the use of their mother tongue by a range of speakers of other languages than to invest all his efforts in acquiring a high level of productive ability in one particular foreign language. On the other hand, the acquisition of study skills by the more intensive study of one language in its various aspects may be more efficacious in producing the autonomous learner capable of learning another language quickly and efficiently when the need arises in later life so as to be accepted, say, socially and professionally in another culture.

This direct practical usefulness cannot of course be substituted by any other curricular subject. It is, of course, conceivable that many curricular subjects might acquire a linguistic dimension. It may become a professional necessity to view one's own special field of activity, whatever it may be, in an international context, so that one would simply expect, say, a geographer at A-level to know the basic terms of his subject in one or more foreign languages. For the foreseeable future, however, one may expect this to be a late specialist addition to a knowledge of the language gained in studying its basic features <u>per se</u> in a communicative framework up as far as, say, threshold level.

To say that in the world which we (with a notable national reluctance) are entering, the study of one or more foreign languages is fully justified in itself, is not of course to lose interest in other values it has in the overall educational process. One of these is clearly to bring a developing child out of a profoundly ignorant ethnocentricity to awareness and acceptance of the variety of human existence. Many aspects of this process can be achieved by other curricular subjects, including particularly the proper study of the mother tongue, which would go a long way to raise the present abysmally low level of public awareness and understanding of language and its many roles in the daily life of a complex modern society. However, a different kind of insight into the complex relations between things, thought and language is gained through confrontation with a differently organised linguistic system - providing of course that teaching has this as one of its objectives. After all, the new mathematics sets out to break the young child's easy

16

acceptance of our decimal number base as being in some way natural. Eight-year-olds seem to find little difficulty in 'translating' into binary, octal, etc. Their parents, who never had their assumption challenged, are the ones bewildered! Similarly, young children quickly learn the elements of set theory and realise the relativity of classifications. Yet these insights are for some reason not transferred to language and are regarded, in that context, as far too difficult for anyone below sixth form level! Of course, the problems of linguistic and cultural relativity are more complex, but the development of full insight into the nature of the problem can be spread out over the whole educational process from infant school to university, passing through different stages and taking different forms according to the maturity and ability of the pupil. Translation, for example, throws up innumerable matching problems, especially where authentic material is used, and the closer the foreign language learnt is to informal conversational exchange (as the communicative method indicates) the more incommensurable the utterances become, and the more impossible - and irrelevant - translation becomes. It is far more than a technical step forward when the pupil grasps meaning in terms of relations within the target language rather than referring particular expressions in the target language back every time to the mother tongue. On the other hand, the attempt to match as exactly as possible, to produce an accurate and faithful rendering of a seriously composed message in another language is an excellent way of bringing young people to handle a language with sensitivity, responsibility and respect.

In the classical education provided by the 'Grammar' schools, a central place was given to the training afforded by the patient, conscious analysis of the network of relations embodied in the structure of the sentences of an unfamiliar language. The tradition goes back to the medieval trivium of grammar, logic and rhetoric, and no doubt beyond that to the Hellenists and the Sophists. It is temporarily under a heavy cloud, since our way of thinking about language is still more under the influence of Romantic concepts than Rationalist ones, that tradition having turned away from natural language to its mathematical offspring. Perhaps it is from that quarter that a resurgence of interest in the fundamental properties of language will re-enter the schools, if mother tongue teaching, which seems to be the proper place for developing this understanding, continues to turn its back on the question. Whether the limited amount of curricular time available to modern languages is best spent in this way is very doubtful. It is not, as Arnold appears to have thought, that it is the classical languages, by virtue of their structure, which are the ideal instruments for the training of the mind, but that addiction to analytic puzzles engenders mental habits which are inimical to fluency in direct interpersonal communication, to which in our present circumstances we may wish to give a higher priority. Nevertheless, there is undoubtedly a type of learner, of high intellectual quality, for whom formal analysis is not only enjoyable, but reinforcing and facilitating to the mastery of language, above all in the use of written language, and after all, we should not react so strongly against the contempt for spoken language shown by adherents of the tradition of classical humanism as to reject literacy in the foreign language. There are strong social and psychological reasons for believing that, almost inevitably, written language will play a proportionally greater role in the use of a foreign language than of the mother tongue.

In general, it will be seen that the various techniques of language study, traditional as well as modern, have valuable contributions to make if their proper ecological niche is identified. Dictation appears in quite a different light if it is understood not as a spelling test but as a training in auditory perception and comprehension. 'Banal' transactional dialogues can lead to enquiry into the nature of social co-operation and the role of language in overcoming blocks. We can see how inter-ethnic misunderstandings and false national stereotypes arise from conflicting interpretations of the pragmatic values of utterances, especially where different politeness conventions operate. Are you expected, for instance, on entering a shop, to greet other shoppers or not? Should you wait for the shopkeeper to address you or will he wait for you to do so?

It may perhaps be claimed that few if any curricular subjects are so well placed as modern languages to demonstrate in action the interplay between the development of skills and theoretical insight, between immediate response to the demands of the situation here and now and the building up of an integrated cognitive system. As such, it has a great deal to offer to all pupils at all stages of their development - especially in counterpoint with the study of the mother tongue. Our task is to find the proper relation of the many parts to each other and to the whole, to respect and foster the different aptitudes to the process by pupils with diverse needs, motivations and abilities.

WHAT PLACE SHOULD MODERN LANGUAGE LEARNING HAVE IN THE CURRICULUM IF IT IS TO CONTRIBUTE TO A SOUNDLY BASED GENERAL SECONDARY EDUCATION?

P H Hoy   Paper II

What considerations govern your view of the secondary school curriculum in England in the 1970's and '80's?

In recent years so much has been written on curricular topics that one is reluctant to add to it, but I would offer the following summary of the considerations which, in my view, should underlie the curriculum of secondary schools, and of middle schools deemed secondary, in the 1970s and 80s:

Preparation for Life in Society

Living with the pupil's peer-group: The pupil should acquire sufficient knowledge and sufficient skills to be respected within his/her peer-group, despite differences in disposition, aptitudes and abilities.

Living in a family: The pupil should be able to live confidently and harmoniously in his family group as a preparation for good personal relationships with others in adult life.

Citizenship: The pupil should be ready, on leaving school, to play a full part as a member of local, national and international communities. He should be aware of his rights, responsibilities and duties as a member of a multicultural national community, and of European and world communities.

Career preparation: The curriculum should have provided the pupils with cognitive, affective and expressive foundations for his choice of a future career and his entry into it. If possible he should have gained suitable qualifications for this purpose. This process should have been assisted by the acquisition of the widest possible knowledge of his local, national and world-wide environment, by some work experience, and by expert advice on careers.

Personal Development

Side by side with the socially oriented development implied in the above sections, the pupil should have opportunities for personal development in the following areas:

the humanities, including experience of philosophical, ethical and religious thought and opportunities for social service aesthetic experience, both active and receptive, in one or more arts such as painting or music

practical skills, eg handicraft, home economics, gardening

physical education

communication skills, literacy, oracy, numeracy; if possible a foreign language

environmental studies, history, geography, science, technology

preparation for the use of leisure.

General Considerations

All the points made above have been influenced by curricular models such as the ones provided in the Schools Council Working Paper 45: 16-19: Growth and response, l. Curricular bases, p 58, and in the Green Paper: Education in schools, a consultative document, HMSO, 1977, p 6-7. The latter model, suggesting educational aims for all schools, appears so relevant to the present brief paper that I reproduce it in full:

(1) to help children develop lively, enquiring minds; giving them the ability to question and to argue rationally, and to apply themselves to tasks
(2) to instil respect for moral values, for other people and for oneself, and tolerance of other races, religions and ways of life
(3) to help children understand the world in which we live, and the interdependence of nations
(4) to help children to use language effectively and imaginatively in reading, speaking and writing
(5) to help children to appreciate how the nation earns and maintains its standard of living and properly to esteem the essential role of industry and commerce in this process
(6) to provide a basis of mathematical, scientific and technical knowledge, enabling boys and girls to learn the essential skills needed in a fast-changing world of work
(7) to teach children about human achievement and aspirations in the arts and sciences, in religion, and in the search for a more just social order
(8) to encourage and foster the development of the children whose social or environmental disadvantages cripple their capacity to learn, if necessary by making additional resources available to them.'

The implementation of all the considerations expressed in all the previous paragraphs must depend on many factors including local needs and traditions, the possibilities of compensatory education, pre-school and primary school experience, and the elements of pupil and parental choice. Despite the desirability of local variations, however, the mobility of families means that some degree of national consensus on curriculum is essential.

What part in the curriculum might be played by a modern foreign language?

A modern foreign language might play the following roles, always with the proviso that the effectiveness of such contributions will depend on the level of achievement to which such study is taken.

Living with peer-group and family

Modern languages tend to become a socially divisive subject in that motivation and achievement are closely connected with the pupil's socio-economic status, as shown by Dr Burstall. This factor may explain the conspicuously greater optimism about language learning in independent schools as compared with maintained schools. To compensate for this divisive tendency particular care should be taken in the maintained sector to establish aims, objectives and expectations which are appropriate for various pupils, and the HMI Green Paper recommends that a modern language should find a secure place in the curriculum for 'as high a proportion as practicable' of all secondary pupils. It might be added that the demand for modern language courses in schools is linked with career prospects. In turn, however, the attitudes of employers towards modern language qualifications may well be influenced by the number of secondary school leavers who have a useful command of a foreign language:

> 'The national obligation to 'export or die' means not only that the needs of industry should influence the teaching of languages, but that we should be training more and better linguists in order to change the attitudes of industry.'
> David Nott, Audio Visual Language Journal 15/1, 1977.

Citizenship

The study of a modern language can scarcely fail to involve pupils in learning something about the lives and character of native speakers of the language, and hence, one hopes in developing friendly and empathic attitudes towards other countries. This process is likely, in the first place, to be concerned with European nations, as advocated by an undergraduate who won the 1978 essay competition organised by the European Cultural Foundation and the journal Europa:

> 'I advocate a Europe with which all members may feel at home wherever they go. This does not mean that each country's individuality must be sandpapered down to a uniform monotony: on the contrary, differences in language, culture customs and ideas should flourish and enrich us all rather than form barriers between people of different nations in Europe. This can only be achieved

through a change in people's attitudes to Europe, brought about by travel and education in the broadest sense.'

Anita Hibbert, Europa, published in The Times, 8.5.78.

Miss Hibbert concludes that Europe could become '...an example of the co-operation and unity of purpose which is possible between different nations'. Michael Hart, who was Headmaster of Mill Hill School and then HMI before becoming Head of an EEC school, has said that

'...the problem of creating a greater awareness of our common European background and heritage ... can only be solved by permeating the whole teaching process by a conscious European orientation, by introducing a European dimension into all subjects, by a liberal programme of staff and pupil exchanges with other schools in Europe, and by giving prominence to language studies.'

M Hart: The EEC and secondary education in the UK. (Published by the Headmasters' Association and the Headmasters' Conference.)

The present writer would suggest that for a pupil to understand something of life in other European countries will help him to understand his own country more clearly, on a comparative and contrastive basis, and also to have more sympathy with the problems, opportunities and potentialities of the Third World, as advocated by supporters of the recent concept of 'development education'.

Preparation for careers

The First Assembly of the NCLE urged that the value of modern languages in the future employment of secondary school pupils should be more widely recognised. In his paper for the same Assembly Mr C V James developed this idea as follows:

'The York exercise (Emmans, Hawkins, Westoby, 1974) was quite invaluable in testing techniques of enquiry, but an actual investigation of the contemporary scene needs now to be carried out. To be of lasting value it should be a process of continuous monitoring, tracing the effect of British participation in the European Community; moreover the influence of the ever-increasing stature of English as a 'world language' needs to be taken into account. Results of a local survey conducted in the West Midlands differ significantly from those of the Emmans report, showing a much higher level of language demands and use, but revealing also quite different patterns' (Ager, 1977).

C V James: 'The role of foreign languages in the curriculum', NCLE, 1978, p 7.

These points are confirmed by two recent papers, one from Eton College, and the other from the Crawley College of Technology. Both of these draw a markedly more optimistic picture than the 1974 researchers were able to produce. The paper which was compiled by the Modern Language Department and the Careers Department of Eton College aims to explain the value of modern languages as a career qualification. It is a broadsheet of only four pages; these contain two dozen messages from prominent members of many professions, summarised in a concluding statement by Sir Oliver Wright, British Ambassador to the Federal Republic of Germany. His remarks end thus:

'So whether you like visiting foreign countries for holidays, whether you travel on business or whether you join the Diplomatic Service, a knowledge of modern languages will increase your pleasure, your profits and your usefulness. You will in addition be a more complete human being since you will understand a little more of that humanity of which we are all a part.'

The document from Crawley is described in the excellent report of a Working Party under the auspices of the West Sussex Education Authority, entitled Modern Languages 11-18. This report says:

'A survey of industrialists in the Crawley area carried out by the College of Technology... revealed distinct interest in recruiting staff proficient in a modern language.... The skills required which were cited most frequently were: conducting business in a foreign language (22), translating foreign correspondence into English (20), dealing with the telephone (19), acting as interpreter for visiting businessmen (17), composing correspondence in the foreign language (17) and reading, understanding and reporting on relevant texts (16).'
(The numbers refer to the proportion of respondents citing each point.)

Thus an encouraging picture of modern languages in employment is conveyed by both the private and the public sectors of education. In addition there is the argument, widely accepted if not yet confirmed by research, that in studying a modern language at school a pupil 'learns how to learn' a language.

Personal development

In an age of increasing leisure more and more British people travel abroad for pleasure; despite the development of English as a world language, many natives of the European mainland, and of countries further afield, do not speak English, particularly those of the middle-aged and older generations. In asking questions of a Finnish railway guard, a Brazilian waiter, or a boatman in Aswan, the writer has within the last twelve months been thankful to possess some competence in one or two languages other than English. But as John Trim has said of the Threshold Level:

'...by far the largest single group of learners, everywhere, consists of people who want to prepare themselves, in a general way, to be able to communicate on straightforward everyday matters with people from other countries who come their way, and to be able to get around and lead a reasonably normal social life when they visit another country. This is not simply a matter of buying bread and milk and toothpaste and getting repairs carried out to a car. People want to make contact with each other as people, to exchange information and opinions, talk about experiences, likes and dislikes, to explore our similarities and differences, the unity in diversity of our complicated and crowded continent.'

The Threshold Level, CCC Strasbourg, 1975, p ii.

Add to such considerations the dividend provided by a knowledge of modern languages in the areas of art, music, literature, current affairs and technology, and it is clear that language study can make a unique contribution to the individual's personal development.

With all these points in mind one is scarcely surprised that the learning of a foreign language is a firm tradition in European education, as indicated by Neumeister in 'Modern languages in school', vol I and II, Council of Europe, 1973. He quotes Austrian practice as a typical instance:

'Pupils learn about the institutions and social, economic and cultural life of the country (or countries) whose language they are studying and about the part it plays in the unification of Europe and the world. It is important that young people should become aware of the values inherent in other civilisations, as this is the best way to prevent them from acquiring prejudices and the best means of developing their critical faculties and making them internationally minded.'

Apart from the excellent section on the roles of language learning in C V James' NCLE paper already quoted, an admirable reply to Question 2 is provided in paragraph 1.19 of the West Sussex report mentioned above:

'To summarise the arguments advanced to justify the place of language in the secondary school, the aims of modern language teaching are varied and should include the development of communication skills, the related insight (through language) into other cultures and ways of life, the lessening of insularity (through personal contact with foreign countries and peoples wherever possible), a deepening awareness by pupils of the nature, functions and structure of language (including the properties of their own language by comparison and contrast), the enhancing of social competence and reinforcement of literacy, preparation for individual language learning at a later stage and, where appropriate, the fostering of specific skills for vocational purposes.'

Modern Languages 11-18, West Sussex County Council, 1978.

Is it possible to identify any elements inherent in a sound general education that can be offered to school pupils solely through the study of a modern language?

Despite the strong case for the inclusion of modern languages in the secondary curriculum, it is difficult to identify elements of a good general education which can be provided <u>solely</u> through the study of a modern foreign language. Many well-educated citizens in many countries have lived happy and useful lives with little or no knowledge of a foreign language. A non-linguist does not necessarily forfeit the respect of his peer-group and family (except in certain multilingual situations), many vocational skills and qualifications can be acquired without benefit of foreign languages, and healthy international attitudes can be inculcated by other means (eg geography, development education, VSO). Nevertheless Professor Hawkins has spoken of 'the handicap of the monolingual', and HMI in <u>Curriculum 11-16: modern languages</u> says:

'The study of a foreign language entails confrontation with a different form of communication and can offer an insight into the structure of language and into the process of both thought and language which the acquisition of English alone does not provide.'

On balance, if modern language study can scarcely be claimed to be the sole provider of certain essential elements in a good education, it can in my opinion claim to provide these more effectively than most other subjects.

If some elements of education are most readily, or even solely obtainable through modern languages, they should clearly, as the Green Papers says, be made available to 'as high a proportion as practicable' of secondary school pupils.

Whatever this proportion proves to be, the effectiveness of the modern language teaching provided for the pupils will depend on the fulfilment of widely agreed conditions for success. These are discussed inter- estingly in the West Sussex report, and include staffing, resources, time allocation and the harmonisation of methods and approaches adopted by teachers at different stages in a pupil's education. Success must also depend on pupils' ability and motivation.

Much recent thinking favours 'compact' courses designed on modular lines to fit given periods of time, eg two years. Such courses might clearly enable a modern language to be introduced at different stages in the secondary course, to suit varying requirements and purposes. If pupils had made a successful 'early start' with a foreign language in the primary or middle school the claims of continuity would usually place the compact course at the beginning of the secondary stage. Otherwise there might be advantages in deferring the secondary language course. A Belgian educational psychologist, Monsieur G Bastin, has suggested that the age of starting a foreign language should be determined 'not by reference to pupils' chronological age... but to their level of linguistic maturity'. Such maturity might, one hopes, be reached more quickly if pupils had benefited by a 'pre-language course' such as the one recommended on several occasions by Professor Hawkins.

Once started, the foreign language course might be continued until pupils' motivation has flagged to the point of counter-productivity. This difficulty might be lessened through the organisation of courses in graded levels, each evaluated by a profile or test. The schematic model suggested in the HMI Working Paper: Curriculum 11-16: modern languages for adapting objectives to pupils' ability and staying power is of great interest in this connection. Nevertheless it is to be hoped that the more able pupils will follow the European tradition of 4 or 5 periods a week for 5 years, together with at least some sixth form work, if we are to establish a cadre of school leavers who possess a sound working knowledge of at least one foreign language.

Is the educational value of modern language study dependent upon the methods by which languages are taught? Are some methodological approaches to be seen as being more 'educational' than others?

Present-day teaching methods, at least as adopted by the best teachers, appear to be settling into some degree of unanimity. They tend to combine the best of the 'oral' methods of the post-war years with a judiciously selected audio-visual element, and they include frequent references to the life of the foreign countries concerned. Published materials follow these approaches and also provide a pupil-centred bias in their subject matter. The British population, in and out of school, is not highly motivated towards the study of foreign languages. Not only do we lack the stimulus of a frontier situation or of a minority language, but the world-wide currency of English as an international language acts as a firm disincentive to language study. Motivation in school therefore depends on bright, imaginative, enjoyable teaching. The recent series Modern Language Teaching, shown on BBC Television, and the accounts of good practice in the otherwise astringent HMI discussion paper Modern languages in the comprehensive school show that, at their best, our teaching methods are as good as any to be found in the world. The same could be said of teaching materials such as 'Actualités Françaises', parts of A votre avis, Longman's Packs, Eclair, and a large range of courses, readers, and enrichment materials. Nevertheless, our decentralised system and the shortage of well-trained modern language teachers at a period of great expansion in the subject have created a situation in which poor teaching is found all too frequently.

If the subject is to make a satisfactory contribution to the educative process, teachers must possess the necessary skills, linguistic and pedagogical, to base their methods on the development of communicative competence and on the inculcation of healthy and well-informed attitudes towards other countries.

26

Has modern language study a specific contribution to make to the 'training of the mind'?

The expression 'training of the mind' raises broad questions of psychology and pedagogy which are beyond the competence of the present paper. Assuming that what is implied is the fostering of a pupil's intellectual powers, I return to the Green Paper, p 6-7, and select three points, (i), (iv) and (viii), as paragraph headings in the following brief discussion of the extent to which modern languages can contribute to a child's intellectual development.

1.   Section (i) of the Green Paper: 'to help children develop lively, enquiring minds; giving them the ability to question and to argue rationally, and to apply themselves to tasks.'

The study of a foreign language ought to broaden mental horizons by presenting the pupil with new environments, new countries, new life-styles. This material should stimulate countless questions, 'Where? Who? How? Why?' and thus lead to a livelier, more enquiring mind in the student. The language itself provides ample material for the exercise of intellectual processes, as suggested in a passage from a Flemish linguist, Van Passel, quoted by C V James in paragraph 1.1.4 of his NCLE paper already mentioned:

> 'Even without going into further details we may say that foreign language learning demands intensive training in task-analysis, in the techniques of observing and selecting facts, in the inductive processes of conceptualisation and generalisation, in the classification and ordering processes, in the deductive rule-governed behaviour, in the formulation of hypotheses and their testing out against the usage of others.'

In developing communicative competence in a new language the student is likely to become interested in the nature of language as a phenomenon worthy of study in itself. A recent article in Modern Languages suggests that more weight should be given to this aspect of modern language courses in schools:

> '...we should set some objectives in terms of improving understanding of the phenomenon of language as well as others in terms of performance of the particular foreign language.'
> M S Byram: "New Objectives' in Language Teaching', Modern Languages, December, 1978, p 204-207.

2.   Section (iv) of the Green Paper: 'to help children to use language effectively in reading, writing and speaking.'

Most modern language teachers would argue that their subject helps pupils towards greater freedom and confidence in using their native language.

3.   Section (viii) of the Green Paper: 'To encourage and foster the development of the children whose social or environmental disadvantages cripple their capacity to learn, if necessary by making additional resources available to them.'

Modern language study could be a useful 'leveller' in that disadvantaged and more privileged children might appear to be starting from a common state of ignorance of the new tongue. But this suggestion, as Dr Burstall has pointed out, ignores the effects of socio-economic background, with its support for the more fortunate child through encouragement, expectations of success and possibilities of foreign travel. Some measure of compensation for the disadvantaged child would be needed, and these might include the type of preliminary course mentioned earlier in this paper. In support of the view that modern languages provide a valuable means of 'training the mind', many examples could be quoted of distinguished administrators whose university degrees were in modern languages, and who give ample proof of the development of such qualities as perceptiveness, the power of organising facts and ideas, and the ability to reason logically and cogently.

Cognitive aspects of language study

Modern language study is a multi-faceted activity, but in a full secondary course (as outlined for able pupils in the HMI paper Curriculum 11-16) the following activities could provide many opportunities for the training of the mind:

First 2 years: Listening with attention, discriminating among sounds and decoding utterances; formulating simple sentences for oral expression; reading; observing new conventions of spelling; formulating, applying and memorising structural rules.

Years 3-5: Refinement of the above skills, plus some writing; meeting foreign nationals; learning about life abroad.

Years 6-7: Reading, writing and conversation taken to near-adult level; experience of creative use of language; appreciation of nuances of expression, application of language to other interests; beginnings of appreciation of the foreign language.

Throughout the course there are opportunities for increasing the pupils' understanding of the nature of language.

The aesthetic aspects of language study

An element which may be underestimated at the present time is the aesthetic pleasure to be derived from the study of a foreign language. Early reports on the French Pilot scheme emphasised the zest and delight shown by young children in learning French. The present writer's personal experience and observation suggest that all stages of a successful course of language learning can be accompanied by intense pleasure and satisfaction. These reactions are partly attributable to the co-ordination of sensory nerves and motor-muscular efforts as aural perception is matched by oral production of speech sounds. There is also the mimic's or the actor's delight in performing a role well. This activity includes the assumption of a foreign 'persona', not only through speech, but by paralinguistic means such as gesture, facial expression and the use of foreign conventions and courtesies ('Skol' - 'Pardon, monsieur' - 'Bitte schön'). This element of role-playing differs from dramatic expression in the native language in that less emotion is usually involved and the ultimate aim is that of clear and harmonious communication with people in other countries.

From the earliest stages the aural/oral skills can entail pleasure in word-games, rhymes and jingles (cf. Opie: The lore and language of schoolchildren). This element can be developed through songs, poems, dialogues and more formal play-acting, and can lead eventually to the appreciation of the subtle word-music of great writing. Those who have heard the very creditable renderings of prose and verse passages at such events as the MLA 'Spoken Word' competition may well reflect that the comptine 'Am-stram-gram...' can after a few years lead to the sensitive and musical speaking of Baudelaire's 'L'Albatros'. Ideas of this kind are developed by H H Stern in his article 'What can we learn from the good language learner?'

> 'The good language learner makes a very deliberate effort in a vicarious way to put himself into the place of (to identify with) the native speaker.'
> Modern Languages in Scotland, no. 11, Sept 1976, p 71-85.

Artistic impulses in a 'good learner' may also be channelled into the writing of verse, plays and short stories in the foreign language.

If the prime purpose of language learning has to do with communication, how important is accuracy of expression, as opposed to communicative competence? What is the place of grammar and translation?

For communication to take place at all, there must be a modicum of accuracy in all aspects of the L2 used - lexis, structure, phonology. Acceptable results in simple, practical matters can usually be achieved even by inaccurate use of the L2, within certain tolerances, but if complex ideas and facts are to be discussed, accuracy of expression is essential. It may be a tenable proposition that, as in the learning of L1, inaccuracy in the early stages is inevitable, and that accuracy is a matter of progressive and incremental achievement. Here is a somewhat extreme version of this idea:

'In general one must murder a language before mastering and part of the murdering process must begin at once.'
    E A Nida, quoted in H H Stern's article mentioned above.

If it is true to say that the experience gained by pupils in school is no less important than the knowledge they acquire, is there perhaps a range of experience which language teachers should seek to offer all their pupils? How important is it that such experience is 'authentic', given that much modern language teaching material is 'artificial' in content and situation?

Assuming that the modern language teacher is dealing with a fairly wide range of ability, he might hope to provide certain common experiences as follows:

(a) the effort to adjust to an unfamiliar means of communication
(b) the parallel effort to understand an unfamiliar country
(c) the satisfaction of attaining goals suited to the pupil's ability.

Further experiences, involving greater subtlety of mind, will presumably be possible only for more able pupils.

Material for the earlier stages is bound to be artificial to some extent in situation and linguistic content. Authenticity should of course be aimed at even here, but can grow as materials become more advanced. Professor Hawkins' distinction between 'rehearsal' (learning L2 under artificial conditions) and 'performance' (using L2 for real, or at least realistic, purposes of communication) is valuable in this connection.

Is it possible to identify any linguistic skills for lack of which a young person at the age of 16+ might be thought to be 'uneducated'? If so, is it essential to study a foreign language in order to acquire such skills?

In L1 the linguistic skills will be literacy, oracy and (some would add) numeracy, together with some ability in 'rapid reading', as suggested in Bullock, p 524, Recommendation 94:

'Flexible reading strategies, i.e. the ability to skim, scan, or read intensively as the occasion demands, should be acquired at school and should be exercised throughout the curriculum.'

In L2 an 'educated' person might be expected to at least be able to read with some ease, to understand the expression of simple ideas or facts in the spoken language, and to be able to ask straightforward questions and to exchange the more usual courtesies. See however paragraph 3.1 of this paper for some reservations as to whether knowledge of an L2 is absolutely essential to a young person who is to be considered 'educated'. Much will depend on the boy's or girl's future work and milieu in assessing the value of L2 to him or her.

30

The aims sketched above for L1 can probably be achieved without help from the study of L2. Nevertheless the L2 might assist progress in L1 in such ways as the following:

(a) ear-training and flexibility of speech organs
(b) clearer understanding of the phenomenon of language
(c) help with structures, lexis, spelling
(d) literary appreciation: sensitivity to the meaning and use of words; understanding of the use of foreign words and phrases used by English authors, eg frequent use of French in Shakespeare.

It is sometimes maintained that one of the aims of contemporary school education should be to encourage the development of 'good Europeans'. Must foreign language study automatically be included in a pupil's curriculum if this aim is to be achieved?

The development of 'good Europeans', as of 'good world citizens' must be dependent on a concerted effort by a school staff to represent the European dimension and the world dimension in all (or most) parts of the curriculum. In an internationally-minded school, a majority of pupils will probably have an unusually high motivation to learn a foreign language. They should clearly be given a chance to study a foreign language at some stage in their school career, always provided that the school has the staff and the resources to enable teaching to be good. Such opportunities will probably increase 'international-mindedness' throughout the school.

WHAT PLACE SHOULD MODERN LANGUAGE LEARNING HAVE IN THE CURRICULUM IF IT IS TO CONTRIBUTE TO A SOUNDLY BASED GENERAL SECONDARY EDUCATION?

D G Smith   Paper III

I think it is unnecessary to summarise the various attempts made by educational philosophers to define the place of modern languages in the curriculum. Nor do I wish to associate myself with any particular such definition. The reader can take his pick among the various models, all easily available. It is perhaps worth stressing, however, that not all educational philosophers appear to be fully aware of what is involved in knowing (as distinct, perhaps, from learning) a foreign language. This paper attempts simply to identify some areas in which are apparent some of the potential contributions of foreign language study to a soundly based secondary education.

Pressures on available time in the organisation of the secondary curriculum are intense. Two things are certain:

- Foreign languages have no more important a place in the curriculum than any other subject for which an equal educational claim can be made.

- Foreign languages have no place at all unless their teachers adduce a valid educational justification which holds up under argument, and unless pupils at the end of a foreign language course can be shown clearly to be 'better educated' in ways to which the foreign language course can equally clearly be shown to have made a significant contribution. 'Better educated' is a vague expression. No specific attempt will be made here to define it.

A VIEW OF THE FUTURE

Children entering secondary schools in 1980 will still be in vigorous middle age in 2015, and will continue to be in paid employment perhaps as late as 2030. A good proportion of today's modern language teachers will still be teaching at the turn of the century. We know little of what the world will be like at that time. Believers in the inevitability of 'progress' will make more optimistic prophecies than those who see a more depressing side to technological and consequent social change. If it is the task of schools to prepare pupils for the material and moral world in which they will spend their adult life, however, some attempt to foresee the nature of that world is essential.

A number of fairly commonplace assumptions can be made. Within the next 30 or 40 years, the world's population will increase enormously. Pressure on living space will become acute - most of us will have to live much closer to our neighbours. Supplies of raw materials, and of food may barely suffice. In our reactions to recent oil shortages can perhaps be read some of the fears and animosities which this might cause. We can only guess at the technological developments which might affect us. Automation has had a far less dramatic effect on patterns of employment than was predicted in the 1950s: the importance of the micro-processor may be much greater, perhaps precipitating the increase in unemployment (or, more positively, in leisure time) which was predicted then. Sections of the public - some much more than others - would find themselves working shorter hours than now, and in many cases needing to re-train, perhaps several times over, to take new jobs for which education so far had made them inadequate. It seems realistic to predict continuing sophistication and miniaturisation of arms, including nuclear arms, the extension of space technology for purposes of both manned transportation and weaponry, and the development of vulnerable sources of energy, including nuclear and tidal power stations. It is difficult to see how the first two of these three developments can fail to provoke anxieties relating to potential use or criminal abuse, and how the third can be conceived without increasing curtailments of personal liberty: armed guards, for instance, seem inevitable.

Teachers perhaps need an unusually high degree of faith in the educability and perfectibility of man. Given this, they may see the suggestions of the previous paragraph as at the worst neutral statements of fact to which quite acceptable answers will be found in time. Changes of this kind do predicate certain features of the school child which will need to be developed, however. These would include tolerance for other people (our cheeks and jowls will be closer even than now); sympathy for other ways of thought and behaviour; a high degree of patience, self restraint, and selflessness; willingness to be hospitable to others, and to share one's resources; the imagination to allow that traditional (or national) systems of organisation may not be the most appropriate in a different social organisation; adaptable, inventive, enquiring minds, in which re-training and éducation permanente in its many forms are seen as normal. As not all technological and social changes can be considered as potentially acceptable, pupils will need, as today, minds which are combative in a positive sense. As the amelioration of social conditions and the widening of some restrictive parental attitudes rarely seem to keep pace with technological change, education will continue to need to exercise what Professor E W Hawkins called a liberating influence, to overcome feelings of insecurity and fear.

There is nothing new in requiring education to do these things. (Nor does the previous paragraph claim to cover more than a segment of the total task required of a sound education.) To produce pupils in whom such manifestly desirable attitudes were developed, however, would be a good first step. Most importantly, this sketchy attempt to face some of the implications of the changes which are likely to occur in the lifetimes of our pupils stresses the often neglected point that in education process is a component part of product: indeed, process may be more important than product. All of us forget the great bulk of what we learn at school - education is what remains when the forgetting has been done. What remains is in a large degree a matter of mental sets, developed more by the process through which the mind has gone than by the product of what it acquires.

WIDENED HORIZONS AND TOLERANCE

Modern linguists often claim that their subject 'widens horizons' or extends mental sets. I believe that such widening can go on in many of the areas touched on above, and that enlightened modern languages teaching can contribute significantly to the humane development of young (and older) people. The modal verb has been used intentionally, however. In order for these things to happen, certain elements need to feature in the modern languages course which are not always present. It will also be apparent that modern language teaching alone will not produce the desirable characteristics concerned. Other components of the curriculum contribute, but in varying degrees. In what follows, no claim is made for the 'uniqueness' of the modern languages contribution, except where a specific claim to that effect is made: it is also arguably unlikely that in the formation of attitudes any other curriculum area can make claims to uniqueness.

Tolerance of other people is compounded of many features: to make them discrete will seem arbitrary. It includes obvious features such as skin colour and smell, dress and diet, personal comportment and family organisation. Radical differences in these areas are apparent in immigrant groups in this country (which include Polish, Greek, Chinese, Italians in the Midlands, as well as Asians, Africans and West Indians - and the point is valid for all of those groups), and in lesser degrees some of them are relevant to the native speakers of the European languages most commonly taught in schools. That they are apparent in lesser degress only is important - personal reactions cover the spectrum from extreme to slight, after all.

Tolerance includes accepting such things as accent, speech defect, low levels of verbalising competence, body language (including gesture), unusual patterns of intonation, a realisation that although Africans often sound rather unusual speaking English, Englishmen speaking Swahili probably sound at least as odd. Nothing of qualitative value at a personal level should be read into unusual speech. Nor, automatically should any such value be read into unusual patterns of behaviour.

Tolerance also includes the willingness to attempt to see the emotional, mental, historical reasons causing different ways of thought and behaviour. The historical mistrust between employer and employee in certain industries gives us one type of example: the unwillingness of certain categories of French people to answer letters, the apparent character change which overcomes Germans at Fasching, the pre-disposition of Arabs to belch while eating are qualitatively equally susceptible of investigation. The ability to understand them, tolerate them in their context, but to see the undesirability of transferring them from their context to that of the learner contribute to a better understanding of the world. Less colourful examples than those above are perhaps required. Let us quote, therefore, the Church/State dilemma in France, the effect of having half their country under Communist rule on the attitude of West German trade union leaders, the results of the teaching of the Koran on Arab attitudes to justice.

CONCEPTS OF CIVILISATION

The paragraphs above are intended merely as an attempt to explain what types of feature would enter into 'widening horizons'. It is debatable, in fact, whether within the classroom most foreign language learners ever grapple with the more complex of the item types mentioned here. There are several inhibiting factors, including time, teacher competence, and the complexity of the concepts involved.

Historically - understandably, defensively - the prime objective of modern language teachers has always been to teach the skills involved in mastery of the foreign language. With study of foreign languages generally occupying at the most something like one eighth of the curriculum time available, even those competent linguists who continue their language study for five years are judged by their teachers to need practically all their available study time to acquire mastery of the foreign language skills. Consequently, very little time is generally set aside for bright pupils to learn about the countries involved in the languages they are learning. A few topics are generally covered by all - types of housing abroad, pavement cafes in France*, life in school, the French wine and cheese areas, some geographical introduction to certain regions of the country. The course materials most frequently used in secondary schools have a 'Frenchness' about them which ranges from virtual zero to a point perhaps halfway across the scale. This is true even of those - few - courses which contain pseudo-authentic French material and items on real French people. Practically without exception, course books concentrate on structure and lexis without ever quite attaining an authentic Frenchness. Even in the case of the courses most frequently used, anything other tham simple surface meaning is sacrificed or ignored for the sake of structure and lexis. Very rarely do these courses contain much material based on actual events in the real life of real people, whether it be in the country whose language is being studied or elsewhere. From a linguistic point of view - from a point of view relating only to language - some horizon widening may occur, and this will be discussed later, but it is rare that such materials give real scope for extending the student's range of concepts on more general aspects of life.

Occasionally foreign language reading materials may give scope for such mental development - although often the content is of an 'adventure' variety rather than being factual. It must be admitted, of course, that certain valid human truths can be learnt from adventure stories. Additionally, some teachers use language teaching materials based on authentic material from France and these materials are potentially more likely, perhaps, to contribute even in tiny ways to the widening process involved. Other teachers seem able by methods difficult to assess to give an authentic foreignness to their course. Perhaps more important still, some teachers teach in the foreign language about real events in the real world - plans for coal mining in the Vale of Belvoir, simplified and taught to a second year class among other reasons to practise the immediate future - and contribute generously to the perceptive as well as the linguistic development of their pupils. Two jobs are done at once.

Paradoxically, however, with pupils less gifted, foreign language courses tend to include increasing amounts of time devoted to work intended less to teach the foreign language than to teach about the foreign countries. The paradox is twofold: that such a course should be given particularly to those pupils who will be least aided by mastery in some degree of the foreign language of the country involved: and that it is predominantly with less able pupils that some of the difficult concepts involved should be broached. No doubt mainly as a result of this second point, teaching about foreign countries seems to consist mainly of factual transmissions (that a French bread shop is called a 'boulangerie', rather than that even in small villages a bakery has a social significance by no means replicated in England).

This may be more directly attributable to the teachers than to pupil competence. If we agree with Bruner that almost any concept can be taught to almost any pupil in some form of educationally valid manner, it may be that teachers have not examined in adequate detail exactly what is implied by 'widening horizons'. There appears to be an undue importance attached to the teaching of facts, and not enough to the making of inferences based on these facts. Facts are unimportant in themselves, and can be looked up or otherwise obtained. What they tell us about the world is much more important.

It must be admitted that very few modern language teachers have received any form of training for the teaching of non-linguistic concepts. It is probably true that most university or college lecturers involved in initial training have little experience of teaching much below the level of grammar school pupils. This has important implications for in-service training, and for the design of teaching materials.

Finally, it should be pointed out that many foreign language teachers, even in comprehensive schools, express doubts about attempting to teach foreign languages to slow learners. It is difficult to reconcile this attitude to the traditional plane of widening horizons, for less able children need this at least as much as the most able. It remains true nevertheless that the kinds of concept involved in this work outside the area of pure language teaching are difficult to teach in a vacuum, whatever the calibre of the pupils involved. Even in those cases where the teaching of facts about the country does lead to the making of hypotheses based on them, it is important to add the final step of verification/amendment of hypotheses. This can be done only by testing hypotheses against reality. In this case, reality is the foreigner in his own country.

DIRECT CONTACT WITH THE FOREIGN COUNTRY

This points to the critical importance in the secondary school foreign language course of providing maximum opportunities for pupils to have contact with the foreign country. It follows from what has been said above that this is at least as important for pupils doing a course with a heavy 'background' component as for those involved in main line language learning, and for those in the early stages of their course as well as for those in the later stages. Such contact is likely to be most effective, of course, if it happens in the foreign country. To some degree, however, it can be of value if it involves pupils in meeting people from the country involved, within the United Kingdom. Some LEAs make extensive provision for opportunities of this kind. Valid claims can be made for brief contacts - some schools organise one-day trips to the continent, from which much of value can result: pupils travel on trains for the first time ever, learn the importance of group cohesion, see that foreigners exist and that they live in their own surroundings. Longer visits must be assumed to be even more rewarding. Some groups spend eight days in a residential centre: again, more group living makes its impact on them, new habits have to be adhered to, new types of food eaten, and more or less probing enquiries can be made into the habits and life styles of the natives of the country. Where home-to-home exchanges are possible - through linked schools, for instance - a much deeper insight into life styles can be gained, and pupils are also faced with the necessity to operate autonomously in a totally unfamiliar environment, to stand on their own feet, to accommodate their own wishes and ambitions temporarily to those of new acquaintances, to attempt to turn those acquaintances into friends, and even to attempt to bend these new friends to their own will, whilst retaining their goodwill. All of these are educationally worthwhile activities: coupled with the testing out of new and incomplete concepts against the reality of the foreign country, they have a convincing appearance of educational validity. It is no exaggeration to say that in some cases, links with a foreign school have brought new dimensions to many areas of the curriculum, in addition to the modern languages area.

If the foreign visit or contact with foreigners are to be regarded as an integral part of the foreign language course, however, they need to be planned at least as carefully as any other part of the course. Agencies are beginning to make big money out of school travel. Experience shows that very many groups going abroad and staying in residential centres are badly underprepared for their visit. Some of them also appear to be horrifyingly under-supervised. If the visit is intended to teach, it must not be assumed that learning will result from unordered, random observation. Again, if it is to be an integral part of the foreign language course, teachers need training - probably in-service rather than initial - to help them carry out this out-of-the-classroom teaching. Some initiation is needed into 'animation', environmental studies, simple observation and simple sampling procedures. Prior acquaintance with the Centre is also essential. All groups from Leicestershire schools going to centres supported by the LEA, for instance, must be accompanied by at least one teacher who has stayed at the centre before. In order to make this a feasible requirement, the LEA organises familiarisation courses in its centres, as part of its normal term-time in-service provision. Strong claims can be made for the value of well-planned visits. No claims should be made for any other kind.

THE NEED FOR FOREIGN LANGUAGE COMPETENCE

Unstated but underlying the paragraphs above is the fairly self-evident truth that finding out about people of another tongue really requires you to have acquired some level of competence in their tongue. It is possible, of course, to rely upon their knowledge of your own, but this limits your contact with them to those areas they are able or willing to deal with in conjunction with you. Clearly it is possible also to learn from what springs to the sense: a friend travelling to France for the first time made to me as his first ever statement on French soil the comment 'France doesn't smell like England'. Carefully prepared observation work based on surface manifestations of the culture can be informative. But to get under the skin of the country, you need some proficiency in the language.

Later sections will examine some of the ways in which language learning contributes to a general education, but for our purposes at this moment it is important to stress the role of language acquisition as a unique facilitator of experience. Through the ability to communicate in a foreign language, pupils have opened up to them areas of experience quite inaccessible without that ability. At a very simple level, a child able to produce 30 appropriate utterances in the French class is experiencing something he would not otherwise experience. Much more so is this true of a child able to converse with a French friend. Incomparably more so is it true of the sixth former spending a term in a French school. Foreign language uniquely makes some experiences accessible. It is in his failure to appreciate this that J P White betrays a failure to understand the difference between mother tongue and foreign language learning. 'Provided that one speaks one language, eg English, one can gain some understanding of what it is for other people to speak another, even though one cannot do so oneself.' Surely this is not so?

Even people who speak a foreign language very well, do not, in a foreign country, experience exactly the same things as they would speaking their mother tongue at home. It is in this area that foreign language acquisition becomes liberating - it liberates pupils from the constraints of their normal mother tongue existence. It should be noted, however, that in order for such liberating experience to be achieved, contact with the foreign country is essential. As the essence of education can be said to be learning from experiences provided or otherwise grasped, foreign language study has an important role to play.

LANGUAGES AND THE CURRICULUM

So far we have suggested that modern languages have a place in the curriculum related to their potential for widening the conceptual grasp of pupils about the world in general. We have then suggested that from the aspect of making certain types of experience accessible, modern languages have a unique role to play. In both these areas, we have stressed the centrality of time spent in contact with the foreign country. It is now time to look in more detail at the more specific linguistic aspect.

In the work of those philosophers of education (the majority) who do accord to modern language study a place in the curriculum, stress is often laid on the way in which foreign languages could contribute to the 'symbolic' education of pupils. Like mathematics, a foreign language is a tightly-organised, infinitely expressive symbol system. What it expresses is qualitatively different from the field covered by mathematics (although a cursory glance at Chomsky's writings may make one wonder). The language course fits, for instance, into the symbolic area of Phenix's 'realms of meaning', ie the ways by which man overcomes the apparent meaninglessness of the universe. Acquisition of foreign language can extend the experiences and conclusions drawn from study of the mother tongue. It requires pupils to notice elements of the foreign language never consciously considered in the mother tongue (adjectives, segments of the verb, stress patterns, for instance) and requires them to make sounds not previously part of their conscious repertoire. In this way it can lead them to realise that language is a variable system of codes with no necessary one-to-one relationships across linguistic/cultural frontiers.

It seems likely that by requiring close attention to sounds, word patterns and functions, foreign language learning can increase sensitivity to language, even in the mother tongue. Although in some cases the mother tongue may be used in ways rather resembling the use of a battering ram, close attention to the requirements of the foreign language tend towards requiring its use rather as a fine cutting tool. Intuition suggests that this can lead to closer attention to the mother tongue. At an advanced level, for instance, it seems likely that close attention to accurate translation, or the attempt to grasp the reasons for the effectiveness of an author's style or the realisation of the potential effect of various word orders, registers, or non-verbal language behaviour (gesture, etc) may well transfer to closer attention to the same area of interest in the mother tongue. It is not suggested that this is invariably so, or inevitably the case, for there do appear to be good numbers of language graduates who are careless, uneconomic, or ineffective in their use of the mother tongue, but intuition/personal experience suggests that the potential is there. It may be that the best way of attending to the mother tongue is by direct operation in the mother tongue, as some writers suggest, but experience in remedial education suggests that diminishing returns can operate: just as, although spelling and counting are important, one would not suggest that a timetable should be completely filled with them. Furthermore, some people have distinct predispositions towards foreign language acquisition, and for them the foreign language appears capable of becoming a vehicle for study and appreciation beyond its immediate context. This is no doubt partly related to the fairly self-evident fact that good knowledge of one language speeds up considerably the acquisition of another. To suggest this is not to wish to accept the full implications of faculty psychology. But within the restricted area of foreign language/mother tongue language usage, transfer does appear to operate.

Thus, although one of the major contributions of the foreign language class will be to teach the foreign language itself, there appear to be other related linguistic benefits. The DES publication Curriculum 11-16: modern languages puts it this way. Foreign language learning can afford 'the opportunity for growing pleasure in the use of words ... develop sensitivity to the sound and rhythms of ... language (and direct) the attention of the learner to the way in which language is organised'. It is hoped that to those who speak one or more foreign languages to a high level these points will appear true: they may even appear banal. Two major questions arise from them, however:

- for whom are the experiences educationally desirable?

- how many pupils gain from foreign language study in all the ways suggested?

LANGUAGES FOR WHOM?

For whom are these experiences educationally desirable? The question will be extended to include all types of experience so far dealt with in this paper.

It is difficult to see any argument other than that the values so far adduced are valid for all secondary school pupils. If any pupils need to develop their sympathy, understanding and tolerance of other people(s) presumably all do. If the experience of getting under the skin of another culture by close contact with it is desirable for some, it is presumably desirable for all. If it is important for human beings ('articulate mammals', as Jean Aitchison calls them) to develop desirably attentive attitudes to their means of articulacy, it is presumably important for all to do so. If one had to decide for which pupils - more, or less - able - the needs in all three areas were greatest, it would be difficult to escape the conclusion that it were for the least able: for the sources of low academic achievement are frequently to be found in low levels of mother tongue attainment and in high levels of anomie.

How many pupils gain from foreign language study in all the ways suggested? In all areas of learning, differential rates of return operate according particularly to aptitude, ability and interest. The question is also made more complex by the fact that suitable courses and materials do not yet appear to have become generally accessible to all levels of pupil, although vast numbers of courses do exist, particularly in French. Tentative impressions can be given, however, but these are purely personal. My own impression is that the foreign visit is crucial. Consider these two comments by teachers. 'Some pupils who went to France without a prayer of a chance in their exams have come back and are covering themselves with glory.' 'The five children in my bottom group who went have astounded their class-mates because of their knowledge of vocabulary which seems to have just come to them.' Without the impetus of the visit, less able - and even middle range - children often seem to make slight progress in the language, and to show little sign of developing interested and acquisitive attitudes to their mother tongue. Often, too, they seem to develop relatively little the sympathetic willingness to go half-way to meeting the foreign culture on its own terms. There are of course notable exceptions - usually taught by exceptional teachers. These serve to suggest that the job is not impossible. One cannot base a curriculum subject on the achievements of exceptional teachers. By definition, most teachers are of average calibre. We must continue, however, to accord foreign languages a valuable place in the curriculum of all children, and continue to seek ways to improve performance in all the areas so far described.

SETTING STANDARDS

It is perhaps legitimate to ask what foreign language standards society should expect of its school leavers. Although it is not self-evident that society knows clearly what it expects of its leavers as far as many other areas of the curriculum are concerned (eg history, geography) it is beginning to become apparent that there may be some grounds for agreement about the standards in some areas such as basic numeracy and literacy. As so many pupils abandon language study well before sixteen, however, variegated objectives need to be set.

There has been a tendency recently for foreign language teachers to fall into a trap partly of their own making. With increased emphasis on oral skills, the temptation has increased for observers to judge terminal performance unfavourably and unrealistically by comparison with the level of the native speaker. The injustice of such comparisons is self-evident. In many cases it has been coupled with pseudo-historical mythology - other teachers claiming with a misplaced and bizarre form of inverted pride that they 'learnt French at school for five years and still can't speak a word of it'. On the basis of earlier claims made in this paper for the capacity of the foreign language course to have beneficial results in other, non-linguistic areas, such a disclaimer for the foreign language course is based on inadequate grounds. Some foreign language teachers have been slow to point this out, perhaps because the non-linguistic benefits are difficult to measure, or perhaps because teachers have still not satisfactorily resolved for themselves precisely what the nature of those benefits is (and thence the appropriate methodology to ensure their acquisition).

In linguistic terms, however, one would hope that school leavers at whatever level would be able to make appropriate efforts to use a reasonable number of elements of the foreign language in truly communicative situations. That sentence is unashamedly vague, because the work currently going into step-by-step teaching and assessment procedures indicates just how difficult and complex are the necessary statements of level.

One thing which is clear, however, is that, welcome as are these efforts to transform the language taught in schools into a type which has realistic communicative intentions, there is a risk that purely functional language teaching will prove difficult and even inadequate. Current attempts to establish functional syllabuses, particularly where they are related to step-by-step assessment procedures, have tended to concentrate in many cases on 'survival language' in situations which are transactional (in the sense of seeking to obtain some form of service from a foreigner), or which relate to a number of contexts, eg railway stations, cafes, where a very small number of possible, but arbitrarily selected, utterances can be predicted. A series of exponents has thus been defined, many of which have relatively little relationship to each other either semantically or grammatically. As a consequence, at least two major methodological problems arise:

- how to teach the exponents

- how to ensure that pupils will stand a chance of understanding a reply to any utterance they make.

There are indications that a tendency is developing to teach the utterances by straightforward translation methods ('to get a plate of chips you say...') followed by parroted repetition, and for the range of possible answers to be learnt by heart. This cannot be considered as real language learning, nor can it have any chance of satisfying those linguistic objectives of school foreign language courses which go beyond the purely practical, and concern development of deeper understanding of the nature of language itself. Graded syllabuses and assessment work currently going on may or may not be founded on an adequate understanding of linguistics and the nature of language acquisition, but it will certainly be necessary to develop a methodology for teaching communicative language competence which may well be different from those methodologies currently employed in secondary schools.

Because many of the items which feature on some of the syllabuses based on communicative language needs which have been produced recently are not inter-related either semantically or grammatically (at least in the order in which they appear on the syllabuses), and because within any one function the exponents can involve a host of grammatical patterns, the graded presentation of grammar which has traditionally formed the basis of even the more enlightened teacher's syllabuses may be difficult to follow. Also - consequently, indeed - those teachers who find it possible with such a grammatically graded syllabus to exclude the mother tongue from their teaching (because meaning does not become unclear in the tiny steps being taken grammatically) might be unlikely to be able to continue the same methods, given a functional/communicative syllabus. There seems to be a danger that mother tongue usage in foreign language lessons will be accepted as an important feature. This would be paradoxical. At the moment, it is fair to say that very large proportions of many foreign language lessons in many schools are conducted with very little use of the foreign language; it may be inferred that this is at least a major factor contributing to the low levels of oral competence frequently reported. It would be paradoxical indeed if attempts to produce communicative competence increased this danger. It is also arguable that attempts to produce communicative competence are unlikely to succeed unless pupils can first communicate in one of the very few areas where the need can be continuously provoked, - in the everyday transactional needs of the classroom. The natural use of the foreign language in the classroom accustoms pupils to using it, and sorting out the meaning of foreign language utterances which they hear, either from the teacher or from other pupils. (Actually, interaction pupil/pupil is apparently very rare: this may be another reason why pupils are not very good at communicating when they need to speak to foreign children.)

Two things, at least, are implied here concerning the methodology most logically consistent with the objectives of teaching communicative competence:

-   The mother tongue should be excluded from classroom usage as rigorously as possible.

-   The grammar of the language will need to be taught, first to allow pupils to make 'novel and appropriate' utterances as required, and also to give them a basic framework against which to lay utterances made to them, which may be utterances never heard before tel quel, but which will need to be responded to.

Attempts to exclude mother tongue from foreign language teaching have implications for the manner by which grammar might be taught. It suggests that the methods should be based on the pupil's ability to operate by analogy and inference, rather than by explicit definition. Such methods are already in use in some (few?) schools. The search for language which produces communicative competence would dictate the elements of lexis taught and the elements of grammar stressed: it might also influence the order in which grammar were presented, but there would be other constraints, such as the wish to operate only in the foreign language, which might equally influence this ordering. It would be necessary at times, no doubt, to pass through some 'non-communicative' phases, in order to lay the foundations for a surer communicative competence later: but 'later' would need to be very much sooner than in the more traditional types of course organisation. The degree to which grammatical depth would be sought would no doubt be one of the factors differentiating the course for learners of differing linguistic competence. Our aims being among others, however, to give some understanding of how a language works, it would be unacceptable for pupils, even of low ability, to be taught without any attempt to produce some measure of the ways in which language remains comprehensible: grammatical accuracy would be one of those ways.

No doubt the attempts to teach language for communication will cause a revised attitude to accuracy, in grammar, pronunciation, intonation. Even for the least able pupils, however, it is clearly essential for teachers to maintain high standards of example and high levels of expectation: it can never be an acceptable aim to teach inaccurate expression, although it will be possible to expect only that measure of accuracy in reply which is consonant with the pupil's highest level of achievement and the possibility of his utterance being understood. (It should be interjected here, perhaps, that grammatical approaches to language teaching have frequently taught misleading and inaccurate language, which needs later to be unlearned, in the belief that this process was easier for the pupils.) Without attempts to produce accuracy, it is unlikely that pupils will be learning very efficiently about how languages operate, nor that their learning will lead to an awareness of the distinctiveness of one language compared to another. It is arguably undesirable for slovenly speech to be accepted in the mother tongue, since it is uneconomical, unattractive, and unlikely to express meaning with any degree of finesse: pupils need to realise that slovenly approaches to a foreign language can have just the same features, and, most importantly, that comprehension can break down much more easily, even through inaccurate intonation. Furthermore, if teachers are to derive help from error analysis, it is important that pupils try not to scatter random error over every utterance which they make. This being said, however, the highest levels of teacher expectation need to be tempered with the need to encourage pupils to articulate foreign utterances, which excessive correction can hinder. Differentiated teacher objectives will need to be established, and no doubt in some cases an acceptance of gross inaccuracy, if this indicates at least comprehension.

It should be said in conclusion that the teaching of pupils to make comprehensible utterances in the foreign language is much more complex than most non-language teachers imagine. It should also be said that if this paper has attempted to place foreign language study in the secondary school curriculum, and to indicate that its contribution potentially goes much beyond the attempt to teach pupils to make such utterances, it is important for language teachers to realise that a course which fails to teach such competence nevertheless makes an incomplete contribution to the curriculum.

* It is found convenient to draw specific examples from France and French teaching. Examples could equally well have been drawn from other countries and languages.

WHAT PLACE SHOULD MODERN LANGUAGE LEARNING HAVE IN THE CURRICULUM IF IT IS TO CONTRIBUTE TO A SOUNDLY BASED GENERAL SECONDARY EDUCATION?

F Weiss   Paper IV

Lorsqu'un observateur étranger considère l'enseignement des langues en Angleterre, il ne peut pas ne pas être frappé par la très grande variété des situations d'enseignement, la diversité des examens de fin d'études et le taux élevé d'abandon de l'apprentissage de langues en cours de scolarité.

Il est évident que, d'une façon générale, les programmes actuellement en vigueur sont loin d'être satisfaisants. Ils sont à la fois trop vagues, trop ambitieux et souvent inadaptés au public scolaire auquel ils s'adressent. Tout comme dans d'autres pays où l'enseignement secondaire est devenu polyvalent et où tous les élèves ont accès à cet enseignement, 'Angleterre n'a pas encore réussi à faire les ajustements nécessaires aux programmes d'enseignement de langues afin de les adapter à ce nouveau public indifférencié.

Afin de sauvegarder le <u>niveau</u> de cet enseignement académique d'un niveau d'abstraction élevé, autrefois réservé à l'élite qui avait réussi à passer l'examen d'entrée à l'enseignement secondaire, on sacrifie souvent des élèves ayant des formes d'intelligence différentes. Les élèves se découragent souvent très vite et abandonnent la langue étrangère a la première occasion possible.

Pourtant on sait que tout et chacun peut apprendre une langue étrangère et on ne peut qu'être d'accord avec Bloom qui affirme que 90% des élèves apprendraient facilement une langue étrangère si les programmes d'enseignement étaient plus souples et s'ils respectaient le rythme d'apprentissage individuel, et si l'on encourageait davantage le travail autonome.

Dans n'importe quel système d'enseignement qui se veut un <u>système éducatif,</u> c'est à ce dernier de s'adapter aux apprenants: tout l'enseignement doit être centré sur l'apprenant, au lieu de l'être soit sur l'enseignant, le programme ou la méthode; et la notion meme d'enseignement sous la forme traditionnelle de transmission, de savoir et d'information devra être graduellement remplacée par celle de facilitation d'apprentissage devant favoriser l'autonomie progressive des apprenants. L'objectif essentiel d'un système éducatif devra être <u>'d'apprendre aux élèves à apprendre'.</u>

Dans la société néo-industrielle (et bientôt post industrielle) dans laquelle nous vivons, les langues étrangères jouent un rôle très important qui s'explique par les caractéristiques de cette société: la mondialisation du marché, la transmission instantanée des informations, les grandes migrations touristiques, la mobilité de la main d'oeuvre (migration saisonnière ou définitive). Dans toutes ces situations, la connaissance d'une langue étrangère constitue un atout majeur, soit sur le plan professionel, soit sur le plan humain.

A mon avis, les deux contributions essentielles de l'apprentissage d'une langue résident dans l'ouverture d'esprit qu'il peut développer et dans la réflexion sur le fonctionnement de l'outil linguistique de la communication.

L'apprentissage d'une langue peut jouer un rôle essentiel dans l'abolition des barrières culturelles et de l'ethnocentrisme.

Dans la perspective de la construction d'une Europe unie, il est essentiel de relativiser et de perdre cet ethnocentrisme qui nous rend imperméables aux influences étrangères et qui valorise inconditionnellement la culture nationale au détriment des autres. Le premier impératif dans l'apprentissage d'une langue étrangère est celui du développement de la tolérance, de l'acceptation de la différence et du droit à la différence.

L'enseignement de la culture ou plutot des 'realités' françaises, allemandes, italiennes, etc fait partie inhérente de l'enseignement de la langue étrangère. On ne peut pas enseigner le français sans apprendre la France. Cet apprentissage est aussi important que l'acquisition de l'outil linguistique et devrait être inclus dans le curriculum. Il devrait faire l'objet d'une approche contrastive sereine et systématique qui viserait à abolir les stéréotypes et les clichés qui sont si souvent répercutés par les manuels et les méthodes meme les plus modernes qui continuent à propager des images figées et des attitudes folkloriques et humoristiques toujours aux dépens des étrangers. Ne pourrait-on pas présenter les réalités étrangères tout simplement comme différentes des siennes propres? La nourriture anglaise ou allemande n'est ni meilleure ni pire que la nourriture française, et elle est simplement différente, elle a une valeur différente, elle joue un rôle différent.

Cette éducation à l'acceptation des différences nationales ne peut être réalisée en profondeur qu'à travers l'apprentissage de la langue étrangère qui seul permet un contact profond et une confrontation intime avec la civilisation du pays de la langue cible qui ne peuvent assurer de la meme façon les études économique, géographique ou historique d'un pays étranger.

Grâce à une telle approche contrastive et objective permettant de garder la distance critique nécessaire, on pourrait peut-être trouver quelques solutions appropriées aux problèmes de l'ethnocentrisme et de l'anomie.

Dans l'enseignement académique classique traditionnel, l'entrainement à la réflexion sur le fonctionnement des langues était assuré par l'apprentissage des langues mortes. Le latin devait nous apprendre à penser clairement et logiquement.

Il est évident que l'apprentissage de n'importe quelle langue vivante peut favoriser la réflexion linguistique aussi bien, sinon mieux que ne le faisait le latin. Il ne s'agit pas simplement d'assurer un apprentissage correct des règles phonétiques, phonologiques et morpho-syntaxiques de la langue cible, il s'agit également de l'apprentissage des règles pragmalinguistiques et sociolinguistiques.

La réflexion linguistique et sociolinguistique devrait mener à l'acquisition progressive d'une compétence de communication permettant aux apprenants de réagir de façon adéquate dans les différentes situations de communication dans lesquelles ils pourront être impliqués. La grammaire normative sera remplacée par une grammaire notionelle. Cet apprentissage se fera également de façon contrastive (pédagogie de la faute) et aura recours à des procédés de découverte et d'heuristique fonctionnelle en vue d'atteindre le stade de la conceptualisation, phase essentielle dans le processus d'apprentissage d'ensemble qui permettra de passer aux suivantes de la production convergentes (application des règles apprises dans des contextes similaires) de la production divergente (application des règle dans des situations nouvelles) et de la résolution de problèmes nouveaux.

Pour illustrer cette démarche, voici le schéma méthodologique pour la fabrication d'unités capitalisables tel qu'il a été établi par notre équipe pédagogique pour la rénovation des cours dans les Instituts Français en Allemagne et en Angleterre.

SCHEMA METHODOLOGIQUE POUR LES UNITES CAPITALISABLES

Remarques

1. Ce schéma est une hypothèse de travail: en tant que tel est sujet à une expérimentation, validation, infirmation, variantes.

2. Dans le cadre du schéma lui-meme, plusieurs déroulements pédagogiques (et supports didactiques) sont possible et souhaitables selon les Unités Capitalisables, le niveau, la demande des études, ainsi que la place dans le processus global d'apprentissage.

Schéma

Phase I: Présentation de la 'tâche'

On crée le besoin d'expression ou de communication (par l'annonce ou l'amorce d'une situation simulée, d'une tâche à résoudre, d'une discussion réelle, d'un échange au sein de la classe): c'est la première phase dite PRAGMALINGUISTIQUE dont le but est de faire surgir la communication des nécessites de l'action et, ce faisant, d'impliquer doublement l'apprenant dans la communication et dans la tâche. Fonction précise de cette phase: justifier les activités de la phase suivante par l'utilisation prévue de la langue dans une situation de communication <u>cible</u>, définie par la 'tâche'.

Phase 2. Compréhension et production dirigées

Mais les moyens (outils) linguistiques de cette communication font partiellement défaut: structures, lexique. Ces éléments linguistiques sont apportés et expliqués aux élèves soit à partir d'un support (écrit, audio ou audio-visuel, selon la nature de la tâche et de l'unité capitalisable), soit au cours d'un jeu ou d'une activité permettant de comprendre et de produire en situation d'utilisation immédiate, réelle ou simulée. Dans les deux cas - point de départ 'réceptif' ou point de départ 'productif', on évite la 'production' purement mécanique (non justifiée par un rôle ou un échange) et la reproduction de dialogues longs, auxquels on préfère des réutilisations immédiates et progressives d'un petit nombre de répliques en situation simulée ou réelle.

Dans cette phase plus proprement linguistique, l'entrainement des automatismes de langage (apprentissage psychomoteur) et la conceptualisation des règles morphosyntaxiques (apprentissage cognitif) ne sont donc pas séparés l'un de l'autre, ni hors situation: la mémorisation ne se fait pas sans PRODUCTION VRAIE, ni l'exploitation sans COMMUNICATION sur de petites séquences.

Phase 3: Résolution de la tâche

On revient à l'activité ou à la tâche annoncée ou amorcée en 1 puis provisoirement délaissée. On la résout en communiquant avec les outils acquis en 2. C'est encore une phase PRAGMALINGUISTIQUE; en outre, avec les progrès des élèves, elle permet une personnalisation de plus en plus grande de l'expression, surtout si on veille, par la diversité des tâches proposées, à varier les situations de communication (rôles assumés par les élèves, thèmes de référence, etc).

C'est la phase de 'transfert' d'un apprentissage réalisé sciemment en prévision de ce transfert.

Phase 4: Variation de rôles, situations enregistrées

On met les élèves en situations de simuler en échange nouveau, ou en leur présentant une réalisation nouvelle à l'aide d'une grille presentant les paramètres situationnels (sociolinguistiques) les plus pertinants à ce stade de l'apprentissage. L'objectif ici consiste à situer la communication amorcée en 1 et realisée en 3 dans l'ensemble des usages sociolinguistiques et à en réaliser d'autres en faisant varier quelques paramètres utiles: ceci permet de montrer l'étroite relation entre les choix linguistiques et les paramètres socio-culturels. C'est la phase de conceptualisation SOCIOLINGUISTIQUE.

49

Nouvelles extensions grammaticales ou lexicales rendues nécessaires par 4 ou désirées par le professeur ou le groupe-classe.

Le schéma méthodologique appelle quelques commentaires. Il est destiné en priorité à des cours pour adultes, mais la démarche pédagogique pourrait également s'appliquer, avec quelques variantes, à l'enseignement scolaire. Il suppose un engagement personnel profond (motivation, implication), beaucoup de travail de groupe, le recours systématique aux documents authentiques dès le stade initial d'apprentissage, ainsi qu'aux méthodes actives (travail sur tâches, fabrication et production de documents et de matériel linguistique.

Le document authentique doit être introduit dès la première leçon. Il existe déjà un grand nombre de documents authentiques simples, utilisables au niveau 1. A quoi bon passer par l'apprentissage d'un français pédagogique neutre et aseptisé qui n'existe que dans les manuels de français pédagogique neutre langue étrangère, avant d'avoir accès au français authentique du code oral et du code écrit?

Nous avons tous éprouvé la meme frustration lorsque nous avons essayé d'entrer en communication avec des étrangers, grâce au bagage linguistique accumulé et qui s'est avéré inadéquat, au bout de la deuxième réplique!

Une approche communicative, telle qu'elle vient d'être esquissée, implique un certain nombre de changements et d'adaptions de la part des enseignants et de la part des élèves.

Une réforme des programmes et des curricula parait necessaire, entraînant une nouvelle définition des objectifs et une réforme des examens de fin de scolarité. Le rôle de l'enseignant ne sera plus uniquement celui d'un transmetteur d'informations, d'un manipulateur d'appareils, d'un organisateur et un contrôleur uniques du travail, il sera surtout celui d'un facilitateur d'apprentissage.

L'enseigné deviendra un 'apprenant' prenant part active et décisive dans son apprentissage. Dans la salle de classe, on cherchera à instaurer un climat de confiance aussi non-répressif que possible, afin que les apprenants aient envie de s'exprimer sans que toute production fautive soit immédiatement sanctionnée. (On ne dira jamais assez les méfaits causés par l'hypertrophie de la correction magistrale.) On aura recours aussi souvent que possible aux méthodes actives, aux exercices de créativité, au jeu de rôles qui permettent aux apprenants de s'impliquer dans la tâche meme, dans le cadre artificiel de la salle de classe.

ON THE JUSTIFICATION OF CURRICULUM CONTENT: A CASE FOR MODERN LANGUAGES AND EUROPEAN STUDIES

D N Aspin

In asking for justification of particular curriculum decisions from someone, one is asking for grounds for adopting one alternative rather than another and the search for such features of a decision, that would constitute convincing and appropriate grounds for taking one course of action rather than another, presupposes that the reasons for taking it are not reducible to authoritarian pronouncement or arbitrary fiat. What is looked for in curriculum recommendations are objective, non-arbitrary principles which are public and general - that is to say, that what ought to be done in one situation by one person ought also to be done in any relevantly similar situation by anyone else - unless of course there are adequate and compelling counter-arguments which so act as to over-ride this general injunction. The idea of justification refers to the giving of reasons which are of a public character, in the sense that the grounds on which they may be accepted or rejected will, in principle, be such as can be understood and internalised by any sane and sensible person. The grounds are generalisable in the sense that if they are seen to be relevant to any decision of that sort upon a course of action, any sane and sensible person could in fact take that decision.

Of the forms of justificatory arguments those that are more commonly deployed are such as the vocational, the motivational, the formal, the utilitarian, the social, the moral or the aesthetic. For Modern Languages/European Studies these may be exemplified thus:

(1) Vocational — Modern Languages are a sine qua non for entry to some professions.

(2) Motivational — Modern Languages provide well for the needs and interests of the learner.

(3) Formal — Modern Languages give a sound training in qualities of mind (and possibly also of character).

(4) Utilitarian — Modern Languages are useful for the understanding of English grammar and vocabulary and are thus a major aid in the learning of other modern languages. It is also useful and necessary for travel and holidays, commerce and industry, especially now that we are part of the EEC.

(5) Social	Modern Languages give the pupil an awareness of the roots of his own culture and an awareness of current social and cultural ramifications, of development and context, all of which enrich his understanding of his place in the world.
(6) Moral-aesthetic	If the aim of education be correctly defined as to give a 'knowledge of all that is noble and beautiful done, thought or said in the world' then Modern Languages - and especially French - are pre-eminently suitable for this.

Now Modern Linguists already know that at least three of these arguments have been, if not straightforwardly controverted, called seriously into question. For example, the vocational argument is only contingently the case and is now becoming less and less operative: one can go anywhere in the world with just English these days. And this is true whether one is talking about tourism or trade: how often does one come across people abroad who are only too anxious to enter into dealings with us in our language. Of course, there may be other reasons why it may be desirable to be able to speak Spanish, French, German or Italian, but that is not at issue here. For as Harry Ree has recently remarked 'continental lorry drivers pick up quite a smattering of Dutch, German, French and Danish - out of school'. The formal argument for foreign language learning was exposed to the elenchus of the critics of 'transfer of training' arguments over fifty years ago and has ceased to be tenable on both conceptual and empirical grounds: even if it were true that there were general qualities of sagacity or competence, the claim that Modern Languages produces them better is open to empirical review. The utilitarian argument has ceased to be considered important, even if it were valid; it too is either an empirical claim or one deriving from historical grounds - a causal connection was hypothesized between success in the learning of English and modern languages only because of the accident that those who excelled in both simply happened to good at learning language in general. The same point holds true for the formal argument. Most recent attempts at giving a theoretically tight account of the place of Modern Languages in the curriculum have accordingly been framed on lines which took no support from those three claims.

I must not do the same, however, before indicating my awareness that there may be some who would assert that the demand for utilitarian proofs has not received adequate consideration or rebuttal. It is true that the modern Headmaster is more knowledgeable in the sorts of grounds upon which curriculum decisions are now based; many have been enlightened by the work of curriculum philosophers and developers and disvalue that sort of demand. They have an enlightened attitude to the whole range of arguments for curriculum choices, have a strong appreciation of the value of a number of clearly non-useful subjects, and are strongly sympathetic to claims for equality of treatment in the provision of staffing and timetable space - and sometimes, too, of financial provision. Nevertheless it is also the case that a contemporary Zeitgeist in the planning of educational curricula is the demand in certain quarters that subjects should be 'useful' or 'relevant'. It is entirely pertinent that we should endeavour to ascertain the precise .meaning of such terms - where they are not merely 'slogans', that is - but the appropriateness of such an undertaking in educational, as opposed to instructional or simply vocational, establishments may be seriously questioned.

Of course, the same question concerning utility may legitimately be raised against many other curriculum activities - poetry, for example, literature in general, history, certainly much of mathematics after the age of about twelve - dare we even say, sociology, too? So if Modern Languages/European Studies falls to that demand, so does almost all of the curriculum. That demand admits of two other criticisms, however; the first is the one of fashion: what is, or is regarded as, 'useful' at one time may not be so at another. I have no doubt that astrology and necromancy were once regarded as 'useful' or 'relevant', but they do not figure on the timetables of educational institutions now. The second criticism follows directly from this; it does not follow, either from the fact of certain fashions, or what is alleged to be a descriptive content of some subjects, that they ought to be taught in schools. There is a disjunction between facts and value here which vitiates demands for courses based on what are alleged to be criteria of utility, relevance or applicability. In terms of the planning of activities for the curriculum, at least two classes can be distinguished: one, of activities which are really worthwhile, the other, of activities which are only worthwhile insofar as they are instrumental to the securing of things which are really worthwhile. It is the difference between curriculum activities that can only be justified as being of intrinsic value and those whose function is instrumental to the acquisition of other goods extrinsic to them but intrinsically valuable in themselves.

Having engaged in such reflections as these, a teacher might think himself on safe ground, when engaging in serious discourse with someone who asks him 'What is the use of it'?, by arguing that such a question betrays a misunderstanding of the nature and purpose of, I should think, the majority of activities included on the curricula of educational institutions. He would, however, be perhaps in some difficulty with another idea which is commonly proposed as a sufficient criterion for the selection and justification of an activity for inclusion on the timetable of our schools or colleges - namely, that it should cater for the 'needs and interests' of the child or student.

I do not wish to spend much time on this particular form of alleged justificatory argument for it seems to me that whatever meaning this well-known formula once had has become lost sight of and possibly devalued in its adoption by people with a particular set of beliefs as to how the educational enterprise ought to be conducted and as to the emphasis that ought to be placed upon the place of the child in this process. Such a view is frequently representative of an ideological commitment of some sort and the 'formula' 'needs and interests of the child' serves as a ritualistic incantation in this particular doxology. The frequency of the use of this phrase, even when not associated with particular methodological prescriptions, has led to its emergence as a piece of educational jargon or as a simple slogan.

The analyses of 'need' and the 'needs curriculum' by Komisar and Dearden have demonstrated the ambiguity in the term: the 'deficiency', or 'psychological' meaning, and the 'evaluative' or prescriptive meaning. These senses are exemplified in statements of the form 'He needs sleep' (a description of a physiological condition) and 'He needs discipline' (a disguised recommendation).

I find Komisar's examination of these points leads to the persuasive conclusion that needs-policy turns out to be sometimes trivial, sometimes indeterminate, and sometimes unsupported, but always unimportant.

Similar strictures apply to the basic hypotheses of the 'interests' policy, which are outlined by Dearden as being such as these:

(a)   The curriculum should start from the child's interests.

(b)   Interest should then move 'onward and outward' from these points, working with the likes and not against the dislikes of the child.

(c)   Interest provides strong motivation for learning.

(d)   To start from the child's interests in this way is the only teaching method compatible with respect for the child.

I do not think I need to spend time on the questioning or the refutation of such contentions as these. It is sufficient merely to underline Dearden's doubts that such views as the above still leave unresolved the crucial question of 'Which new interests is the teacher to stimulate or selectively to encourage? Which basic skills are to be harnessed to existing interests?' And, perhaps most important, 'How far is one justified in identifying what children are interested in with what is in their interest?'

Such reflections as the foregoing are, I believe, sufficient to give the teacher pause before giving credence to any argument for the retention of his subject on the curriculum framed in terms so ambiguous and unclear. But I hope it will be thought that my treatment of them here does at least give an adequate account of the most frequently argued, or at least encountered, claims advanced by teachers of some subjects for their subject. And I take it that, in treating of these various forms of supposed justification, I have dealt with curriculum arguments which may be appropriately assigned to that logical category which may be referred to as 'the prudential' - arguments of an 'If-then' character. This still leaves moral and conceptual arguments to be considered.

Probably the best-known example of what we have called a 'conceptual' justification of curriculum activities is that advanced by R S Peters in relation to his concept of 'worthwhile activities' in Ethics and Education. This argument (though it is one in which no reference to Modern Languages appears) rests upon his own 'analysis' of what it means to be educated and proceeds via what he calls a 'Kantian-type' transcendental deduction of theoretical activities as the worthwhile ones. A similar form of this argument can be found in Hirst's account of liberal education and the nature of knowledge, in which it seems that Modern Languages has no place either.

It would be tedious to go through Peters' argument at length, especially so since it is widely familar now, and since anyway summaries of it may be found in the works of those who have attempted the task of criticising it. Dr Powell's is perhaps the clearest of these and might be cited:

'If 'education' is construed, as suggested by Peters, in terms of the initiation of young people into intrinsically valuable theoretical activities then there is a problem in deciding which activities are to be taught ... (Peters argues that) if someone is wondering how best to spend his time and searches for reasons for engaging in one activity rather than another then he is clearly allowing that there are features of activities which make for worthwhileness, and that these hold a strong attraction for him. Among such features would probably be the capacity of the activity to hold his attention for a considerable span of time, the challenging opportunities which it offers for the exercise of skill and resourcefulness, and the exacting nature of the standards of performance which are appropriate to it.

Any one, therefore, who is thinking seriously about how to spend his time cannot but go for activities which afford rich opportunities for employing his wits, resources and sensibilities in situations in which there is a premium on unpredictability and opportunities for skill - and a sense of the fitting.

But an immense number of activities could well satisfy these requirements and could thus be open to anyone who was wondering how best to spend his time, so there must be further considerations which justify the special place accorded to theoretical curriculum activities in educational institutions ... Peters ... concludes that the most important ... concerns the extent to which an activity is bound up with the pursuit of truth and understanding ... It is this connection with truth and the importance which is attached to it which marks off educational curriculum activities from a host of others which, although they may be worthwhile, lack the capacity to illuminate human experience and extend knowledge. Anyone who asks 'Why do this rather than that?' is therefore bound to be led into an exploration of this special class of theoretical activities since it is only through them that he will be able to find the answer to his question. Furthermore, the very posing of the question pre-supposes a measure of commitment to the central feature of all such activities, namely, the pursuit of truth. It is here that the transcendental deduction really gets a grip for if someone questions the pre-eminent worthwhileness of scholarship he must already possess to some degree the deep concern for truth which characterises all scholarly activity. So by seriously questioning the value of scholarship, he reveals a commitment to what is supposedly in doubt since '... he must already have a serious concern for truth built into his consciousness'. The justification of the pursuit of knowledge is thus presupposed by any serious attempt to question it.'

According to the argument, the 'serious' theoretical activities, whose pre-eminent claim for inclusion in the curriculum rests, for Peters, on this transcendental argument, possess the following features: they are essentially

(1)   cognitive - they have 'wide-ranging cognitive perspective'

(2)   transformative - in that they (a) contribute to the quality of living; and (b) explain, assess and illuminate the different facets of life; and thereby transform how the person committed to them sees things

(3)   they are incapable of being hived off or confined to limited times, places, moods or physical states or conditions, or being the objects of jealousy, envy or competition.

The argument is highly technical and sophisticated, and, as Peters' critics have found, extremely difficult to rebut. But when Peters proceeds to predicate worthwhile activities in terms of the various 'distinctive forms of knowledge, such as science, history, mathematics, religious and aesthetic appreciation, etc' and tells us that to have a mind 'is to have an awareness differentiated in accordance with the canons implicit in all these inherited traditions' we may perhaps hesitate. For to equate these 'traditions' with 'worthwhile activities' is again to stipulate. He has not, I believe, justified their worthwhileness, nor has he shown that, as activities, these are more worthwhile than other activities. He states that the task of the teacher is to try to get others on the inside of a public form of life that he shares and considers worthwhile'. While we may agree with this in formal terms, the particular content which Peters proceeds to pack into this 'form of life' is shot through with value considerations of one sort or another. He has not informed us by what criteria these activities are objectively worthwhile, though he has previously argued that critical procedures (of assessment and justification, one presumes) contain public criteria which act as impersonal standards. To this extent, we may conclude, Peters is not obeying his own rules in relation to objective standards, when engaged in theorising of his own.

I do not wish to labour the point; the case for the idea of education as being concerned with the transmission of worthwhile activities in general is certainly made out; but Peters' case for only a <u>certain set</u> of <u>activities</u> is in need of support. His use of rationality as a plea for rational activities is unsatisfactory because it involves us in circularity. Our criteria of judgment must be, not only impersonal and objective, but also logically valid. We may therefore ask is there any other way in which we can attempt the difficult task of laying a defensible base for compelling pupils to study subjects other than those to which they are personally attracted? - among them such subjects as Modern Languages and/or European Studies. Some have argued for this on the basis of the slogan 'education for democracy' or 'education for citizenship'. I shall try to see how far we can get with the idea that 'being educated is to learn to become a person'. For it is on this basis that I believe we may attempt a derivation of some activities which are worthwhile for everyone.

The word 'worthwhile' is clearly part of one of these forms of talk and I take to refer to pursuits and activities that are held to be of value either in themselves or for some external end. They are worth spending time on. By itself the word 'worthwhile' tells us little. Sitting in a locked room all day is only of value insofar as one wishes to remain totally undisturbed or to avoid someone. Thus to pin down 'worthwhile for everyone' we need to refer to the idea of the importance of the institutional contexts within which such discussion and discussion-making has to take place, relate it to the creatures whose life is constituted of such frameworks, and give a formulation of moral justification which depends upon that truth. That will enable us to deduce some activities that are as a matter of fact worthwhile for everyone.

The feature which makes human beings categorically distinct from other creatures is straightforwardly their possession of rationality and this is inextricably connected with their possession of the ability to articulate that capacity in precise and sophisticated forms of communication with members of the same species (though of course there may be other less central distinguishing characteristics). So human being in physical form and human being-become-person is discernible in these important respects: language and rationality. This point was well expressed by Julian Huxley in <u>The Uniqueness of Man</u>. He wrote:

'The first and most obviously unique characteristic of man is his capacity for conceptual thought; if you prefer objective terms, you will say his employment of true speech ... True speech involves the use of verbal signs for objects, not merely for feelings. Plenty of animals can express the fact that they are hungry; but none except man can ask for an egg or a banana. And to have words for objects at once implies conceptual thought, since an object is always one of a class. No doubt, children and savages are as unaware of using conceptual thought as M Jourdain was unaware of speaking prose; but they cannot avoid it. Words are tools which automatically carve concepts out of experience. The faculty of recognising objects as members of a class provides the potential basis for the concept: the use of words at once actualises the potentiality.'

Thus language and conceptual thought, inextricably inter-connected, are not only propria of human being status: they are its prime determining and defining characteristics. Potential persons therefore have an interest in coming to have language and rationality: without the possession of these what Strawson called their 'P'-potentialities remain unrealised.

On this secure and indisputable ground we may claim that human beings have an interest in maintaining and developing their ability to communicate in language in its developed forms, for otherwise they cease to be, at least in major part, persons; without language and rationality their world as human beings would be that much more the less if, indeed, it were tolerable at all. Thus, there is clearly better reason for pursuing activities which maintain and develop the status of being human than not doing so.

By itself, however, to say that persons are distinguished from other categories of organic and inorganic entity by their possession of, inter alia, language and rationality, and that therefore to be educated is to be brought into that form of life which is constituted of and characterised by the various forms of these and to get progressively better at them, is not to say very much. There has to be a purchase point for the notions of language and rationality: we cannot speak of them in vacuo but can only properly refer to them as linguistic expression of something, certain forms of rationality which are predicable in terms of certain sets of characteristics. It is uninformative to speak of 'language and rationality' as though they were some sort of general facility or capacity; such a locution is quite vacuous. The notions of 'language and rationality' only get a purchase when we speak of them in terms of their various particularised exemplifications: the language of the arts, the language of dance, the languages of science, mathematics and the rest, and their associated nets of rationalities. And this sort of distinction does, of course, rest upon the possession of 'language' - one's mother tongue.

Of course it is easy enough to speak of certain sorts of language or rationality; that will most probably be conceded readily enough. What is more difficult and controversial is to decide upon the criteria by which we can differentiate one sort of language/rationality from another. There is considerable difference of opinion amongst thinkers on this matter; particularisations in respect of certain formal features of cognitive operation, or in respect of something so basic as characteristic content are merely two of the distinctive criteria that have been suggested. So P H Hirst, for example, distinguishes between a number of irreducible modes of knowledge and experience on the basis of their use

58

of concepts of a sui generis nature and their distinctive types of test for their objective claims; J J Schwab agrees that distinctions can be made between areas of knowledge and experience but suggests that they will rest on such criteria as their different bodies of content, the statements of which have a radically different syntax, the skills of their practitioners, and the sort of outcomes at which they aim.

The general, fundamental argument of all this is, however, the same: human cognitive activity and perceptual experience is radically discrete and only discernible in terms of its different constitutive forms and focuses, the different modes of expression and public discourse in which human language and rational thought is conceived and articulated. The different ways there are of looking at things are the forms and focuses of language and rationality and they constitute the whole of human thought and reality. It follows that one only becomes a person insofar as one develops the ability to engage in and operate according to the criteria of the various sorts of languages and rationalities that there are.

W D Hudson summarised this thesis well:

> 'The life of a human being, as such, ... consists, not only in possessing a certain physical constitution, but in participating, within human society, in a number of universes of discourse or 'forms of life', as Wittgenstein might have called them. For example, moral and aesthetic judgments ... Ability to participate in such universes of discourse, at least to some minimal extent, is part of what it means to be a human being. Someone who did not at all understand what moral obligation is, or who had no conception whatever of what beauty is would surely, to that extent, be sub-human. If, then, participation in these universes of discourse is part of what it means to be a human being, (then), insofar as 'education' means learning to be a human being, it logically implies initiation into these universes of discourse.'

The question of how one is going to acquire all this cognitive expertise and the ability to communicate in all these distinct symbolic codes is an empirical and methodological one which different practitioners may prefer to solve for themselves. Clearly mathematics is different from science, from literature, from religion; and it may well be that their appropriate methods and concepts which are characteristic and constitutive of them will call for different teaching techniques. That some disciplined forms of thinking - some 'languages' are distinct and differentiable is widely agreed; but it is also held that there are, as well, certain 'subjects', 'fields' or 'domains' that do not appear to admit of being defined in a 'single discipline' way: Geography, Engineering, Politics and Economics. These are subject 'areas', or 'domains' that give their students an insight into and require them to be able to operate according to the criteria of that set of distinct disciplines which makes them the universes of discourse that they are. It is the claim of this paper that Modern Languages and European Studies constitutes just such a 'domain'.

Let me try to summarise this in another way. When we talk about the notion of 'education' we are looking for ways in which we can give our young an introduction into the values and typical modi operandi of, let us say, the analytical, the empirical, the moral, the aesthetic, the religious, the philosophical, the interpersonal modes of discourse, cognition and enquiry. But that is only one aspect of their cognitive life; for there are certain domains of cognitive concern which are of central importance in a person's life, both public and private: one thinks of such areas as the Law, Business, Politics and Economics, and all those areas in which matters of crucial practical import and consuming theoretical interest to the individual and society arise - all those things that have to do with preparation for life as a citizen in a democracy and the wider world; and for gaining of access to sources of personal richness and satisfaction. In this connection Art Education is as important as Physical Education, as Medicine, as Moral Education. And in this general class of what we might describe as Human Studies - subjects vital to our lives as members of our community, as individuals with opportunities for great personal and public enrichment - I consider that for us European Studies should be placed.

Why do I therefore insist on the presence of what I call European Studies in the curricula of educational institutions of our culture and society? It is because, not only do European Studies qualify for inclusion under the heading of those subjects which are both instrumentally valuable and also worth doing for their own sake and the satisfactions that are inherent in them; not only do European Studies, as a domain of cognitive concern, exemplify a number of the diverse forms of thought and awarenss that can be distinguished in human thinking - the aesthetic, the moral, the religious, the philosophical, the interpersonal, for example - and indeed may be said to exemplify them pre-eminently or even paradigmatically. Those considerations are, to my mind, powerful and persuasive; but my argument is also that the subjects of study in this domain actually, in many instances, lie at the very root of those differentiations and of the different ways of thinking within the sui generis forms; they may also, in one or two cases - perhaps the aesthetic and the philosophical - be said to be still constitutive of them. One thinks of the importance of drama, literature and poetry; of 'belles lettres' and historical writing as being of the very stuff of 'literature and the arts'; while the philosophical problems tackled by Descartes, Kant, Rousseau and Hegel still figure prominently in philosophical discussions today. Further: what of different European concepts of God? Of Law? Of moral or political theory? All of these are not only germane to our English thinking in those fields of interest in instrumental terms; they actually lie at their very root and are presupposed by all further attempts at sophistication in them. For this reason, it is argued, the curricula of our educational institutions must in some measure make the attempt to bring the growing person into contact with the values, attitudes, beliefs, concepts and skills that are found in European Cultures and Societies, for they are so much a part of our own that they form a fundamental part of his human heritage.

This move enables us to anticipate and provide an answer to the question 'What use is Modern Languages/European Studies?' On my analysis I argue that, for one thing, Modern Languages/European Studies is just as much a subject worthy of study in its own right and for the joy of the enrichments that are internal to it as any other form of cognitive activity, whether mathematics (which is generally held to be highly instrumental in character but is in fact not) or technology; though to appreciate what those enrichments are one must first have them pointed out to one and must then attempt to engage in them, from the inside, in order to determine if the sorts of satisfactions which are inherent in the subject are such as one might oneself select as part of one's life options.

My point here is the further one, however, that Modern Languages/ European Studies is also worth studying because of the context in which it comes to us - as part, not only of the foundations, but also of the very fabric of many of our modes of thought and expression, of many of our modern institutions, and of those activities by which the individual may seek to expand his horizons and enrich his life. I want to emphasise the crucial and central role of European models and modes of thought and understanding as part of our civilisation and culture. On that basis we have to stress the distinctive nature of the contributions made to our lives by our neighbours across the Channel and point to our fundamental and ineradicable rootedness in and relationship with European values, institutions, thought and language. On these grounds we may judge these studies more worthwhile and justifiable as elements in educational curricula than, say, the study of Chinese, Egyptian or Persian civilisations. For these cultures are underpinned by concepts and schemes of a different kind, from a different time. They involve radically different 'forms of life'. It is for the reason that our form of life is constituted, in very large measure, of elements that are basically European that I seek to justify their inclusion in the curricula of the educational institutions promoting and initiating our young into that form of life.

My conclusion then is based on the idea of education as the progressive development of 'persons' - their engagement in and necessary commitment to a particular form of life, their ability to do so being a function of their competence at operating within the various 'universes of discourse' that characterise and indeed actually constitute it. I do not wish this to sound in any way mystical - though there are some who would describe the Wittgensteinian metaphysic on which it is based as poetic. These languages of ours are quite the ne plus ultra of our being: language and rationality are the constituent parts and public manifestations of our personae, and, in the final analysis, that they are our reality and the only reality, is my case. What distinguishes us, as human beings, from all other forms of organic existence is that we have these symbol systems, these codes of communication that are quite distinct and make us quite distinct - our languages. All we have in which to make sense of our place in the world are our human linguistic capacities. And it is only in terms of these that we have constructed the world, under all the various sorts of description that we have gradually worked out to give expression to our appraisals of it.

'Education' therefore comes down to trying to get people-persons still developing - on to the inside of as many modes of discourse - as many forms of language as there are. In terms of our schools' endeavours, that means that we must attempt to chart and 'map the geography' of all the domains of discourse that there are in the endeavour to help our young actually to enter into a wider world for themselves. My point is, of course, an evaluative one to do with (at bottom) the value I place upon the ideas of 'width', 'diversity' and inter-personal and inter-cultural understanding. For many people, operating within a severely restricted number of forms of inter-personal communication, the universe is that much smaller than that of people who have access to and can operate within the wider range of a greater number of forms of talk. There is no moral evaluation of 'better' or 'worse' people here; I seek only to make a logical point about their wider or narrower universes. But that it is a value judgment that it is better to have a wider universe and to have access to great ranges and sources of inter-personal and cultural understanding I am perfectly ready to concede. For having ability in a wider range of universes of a discourse means, in a sense, being more of a person. As the proverb has it 'So viele Sprachen Sprichst Du, So häufig lebst Du'.

The point is that one can only get on the inside of all these various forms of discourse and modes of thought and communication by actually engaging in them - for they are skills, at rock bottom. So this means not just having the propositions and criteria of the various languages and forms of perception and understanding paraded before one, to be learned off parrot-fashion; it also means actually 'getting one's coat off' as it were and taking part in them, learning the procedures typical of them, struggling to grasp the concepts and skills basic to them and trying to achieve mastery with these so as to reach standards of acceptability and excellence in one's operation of comprehension and communication skills within it.

To be a person in our day and age one has to get on the inside of and be able to operate with an increasing number of worlds of talk; and sometimes, if, for example, one changes countries or political (ideological) environments, one has to learn to become, in a decided sense, a different person. But it is my argument that to learn to become a person in our culture, with all its characteristic modi vivendi and cogitandi, is to have to become acquainted with and to come to make one's own all those forms, tradition and institutions that help to define it. These are the stuff of our civilised, European form of life and will thus require us to study in our educational institutions those subjects of study which we set down as coming under the heading of Modern Languages/European Studies.

The justifications of Modern Languages therefore are primarily twofold: intrinsic and extrinsic. So far as the former is concerned, one of the chief reasons for doing the subject will be an argument of an 'Everest' character: it is good to do it because it is there. This means that there will be an allure and fascination about the subject and the way in which it is presented that will itself generate a reason for doing it; the satisfaction of struggling to achieve mastery of the various skills, concepts and truths involved will be worthwhile doing for their own sake. In this sense the intrinsic value of doing the subject will have the same sort of status as that which Plato assigned to the top of his scale of values in the Phaedo: the value of doing a subject will be the 'underived first principle' that functions in the way that Aristotle stated his First Principle moved - by the attractions internal to it. There will also be, however, satisfactions of an extrinsic kind and these relate to the moral values to be attached to the ideas of inter-personal communication and inter-cultural understanding. The whole point and purpose of the enterprise thus will lie outside itself and in asking seriously the question 'Why should we study Modern Languages/European Studies?' we should be seriously asking for guidance and want to know what we ought to do in terms of seeking a moral criterion upon which to base the whole of our educational endeavours. Such a criterion resides in the idea of inter-personal discourse and inter-cultural harmony than which, in my view, no higher moral value can be found. To put it in a nutshell, the aim and function of Modern Languages is to promote cultural harmony and to inhibit racial discord. Its purpose is thus profoundly moral.

There is a sting in the tail of this argument however. Given that we subscribe to these moral norms and are concerned to do all we can to promote them, it still remains an open question as to whether we need actually to engage in the speaking of a foreign language in order fully to implement these ends. There are massive differences of opinion over just this issue.

On the other hand, there are those who believe that it is possible to promote inter-personal communication and inter-cultural understanding without necessarily having to speak other people's languages at all. J P White is one of those who assigns the study of Modern Languages to his Category 2 activities - those activities in respect of which understanding is possible without necessarily engaging in them. On this thesis it is possible to understand what it is to communicate in French, German or Spanish without necessarily having to speak any of these languages at all. There are also those who would argue that, since it is possible to struggle with the sophistications of understanding Kant in an English translation there is no need to bother to learn the German. Other people again argue that, since English is the lingua franca of the world today it is possible to go for these entirely morally laudable ends without having to exert oneself outside ones own linguistic community.

There are, on the other hand, those who would attach the greatest significance and importance to the deep meaning of the Wittgensteinia aphorism: 'Die Grenzen meiner Sprache bedeuten die Grenzen meiner Welt'. They would maintain that it is not possible fully to enter into the heritage of any linguistic community and to gain full value and meaningfulness from engaging in discourse with members of it except in terms of their own language. The untranslatability of such concepts as: in English, 'fairness' and 'xenophobia'; in French, 'panache' and 'savoir faire'; and in German 'Gestalt' and 'Weltanschauung' is eloquent testimony to the truth of the fact that concepts and beliefs that serve to define a particular linguistic 'form of life' cannot be carried across cultures. It is impossible, so such people would argue, fully to capture the particular 'flavour' that links one up to the whole complicated pattern of values, attitudes and beliefs that lie at the root of any particular form of modern European civilisation, without actually having to enter it linguistically oneself.

It is at this point that scholars divide and there is clearly a great deal of work to be done, not only on the important issue of whether complete inter-cultural understanding is ever possible without learning someone else's language, but also as to whether there are or not any absolute criteria of truth, meaningfulness and objectivity that underpin and are pre-supposed by linguistic communication in any 'form of life'. There are those who argue that principles such as those of Identity and Non-contradiction are inherent in every language system we know of; there are also those who argue that there are linguistic cultures the rationality of which we cannot ever in principle begin even to conceive of. The solution of these and their related problems clearly merits and requires separate and extended treatment.

But as a prelude to that we may note what seems to me to be an absolutely clinching argument for the place of European studies and Modern Languages as an indispensable element in the curricula of our community's educating institutions: the value of inter-personal understanding and inter-cultural harmony is not only pre-supposed but also preferred as a prime moral principle by the emphasis placed upon it by the continuing influence of such bodies as NATO and the EEC, not only as a means of perpetuating our European values, beliefs and attitudes at all but also as a means of enhancing and enriching the cultural tradition in which the various members of those communities all so signally share.

SECTION II: LANGUAGE POLICIES IN SCHOOLS

Report of Working Party B

A study of language policies in schools with special reference to co-operations between teachers of foreign languages and teachers of English.

REPORT OF A WORKING PARTY COMPRISING:

D W H Sharp (University College of Swansea), Chairman
B C King (Somerset Education Authority)
Hilary Minns (Clifford Bridge Primary School, Coventry),
    Corresponding member
Dr W H Mittins (formerly of the University of Newcastle upon Tyne)
G E Perren (formerly of the Centre for Information on Language
    Teaching and Research)
A J Tinkel (Southlands School, Reading)
Helen N Lunt (Centre for Information on Language Teaching and
    Research), Secretary

1.   The members of the Working Party each took an area for study in depth and prepared a paper giving the results of that study.

2.   A review of the relationship between teachers of English and teachers of modern languages during the last seventy to eighty years traces the divergent parts in this century of teachers of foreign languages and teachers of English (G E Perren, pages 69-78).

3.   An attempt to establish theoretical bases common to both the teaching of English mother tongue and foreign languages proved to be the most difficult aspect. It was not possible to discern any such common bases in the present state of knowledge. The topic deserves and needs further extensive and intensive work. What we do present is an examination of the concept of a school language policy, taking English as the language in question (Dr W H Mittins, pages 79-90).

4.   In contrast to the rather bleak picture of divergence up to now is an investigation of the differences and similarities between foreign language teaching and mother tongue teaching, which identifies possible points of contact between the two groups of teachers, as well as outlining the areas considered to be non-productive (B C King, pages 91-105).

5.   A controversial area, but one which might both link and support mother tongue teaching and foreign language teaching, is the study of language as such; its relationship with the learning of languages was examined, with suggestions and detailed, practical proposals (A J Tinkel, pages 106-120).

6.   Samples of language policies in schools have been collected and examined, a task which revealed a comparative lack of activity following the Bullock Report recommendation in 1975 that every school should formulate and implement a language policy across the curriculum - nevertheless important features emerged, as did some of the benefits to be gained from language policies (Derrick Sharp, pages 125-138).

CONCLUSIONS

There are obvious problems of agreed definitions and their interpretation, especially of the term 'language policy' - which has acquired widely differing meaning among the professional public, whose views are necessarily reflected in the evidence assembled. The Working Party concentrated on 'language policy' in the Bullock Report sense, which is essentially a policy for the use of the mother tongue (in this case English) as the medium of learning and teaching in all areas of the curriculum. It was aware of other aspects, such as which foreign languages should be included in the curriculum at which stages, but was not able to cover all possibilities.

Some would no doubt prefer to work from initially clear and exact definitions of terms and curriculum areas, while others believe that by starting from vague and generalised notions, they will, by discussion, achieve increasing precision directly related to practical problems. (There are also those undoubtedly, who reject the whole concept of a policy for language across the curriculum and others who think that schools have more important matters to deal with!)

The Working Party was very much aware of the complexity and range of the subject, which affects the whole curriculum beyond the boundaries of any subject specialisms. It believes that certain entrenched positions taken by some teachers should be abandoned. Teachers of English and teachers of foreign languages do not, at present, often seek or offer each other co-operation. We believe that they can and will agree on a common approach to language work of all kinds in schools when they fully perceive its relevance and value to their own subjects. (It should perhaps be noted that while this relevance becomes most obvious in schools containing a high proportion of non-native speakers of English, for reasons of time the Working Party decided not to undertake a special study of such situations.)

Inevitably the Working Party wishes to make recommendations for further investigation, putting forward at the same time a number of specific questions which have arisen from its work and which deserve debate:

RECOMMENDATIONS

(1) Teachers of English and teachers of foreign languages need to clarify and co-ordinate their views about the nature of language and about children's acquisition and development of language skills.

(2) At present pupils receive conflicting and confusing messages about the nature, function and use of language from teachers of English and teachers of foreign languages. To avoid this, specific areas of school work where co-operation and co-ordination betwee the two is necessary should be agreed and defined.

(3) Old-established differences, often arising from historic subject allegiances, exist between the two groups of teachers. In encouraging co-operation, these should be understood rather than ignored.

(4) While Working Party members arrived at no agreed view about the value of 'language' as a separate curriculum study they consider that carefully monitored experiments in its teaching would be justified.

SPECIFICALLY DETAILED QUESTIONS FOR FURTHER DISCUSSION BEFORE AND AT THE SECOND ASSEMBLY

(1) What does a language policy provide which is not equally well given by a curriculum policy or by the work of a sensitive teacher?

(2) Is language study a necessary (or desirable) link between English and foreign languages?

(3) Should foreign languages and English (mother tongue) be taught by the same teachers, at least in the lower secondary stages?

(4) What aspects of language study/linguistics have relevance to the educational process? How do they, and how should they, figure in the initial and in-service training of teachers of foreign languages and of English?

(5) Does a language policy necessarily involve the whole staff of a school or a majority of them?

(6) Are there areas of the curriculum to which language across the curriculum does not, or should not, apply? Is modern languages such an area?

(7)   Where does language policy come on a list of priorities? Is a school department justified in deciding that it has enough internal organisation and development to do, and therefore cannot consider the wider issues of language across the curriculum? Is language policy so fundamental that it should be determined before, for example, interdisciplinary curriculum schemes, given that resources of time and energy are always limited?

(8)   What are the practical measures needed to improve co-operation in language policy work, (a) within a school and between schools, and (b) specifically between teachers of foreign languages and teachers of English?

THE RELATIONSHIP BETWEEN TEACHERS OF ENGLISH AND TEACHERS OF MODERN LANGUAGES DURING THE LAST SEVENTY TO EIGHTY YEARS

G E Perren

Originally it was hoped to attempt a review of 'the literature of the subject' (ie language policies) on historical lines, which might cover the last hundred years and thus provide a helpful background to the discussion of more recent views. For education in England, like many other social activities, is intensely traditional - as much as ever today. Although the country is now seeking a new and acceptable national image, what Lionel Elvin once called the 'mature snobocracy' of English education retains deep roots and old prejudices are slow to die and quick to revive.

However, a preliminary search of likely sources soon revealed that there is no literature of the subject - unless one makes very arbitrary extensions of the meaning of 'language policy', and takes a very tolerant view of what constitutes co-operation.

It has been assumed that 'language policy' is a convenient short form for the Bullock Report's 'policy for languages across the curriculum', as explained, not very precisely, in its chapter 12 in relation to secondary schools. But as those six pages make no mention whatever of foreign languages, co-operation between teachers of English and teachers of foreign languages is presumably neither envisaged nor deemed relevant. So what is meant by language policy in this paper is something wider than that adumbrated by Bullock. In passing, it is worth noting that the earlier (and perhaps more influential) Newbolt report of 1921 was less exclusive in its treatment of what it called 'the true relation of English to other studies' (1). It is true that Newbolt's references to the relationship between English and other languages concentrated on the need for a common grammatical terminology and on the value of translation as an aid to English composition. But it should be remembered that in 1921 both grammar and accurate expression were very highly rated. To appreciate the implications today we should probably have to substitute phrases such as 'linguistic insight' or 'cross-cultural understanding' for grammar and translation. A collection of tentative studies concerning possible relations between English and foreign languages has quite recently been published (2), but this does not reveal many examples of co-operation and merely suggests rational bases for it - without a great deal of conviction.

General educational writers in the past did not often concern themselves with the interrelationships between 'subjects', normally regarding each as self-sufficient, nor, until Newbolt, did they discuss the extension of teaching English skills 'across the curriculum' or through other subjects in secondary education. Perhaps the problem did not arise when secondary education was limited or highly selective. But in elementary or primary schools it has been more readily accepted that all subjects or activities should and could contribute to the improvement of reading, writing and speaking English. Thus the Newbolt Report stated 'every teacher is a teacher of English, because every teacher is a teacher in English' with a brevity and clarity hardly equalled by Bullock (3).

From the mid-nineteenth century onwards certain assumptions about the role of English, the place of foreign languages and the linguistic virtues of the classics in schools, were made by the universities, accepted by the training colleges, and ultimately received by the public. One must remember that the influence of university opinion was exercised not only through teachers, but through administrators and politicians, most of whom were products of the public schools and Oxford or Cambridge. It is worth looking at these views, certainly not as favourable auspices for language policies or for co-operation, but as factors which have militated against co-ordination and which have often inhibited collaboration between teachers. Tradition persists: past attitudes (often re-styled as values) even now incongruously co-exist with those generated by recent social changes. For examples one has only to look at the painful marriages of old grammar schools with newer modern schools and the curricular problems which result. Particularly the rationale of teaching modern languages often shows an unresolved conflict between older cultural and newer vocational aims. No doubt in some schools there has always been effective integration of all language teaching, including foreign languages, across the curriculum simply because there have always been strong-minded heads who have insisted that their assistant staff work as a team beyond the boundaries of their specialisms. But this has been less the result of conscious theory than of pragmatic intuition. On the whole, unless directed, subject teachers have gone their own ways.

Until quite recently, doctrine about what should be taught in secondary schools, and why, has been dominated by the views of the mandarins of the senior common rooms, who seldom admitted to their innermost conclaves such upstarts as professors of education. For long, professed 'educationalists' were deemed to be only superior masters of method, concerned wholly with the 'how' of teaching and with the development of techniques unfortunately necessary for the uneducated to teach the unwashed - or for females to instruct the young. Education was certainly not accepted as an academic discipline or even regarded as a respectable scholarly study unless disguised as history. Such donnish elitism was most obvious at Oxford and Cambridge, but it had its supporters in the nascent provincial universities. In the later nineteenth century and after, HMI were supposed to bridge this gap betwee the university etablishment and the trained non-graduate teacher. But by class and education the sympathies of Inspectors lay with the high culture of the older universities, and at best their role was not unlike that of missionaries to darkest Africa. Indeed it was noted of the

Department of Education around 1890-1900 that:

> 'its staff of distinguished and aristocratic scholars from the universities treated elementary education and elementary teachers with contempt. Their cherished creed was that no education mattered or was of any real value except Classics and Mathematics....'(4)

No doubt graduate teachers might be admitted to a place above the salt, but unless they taught in the 'great' public schools, only as poor relations. When trained graduates began to appear in the 1920s and 1930s they were regarded as potentially most useful in elementary rather than secondary schools. (5)

WHAT IS A LANGUAGE POLICY?

Modern reports on education often seem to strain anxiously to produce catch-phrases and slogans for popular currency, and for use by such bodies as the Schools Council which need a kind of programmatic shorthand. So 'a policy for language across the curriculum' (not, be it noted, a term invented by the Bullock Committee - its use since 1969 was acknowledged) has been offered as a nostrum to regenerate English teaching, it being assumed that everyone understood what was meant by both language and policy. The use of 'language' deserves examination. In educational parlance it has come to mean exclusively English used as the language of intruction. (Only very recently in England has it been realised, much less recognised, that this may not be the pupil's mother tongue.) Rather like the use of 'religion' to mean exclusively Christianity, 'language' has been assumed to mean only English even where other languages are taught. Bullock maintained this chauvinism to the annoyance of some foreign language teachers (6). Such semantic sleight of hand or imprecision would, a hundred or even fifty years ago, have brough down the thunders of the classicists and the contempt of scholars. Today even the linguists hardly murmur at all.

But whatever we call it now, English in schools began with the need to establish literacy - the skills of reading and writing - on which all subsequent learning had to rest. When 'English' first achieved a place in the elementary school timetable, before secondary education became a public charge, it inherited this prime responsibility.

To nineteenth-century educationalists the classics may have seemd the only acceptable exponents of formal linguistic values, whether these resided in the logical concepts of grammar or in the cultural content of literature; but at less exalted educational levels the other great linguistic and cultural reservoir was the English Bible. The first and main purpose of teaching reading to the majority was to provide access to this. Long before it ever got on to the timetable as a separate subject, English literature had enjoyed a head start for centuries under the guise of scripture or divinity. 'Sufficient literacy to read the Bible' was no small aim, even with the ultimate sanctions of salvation and hell-fire to assist.

The idea of English as central to cultural and social education grew apace with the development of state education. English became the repository of values - many already obsolete - which had been assumed to rest in the classics and divinity by the endowed and public schools of the nineteenth century. Matthew Arnold praised the teaching of English grammar because it provided a useful mental discipline and even went so far as to favour it as an examination subject because (to him) its subject matter was exact and could be stated as a law rather than a theorem (7). The wider claims of English to educate, far beyond functional literacy, owe much to Arnold, Newbolt, Sampson, and latterly to Newsom and other reports up to Bullock. They originated in elementary schools and have spread into universal secondary education. They were reinforced by the demise of Latin as a principal 'cultural' subject at the very time when nineteenth-century public school standards were being used as a model for new twentieth-century maintained schools. The change in terminology from 'English' to 'language' has coincided with the extension of cultural, moral and social claims for the process assumed to be covered by its teaching.

As personal religion has been replaced by the less demanding social conscience which exhorts us to worry more about other people's morals than our own, the ancient holy alliance between literacy and divinity (or scripture) has given way to more fashionable and less formal relationships. Now that sociology rather than sin explains our problems, English has moved with the times and made new liaisons.

One must also beware of the use of 'policy' in the phrase under discussion. In chapter 12, Bullock does not dare to suggest that it might refer to a written plan, although the report does later admit that a 'cumulative and slowly changing document' might be acceptable as an 'instrument of policy' for the English department in schools (para 15.30). But among these cloudy and extended phrases no clear meaning of 'policy' can be discerned. One may perhaps recall that the NED records 'the chief living sense' of the word policy as 'any course of action adopted as advantageous or expedient'. But expedient for what? - one might ask. Again Newbolt was much more explicit:

'The undue isolation of English has often made the teaching, not only of English but of other subjects, ineffective. It is impossible to teach any subject without teaching English; it is almost equally impossible to teach English without teaching something else.... We wish to see English constantly overflowing its own compartment, and penetrating into all the rest.' (8)

No catch-phrases, no 'policy' and no equivocal use of 'language' here, but straightforward curricular imperialism. But as it overflowed, doubtless English became somewhat diluted.

THE PLACE OF MODERN LANGUAGES

By contrast with English the growth of modern language teaching and of its claims has been far more controlled and limited. Foreign languages could hardly overflow or penetrate other subjects unless they were to be used as media of instruction. (True, we have a few <u>sections bilingues</u> today, but they are very rare.) In terms of curricular aims their role has never been without dispute. Initially, in the nineteenth century, a modern language could well be regarded as an inferior substitute for the linguistic discipline imputed to the classics, particularly through the teaching of grammar; as a cultural surrogate, through literature; ˉs an adjunct to the development of style, through translation or, for those who would seek a 'place' in commerce, it might confer a possible vocational advantage. These various aims had a kind of social grading. Learning to speak a foreign language at school was not rated very highly; learning to read it was better. Reading French certainly offered insights into elegancy of expression, and reading German could be a key to profundity of thought no less than to a great deal of useful information of a more material kind. One of the difficulties, of course, was that the speaking skills had to be taught by foreigners (necessarily inferior beings) while the rest might be easily within the compass of British classics graduates. Not for the only time in England was the status of the subject or skill determined by the status of its teachers. It is therefore interesting to note at length the views published in 1920 by Atkins and Hutton (9). (It will be remembered that these were contemporary with the first great report on modern languages (10), as well as with Newbolt.)

After deploring the fact that modern languages were still regarded as poor relations of the classics, the authors noted that their status was lower when foreigners were employed to teach them.

> 'The first and essential step towards a reform of this state of affairs is to place the work in the hands of Englishmen of the right type, and everything else, system, method and prestige is bound to follow.'

But, they thought, the teacher of French must be able to deal with the history and geography of France and with the parallel growth of two languages, English and French. Furthermore he must also understand the aims and content of the study of English: literature and language, grammar and composition. Finally:

> 'I have insisted on the unity of the timetable as a whole, and I must insist still more strongly on the unity of the linguistic group of studies as a whole. If the group contains one or more modern languages, one or more ancient languages, even if it contains one or more representatives of both, we must still assign to the mother tongue a greater importance in any scheme of national education.... The foreign language teacher cannot say to himself 'this is no concern of mine'. Such an attitude is the pride of the narrow

specialist in his ignorance of other specialist studies and activities. He is a language teacher before he is a foreign-language teacher: he is an Englishman before he is a teacher.'

One must make allowances for emotions generated by the 1914-18 war, and perhaps for the emphasis on French, but the case of the unity of language teaching had rarely been put with such conviction. Much more common were endless negotiations - and reservations - about who should teach the terminology of grammar (11), or complaints by language teachers about the 'grammarless beginner - beginning modern languages in a state of primeval innocence as regards the elements of the subject' because teachers of English had neglected it (12). In return English teachers began to regard modern language teachers as remote from social reality and as crusty traditionalists.

Modern language teachers have certainly been less ready to accept the challenge of changing social conditions and purposes in education than teachers of English. Largely content to inherit the vacuum left by the classics, it was not until the sixties that they perceived a contemporary political and social dimension to their subject in schools. Literature had been their principal stock in trade, largely interpreted in English. Even as late as 1954, the Ministry of Education's Language, some suggestions for teachers and others, could state:

'...it is difficult not to conclude that our tradition of approaching French and German in a deep and scholarly way through literature as well as language has been right. Most educated Englishmen would not exchange their knowledge of French or German literature for mere conversational fluency...'(p21)

This attitude is in the direct line of descent from Matthew Arnold, who also regarded speaking a foreign language as rather meretricious. Often unable to reconcile vulgar vocational with more lofty educational aims, modern language teachers were well aware of the difficulties of explaining what they were up to. A memorandum of 1949 deplored that few grammar school pupils regarded modern languages both as of later utilitarian value and as useful in developing 'habits of careful thought':

'How much the schoolboy, even of high ability, can understand these aims is open to doubt... It is this blindness of the young that gives to the modern language teacher his greatest difficulty.' (13)

With the sixties came an improvement in morale and a new youthful vigour of action, stimulated by the joint promises of technology and applied linguistic theory. Aware of Britain's potential new role in relation to Europe, modern language teachers began to see themselves as participants in a new and rather glossy international educational purpose. Introducing French into primary schools was an offering of manna to the multitude, which, it was hoped, might give modern language teaching a wider social coverage and perhaps soften its 'academic' image. But this had little in common with the English teachers' increasing commitment to social equality of opportunity - arising from changes in the structure of education and reinforced by the claims of English to be 'coexistent with life itself' (14). Thus teachers of English could highly resolve that they 'were all working to make their society a more democratic one, and they were all convinced that English was an important basis for the changes to be made...' (15). Teachers of foreign languages certainly had no such messianic aims although they did claim to contribute to the development of the individual by providing a new freedom in the world as it actually existed (16) and hinted at ensuing material benefits. While English teachers still sought the new Jerusalem, modern language teachers came to terms with Mammon. Each group regarded the other as unrealistic, and both went their ways. But if community of educational purpose seemed remote, both have been deeply affected methodologically by latter-day developments in linguistic - and especially in the case of English, socio-linguistic principle, but it may form the basis for collaboration in practice. However, the value of some form of linguistics as a linking subject between English and other languages in schools is far from being generally accepted, although it now appears in various forms in teacher-training courses.

SOME CONCLUSIONS

It would be wrong to draw too many conclusions from such limited observations as these. Hitherto, teachers of English and teachers of modern languages have shown little disposition to co-operate and have perceived no great practical reasons for doing so. The reasons are partly historical, partly psychological. While English teachers have been extending the boundaries of their subject, modern language teachers have been defending a largely static perimeter. There are suspicions on both sides.

One must accept that to most teachers, except modern language teachers, language means English, and a language policy means an English policy. All subject teachers who teach in English have a more obvious concern with this than those who specifically claim not to teach in English.

The comparatively short history of university departments both of English and of modern languages must be remembered. Since around 1900, both have had to establish themselves as purveyors of respectable disciplines, and during the early twentieth century a good deal of conscious self-importance rubbed off on to the graduates of both, who then went on to teach in secondary schools. To both groups literature had usually been presented as the most attractive part of their studies, and one which could most fittingly be passed on to the schools. The Newbolt report canonised English Lit in schools, while foreign literatures received such minor beatification as befitted their provenance. But while English (and its literature) was clearly for all pupils, modern languages (and theirs) were equally clearly only for some. It might be added that the impact of any foreign literature was to some extent dependent on English, while the necessary underlying skills of extended reading and elementary critical awareness could only be acquired through English in the first place.

English teaching in schools always had and still retains one major educational role: the establishment and development of literacy - from the teaching of reading and writing in the primary classes to more advanced levels of comprehension and expression required by all kinds of subjects, and possibly also to the conscious appreciation of language and literature proper to sixth forms. Whether or not such tasks are exclusively the responsiblity of English specialists is irrelevant: the total process is an educational function of the whole curriculum. In this sense English skills are paramount.

While no-one will dispute this, yet as the Bullock Reports shows, there is ample need for the definition of immediate objectives and for discussion of the techniques and methodology to achieve them. And whatever wider claims are made by English teachers for the social relevance of their subject they cannot abdicate responsibility for their part in developing literacy in the fullest sense.

Modern languages can claim no such responsibility. However desirable it may seem for all pupils to have the opportunity to learn a foreign language, it is clear that only a small minority actually do so with much benefit. This is not to say that modern language teachers may not have much to offer in the formulation of a policy for English across the curriculum. They may have technical insights simply because they are constantly concerned with their pupils' understanding and accurate use of words, structures and associated meaning as well as their apprehension of language in general. But it would be idle to claim that a language (= English) policy should necessarily be a joint creation on terms of equal participation by teachers of modern languages and teachers of English, or indeed that the former have a greater interest in its effectiveness than teachers of any other subject.

On certain matters of curriculum design and methodology, there are common interests which deserve greater recognition than they now get, and where some co-operation would benefit subject interests as well as any overall policy. For example, both English and modern language teachers are now rather warily toying with the idea of elementary linguistics as a schools subject. In a sense this may be a modern version of the old problem of who teaches grammar; it probably results from the need for clearer descriptive terms for language as a social phenomenon (by English teachers) or as a system (by modern language teachers). Both sides are perhaps seeking a new taxonomy which will serve their subject purposes, and if one is to be developed, then clearly it would be less confusing to all concerned if it were agreed. Who actually should teach any such basic course in linguistics seems of less importance than that its content should be equally valid for the purposes of teaching English and any other languages in schools (including the non-English mother tongues of substantial numbers of pupils).

If, as is sometimes, claimed, it is beneficial for the same teacher to teach both English and a foreign language to a class, there is obviously a need for him to have consistent and congruent bases for his everyday judgements of correctness, error, acceptability, etc in both languages. It is not uncommon at present to apply more rigorous criteria to a foreign language than to English in such matters. Pupils may be able to accept this when there are two different teachers, but it might seem confusing from one. There are implications here for teacher training as well as for linguistics in school.

In higher forms, where the main substances of English and foreign language courses may be literature, there seems a clear case not only for co-ordination in the choice of texts (so that these may complement, support or contrast with one another according to whatever curricular policy is currently favoured), but also for employing compatible criteria in encouraging (or imposing) such embryonic critical judgements as may be expected of pupils.

Modern language teachers are often accused of conservatism, academicism and elitism. This is not surprising since many today see their task as not very different from what it was fifty years ago - only the pupils have changed, which makes it more difficult. Many would undoubtedly benefit from understanding more clearly what their English-teaching colleagues are at. This is no easy task, and is certainly not the same in every school. But the starting point of all foreign language learning must be the pupil's own language and his own concepts about language derived from his own experience of using it. As this is what the teacher of English claims to know most about, he is particularly well qualified to advise the modern language teacher about the initial aims (and even content) of a modern language course. But to do this, the English teacher must in his turn be ready to understand the special problems of teaching a new language, and particularly how this task differs from his own work of developing skills in the use of the mother tongue.

REFERENCES

1. The Teaching of English in England, 1921 (the 'Newbolt' Report). Ch. IV para. 110.

2. The mother tongue and other languages in education, CILT, 1979.

3. The teaching of English in England, p 63. Unlike Bullock, conviction is matched by conciseness here.

4. Kekewich, GW: The Education Department and after, 1920, p 10. The author was Permanent Secretary of the Department 1890 - 1902.

5. The teaching of English in England, p 189.

6. cf. Hawkins, E W: The linguistic needs of pupils. In: Foreign languages in education, CILT, 1979.

7. Arnold, M: Reports on elementary schools 1852-1882, 1889, passim.

8. The teaching of English in England, p 63.

9. Atkins, H G & H L Hutton: The teaching of modern foreign languages in school and university, 1920, passim.

10. The position of modern languages in the educational system of Great Britain, HMSO, 1918. (Report of the Prime Minister's Committee.)

11. cf. Report of joint committee on grammatical terminology, 1909, and IAAM Memorandum on the teaching of modern foreign languages, 1929, p 181.

12. Brereton, C: Modern language teaching, 1930, p 67.

13. IAMM: The teaching of modern languages, 1949, p 20.

14. Mathieson, M: The preachers of culture, 1975, p 1.

15. Squire, J R and R K Applebee: Teaching English in the United Kingdom, 1969, p 139.

16. See James, C V: Foreign languages in the school curriculum, in: Foreign languages in education, CILT, 1979, for a comprehensive summary of the expressed aims of modern language teachers in recent years.

THE CONCEPT OF A SCHOOL LANGUAGE POLICY

W H Mittins

There is a possible ambiguity in 'school language policy'. It could mean either

(a)   a policy for the teaching in schools of languages or
(b)   a policy for the use of language in schools.

Though meaning (a) would clearly be of great interest to the National Congress on Languages in Education, and though to some extent it is included in meaning (b), it is meaning (b) that is the concern of this paper. This meaning is equivalent to that of 'language across the curriculum', which was the title both of the document produced by the London Association for the Teaching of English in the last 1960s (and printed in Language, the learner and the school (1) and of the 1971 conference of the National Association for the Teaching of English. It is also the title of Chaper 12 of the Bullock Report (1975), which acknowledges the provenance of the notion and advocates its implementation in one of its major recommendations (2). In other contexts, 'language' is not necessarily confined to English. (For example, CNAA regulations for the first degrees identify 'language in education' as 'at least one official language of the United Kingdom'.) But, for the purposes of the Bullock Committee and for this paper, the language under consideration is English.

Putting together 'school language policy', 'language across the curriculum' and a restriction to English, my title may be expanded, therefore, to 'the concept of an English language policy across the school curriculum'. if a large number of schools were already operating such a policy, it might be possible - assuming some areas of similarity - to abstract from actual practices the theory underlying them. But in fact there are comparatively few coherent policy statements and, even in schools with policies, very varying practices. Some of the variation may arise through a narrow and shallow interpretation of the undertaking. One school may confine itself to an agreement to tackle spelling in all relevant subjects; another may, less trivially, seek to equalise the readability of textbooks; a third may try to establish a consensus on the appropriate 'register' for classroom speech; and so on. Obviously, at this level no single concept is likely to emerge. To arrive at an agreed total concept, one must go well beyond spelling/writing/reading/comprehension/readability, etc in all subjects and think both more broadly (following the Bullock Committee's belief that 'language competence grows incrementally, through an interaction of writing, talk, reading, and experience, the body of resulting work forming an organic whole' (3)) and more deeply, drawing on general principles of psychology, sociology and linguistics.

This latter is a very tall order. The subject-matters of these disciplines are complex. Wallace Chafe has remarked that 'Language is, without doubt, an extraordinarily complicated elephant', (4); others might well say the same of psychology and sociology. Add to this complication the inter-disciplinary ramifications of social psychology, psycholinguistics and sociolinguistics, and theorising of any kind begins to look extremely daunting. To make things even worse, all three disciplines, if sciences at all, are 'soft' human behavioural - and therefore imprecise - sciences rather than 'hard' empirical physical sciences, and all three (if we take linguistics synchronically and exclude the diachronic or historical dimension) comparatively young and immature.

Education has never been able to wait upon reliable evidence from its contributory disciplines. Perhaps one day psychology will provide a single persuasive learning theory which teachers can adopt; perhaps sociology will similarly supply an agreed theory of social class and power distribution to help in organising a rational school system; perhaps linguistics will come up with a full, coherent explanatory description of the English language to 'underpin' a school language policy. Equally, perhaps not. Meanwhile, educational decisions must be taken on the best evidence available, with common sense, teaching experience, critical reflection and imagination compensating for theoretical inadequacies.

Considerations like these, especially in the areas of linguistics and psychology (the former seen by him as a branch of the latter), led Chomsky, talking about linguistic theory and language teaching, to say that 'well-established theory, in fields like psychology and linguistics, is extremely limited in scope' and that 'There is very little in psychology and linguistics that he [the language teacher] can accept on faith'. He doubts the relevance of psychological theory to the acquisition of language. 'The applied psychologist and the teacher', he says, 'must certainly draw what suggestions and hints they can from psychological research, but they would be well-advised to do so with the constant realization of how fragile and tentative are the principles of the underlying discipline. Turning to linguistics, we find much the same situation' (5).

Similar considerations may account for the shortness (four pages) of the Bullock Report's Chapter 4, the chapter that is intended 'to provide a theoretical foundation for the chapters that follow' (6). (The following chapters include, of course, the one on 'Language across the curriculum'.) Chapter 4 takes as its title 'Language and learning' and draws on extensive writing on this topic, specifically naming Vygotsky, Luria and Vinogradova, and Chomsky 'and his associates'. It does not mention James Britton, probably because, as a member of the Bullock Committee, he had a large hand in writing it, but the chapter-heading is the same as Britton's book, published in 1970. This book (7) distils from formidably wide reading the essence of the most important thinking about language and learning. It also looks virtually certain that the epigraph heading Chapter 4 comes from the same source. Britton has quoted elsewhere Georges Gusdorf's succinct generalisation that 'Man interposes a network of words between the world and himself, and thereby becomes the master of the world' (8).

When Bertrand Russell remarked that 'The purpose of words, though philisophers seem to forget this simple fact, is to deal with matters other than words' (9), he probably had so-called 'linguistic' philosophers in mind. He could have bracketed with them linguisticians. The extra-linguistic objective in schools is learning. That means making sense of experience, both the learner's own (in the classroom and outside) and that of others as encapsulated in the curriculum. It is in the process of pursuing this objective of ordering otherwise chaotic experience that language is inextricably involved. As Peter Berger puts it, 'The fact of language can readily be seen as the imposition of order upon experience. Language nomizes [creates conceptual order] by imposing differentiation and structure upon the ongoing flux of experience' (10).

Before looking at this large claim in more detail, it is important to clarify its use of the term 'language'. Berger may mean solely verbal language. Alternatively, he may include non-verbal symbol-systems. In either case, it is the symbolising function that is crucial. Man, as many scholars have insisted, is distinctively a symboliser, a symbol-maker and symbol-user. According to Suzanne Langer, 'This basic need, which certainly is obvious only in man, is the need of symbolization. The symbol-making function is one of man's primary activities, like eating, looking, or moving about' (11). Man has at his disposal many symbol-systems besides the verbal one - mathematical and scientific signs; colour, line and shape in the plastic arts; the sounds of music; movement, gesture, and so on. But however useful and important these may be, the verbal system remains the broadest, most flexible, most resourceful of all. It is surely no exaggeration to assert, as the Bergers have done, that:

> 'Language [sc. verbal language] is very probably the fundamental institution of society, as well as being the first institution encountered by the individual biographically... The state, the economy and the educational system [my underlining], whatever else they may be, depend upon a linguistic edifice of classification, concepts and imperatives for individuals' actions - that is, they depend on a world of meanings that was constructed by means of language and can only be kept going by language.' (12)

The relevance of this to teaching is exemplified at various levels by many people. If Bruner is right in crediting the anthropologist Ruth Benedict with having 'actually presented the Japanese culture by attempting to give the meanings of a few Japanese words' (13), the extraction of meaning from English words should be indispensable to the transmission of our culture. At the particular level of the classroom, we have William Gatherer's view that ' learning physics is as much a process of learning to talk physics as anything' (14). This observation could be applied to other subjects, as it is by the teacher quoted in the Bullock Report as saying: 'It is not just that language is used in mathematics, rather it is that the language that is used is the mathematics' (15).

How does language operate in making sense of experience in general and of school subjects in particular? The answer turns to some extent on the relationship between language and thought. This is an old but persisting and controversial matter ('the last and deepest problem of the philosophic mind', William Urban called it). The term 'thinking' is itself problematical; let us assume for our purpose that it covers, not only the intellectual ratiocinative processes that come first to mind, but also reflecting, imagining, remembering, speculating, intuiting, and the like. Behaviourist psychologists like Watson actually identify thinking with verbal language; 'even thinking is but sub-vocal talking' (16). We do not need to agree with such an extreme view. Even if, as it is plausible to assume, there are non-linguistic ways of thinking, and even if we allow a sizeable role in thinking to non-verbal symbolic systems, we are left with the predominant part played by words in most of our thought.

Thinking is often equated with having ideas and manipulating meanings. In some ways these terms - 'ideas', 'meanings' - are even more slippery than 'thinking'. What is more serious, they carry dangers of reification. The notion that an idea or a meaning (or for that matter a thought) has an existence independent of the symbol which is associated with it is naive and misleading. Symbol-making and symbol-using are inseparable activities. The old metaphors by which language is represented as a mould into which meanings are poured or as clothes donned by ideas are even less helpful than the behaviourist treatment of language as laryngeal habit. Much more persuasive than the cloak and mould theories is the view that 'language does not simply symbolize a situation or object which is already there in advance; it makes possible the existence or the appearance of that situation or object' (17). Vygotsky has reiterated and expanded this view: 'All the higher psychic functions are mediated processes, and signs are the basic means used to master and direct them. The mediating sign is incorporated in their structure as an indispensable, indeed the central, part of the total process. In concept formation, the sign is the word, which at first plays the role of means in forming a concept and later becomes its symbol' (18).

The term 'concept' is a useful addition to the terminology of language/ thought debate. Concepts themselves are 'essentially non-linguistic (or perhaps better alinguistic)' (19). They are 'the coinage of thought' (20). They categorise, sorting out classes of things and events from the amorphous mass of experience and carving up the continuum with boundaries. These boundaries are drawn with words, which, because language is discrete, 'select and group elements of our experience of the world' (21).

But the notion of 'concept' carries with it something of the same danger of reification as the notions of 'idea' and 'thought'. Because both concept and word segment a moving mass into separate manageable units, and because it is much easier to think and talk about small, relatively stable 'things', it is only too easy to give excessive prominence to isolated named concepts. Naming in this simple labelling sense is, of course, an important function of language. The botanist Linnaeus recognised this in the eighteenth century: 'Nomina si nescis, perit et cognito rerum' (If you don't know the names, even knowledge of the things themselves will pass away). More recently, George Orwell has exploited this same possibility; in Newspeak, the '1984' new language, undesirable ideas such as freedom and democracy are to be eliminated from minds by eliminating their names from dictionaries. A more positive, though perhaps no less pernicious, use of the same phenomenon was made, according to Daisy Jones (22), by an American lobbyist who circulated a letter to legislators debating a proposed large appropriation for a state college:

Dear Congressman,

Before your cast you vote on Senate Bill N. C-192-a, please give careful consideration to the following facts gleaned from the campus. You should know that up at the state college the men and women use the same curriculum. The boys and girls often matriculate together. A young lady student cannot get an advanced degree until she shows her thesis to the male professors.
[Signed]   Bill Smith, Lobbyist for Economy
in Government

If it is at all true that this letter contributed to the overwhelming defeat of the senate bill, then it testifies to the enormous power of three words disingenuously used.

Nevertheless, however powerful individual words may be, lexation is only part, and probably not the major part, of language. It is the part that teachers are commonly more ready to accept as deserving of attention. They can then present their subjects as primarily sets of concepts identified by key-words. To the extent that they do this, they are accepting a simplistic 'building-block' view of language as a mere repertoire of words, a vocabulary or lexis. Such an impoverished view may be adequate for the language - 'Me Tarzan, you Jane' - of personal contact in the jungle, but it is quite insufficient for the more advanced purposes of school learning. Single concepts are less important than the networks that make them into systems and schemata; entities are less significant than the relations that connect them into events; vocabulary is less fundamental than phrase, clause and sentence structure.

In the late 1950s, a metaphor that attempted to place emphasis on the network rather than on the words netted compared language with 'a kind of grid, or series of grids, through which we 'see' the world, dissected along lines laid down by the systems of the language' (23). Randolph Quirk pointed out at the time that the view of 'language as a grid interposed between speakers and reality, a grid which provides them with their segmentation of reality, [is] partly a misconception, partly a convenient abstraction, partly arbitrary and partly realistic' (24). Obviously, any mapping of language on to experience needs to be less static than the metaphor of the grid allows. Nevertheless, the metaphor at least emphasises that language 'provides a fundamental order of relationships by the addition of syntax and grammar to vocabulary' (25). The point of this congested sequence of quotations is neatly made in yet another; Herbert Read has somewhere summarised my laborious argument in the remark that 'no difference between man and beast is more important than syntax'.

Importance, however, is not the sole criterion for selecting what to teach and how to teach it in schools. If it were, we should presumably teach (and examine!) breathing and eating. It must be conceded that by a very young age normal children have naturally mastered most of the basic syntactic structures of their mother tongues. They can use a variety of phrases, clauses and sentences to make their meaning clear and to get their own way. But it is wrong to assume that they have therefore mastered the range of structures they need for purposes of study - for listening, reading and writing about the subjects of the curriculum. It is even more dangerous to assume that continued personal growth on its own brings continuing language acquisition, going beyond the basic structures of expressive child speech to something like control of the full range of the language's syntactic resources. Many teachers would agree that the major weaknesses in students' use of language are not matters of particular grammatical or lexical inaccuracies so much as a more general lack of resourcefulness, a threadbare limitation to comparatively few and simple structures. The writer - and to some extent the speaker, listener and reader - too often fails to attain to or to appreciate closeness of match between word-sequence and the flow of meaning. The remedy for this weakness is not study of grammar (though this may help with older and abler students) but constant and varied practice in matching language to a whole gamut of meanings 'across the curriculum'.

Study of classroom language increasingly and persuasively indicates that this matching process - learning how to mean with words - is hampered by excessive lecture-talk by the teacher, by over-emphasis on writing, by dictation of notes, by questioning that requires the reading of teacher's mind for 'correct' answers, and by other ways of 'playing teacher's word-game'. It is hampered further if the quality of the word-game is diminished by a teacher's unrealistic assumptions about language - assumption such as that meaning inheres in words instead of being put there by users, that words can have precise single meanings (known, of course, to the teacher), that writing is a more proper and prestigious use of language than speaking, that pupils should talk written English, that 'hesitation phenomena' in speech are signs of weakness, and so on. The evidence of recorded classroom discussion, and especially of small-group talk, strongly suggests that (pace Stuart Froome (26)) informal talk marked by considerable tentativeness and groping for meaning can be a most productive method of learning in itself and an invaluable adjunct to other methods. Obviously, if and to the extent that this is true, the effectiveness is likely to be greatly enhanced if the method is applied across the curriculum. The various subjects are bundles of diverse meanings. The kind of teasing-out of meaning through talk appropriate to history is different from that needed in science or mathematics or geography. Together they may add up to a strong programme of mutually reinforcing learning experience.

Recognition of the power and resourcefulness of verbal language, oral and written, as an agent of learning is the main thrust of the 'language across the curriculum' movement. But power can only be obtained at a price, as Faust came to learn. It is significant that, in Goethe's version, it is Mephistopheles who urges the learner to cling to words and not to worry overmuch about meaning:

'Mephist: ...To words stick fast!
Then through a sure gate you'll at last
Enter the templed hall of Certainty.

Student: Yet in each word some concept there must be.

Mephist: Quite true! But don't torment yourself too anxiously:
For at the point where concepts fail,
At the right time a word is thrust in there.
With words we fitly can our foes assail,
With words a system we prepare,
Words we quite fitly can believe
Nor from a word a mere iota thieve.' (27)

There is no 'templed hall of Certainty', nor any 'sure gate' into it.

Language is vulnerable to Mephistophelean 'mere verbalism'. It also gives humans their distinctive ability to lie and deceive, as Bill Smith's letter shows. With lying George Steiner associates the perhaps more serious offence of obscurity: 'We live under a constant wash of mendacity. Millions of words tide over us with no intent of clear meaning' (28). To Otto Jespersen's ironic enumeration of the functions of language as (1) the communication of ideas, (2) the concealment of ideas, and (3) the concealment of the absence of ideas, J B Newman has added a fourth category, 'the communication of the absence of ideas' (29).

It is unlikely that teachers in their teaching often use language deliberately to deceive. But learners do need help in extracting intended real meanings from verbal formulations. There is some evidence that young children come sometimes to regard the old 'kerb drill' (now, I believe, discredited), not as a directive for safe behaviour but as an incantation to ward off danger. Adolescents often evince a reaction against the use of words for rational dialogue because of the hypocrisy and euphemism with which language is officially used. The savagery of military operations in Vietnam, for instance, was to some extent masked by the bland language of 'escalation', 'defoliation', 'pacification', etc (30). More subtly, a Feiffer cartoon caught the same process at work in a civil context; the text ran:

> 'I used to think I was poor. Then they told me I wasn't poor. I was needy. Then they told me it was self-defeating to think of myself as needy, I was deprived. Then they told me deprived was a bad image. I was underprivileged. Then they told me underprivileged was overused. I was disadvantaged. I still haven't got a dime, but I have a great vocabulary' (31).

Teachers of all subjects have as language-users a responsibility to build up learners' defences against these abuses of language, against deception, blurred distinction, opaqueness, sheer muddle. This is not just a matter of the teacher of English inducing students to detect, for example, the deceptive use of language by advertisers. (In any case there may be a grain of truth in the allegation that the only real difference between teaching and advertising is that the advertisers know what they are doing!) The task is not detachable from the general subject-teaching undertaking. The negative business of cultivating an alertness to wrong or bad thinking-in-language can best be tackled in school by the same process that serves induction into subject-disciplines, that is, the constant wrestling with strings of words to get at meanings, detecting and discarding the false and irrelevant, and refining to suitable precision the accurate and true.

In order to develop a single theoretical statement embracing all aspects of language and learning, I have found it necessary to operate at a level of abstraction and generalisation that may seem to have lost contact with the particularities of language in school - the skills of listening and speaking, reading and writing, the issues of correctness and convention in spelling, punctuation, usage and grammar. For the teacher the bridge between the large theoretical framework and these particularities is what the Bullock Report sums up as 'a more complete understanding of language in education than has ever been required of them in the past' (32). The Report gives two examples of a basic language course for pre-service teachers designed to develop such an understanding. They are only examples to serve as agenda for discussion in institutions planning their own teacher-training courses. Unavoidably they need explication and, probably, pruning. That is essentially a job for teachers to do. Whatever programme is the outcome of discussion, however, it would seem necessary for it to include study of at least: the nature of language as an instrument of thought, expression and communication; the functions of language; the varieties, dialectal and diatypic (registral), within a single language; speaking and writing; reading, readability and comprehension; correctness and appropriateness; syntax and lexis;

grammars; usage and convention; and, of course, language across the curriculum.

The complaints in Chapter 1 of the Bullock Report about the English, especially the written English, of school-leavers going into industry, other employment, further/higher education or teacher-training raise the question of whether at least able students (including, one hopes, those contemplating careers in teaching) should not begin their studies of language before they leave school. The evidence claiming to establish that studying language has little or no effect on the quality of language used needs re-examining. It may be that much of it is less than conclusive. To the extent that studying language has in the past meant not just studying a traditional Latin-based grammar but often studying the more questionable features of that grammar (eg parts-of-speech classification, stereotyped clause analysis), it could be that research has merely demonstrated that teaching bad grammar badly does not improve composition. It hardly needs research to tell us that. It could still be that real understanding of how language works was not sufficiently inculcated by the now discredited old grammar and that W P Robinson is therefore right in saying that 'The possibility that understanding might facilitate use has hardly been explored' (33). In the United States, post-sputnik concern about standards in the use of English - standards which, as in this country, may not have been falling but certainly aren't high enough - led to the extension of 'college freshman' courses in English in colleges. Reasonably, the Bullock Report found this curative measure the least attractive of any mentioned (34). It was none the less in 'bonchead English' teaching that the late Mina Shaughnessy seemed to have had marked success in raising levels of performance, and in her record of the work (35) she constantly stresses the value - indeed the necessity - of both students and teacher knowing something about the grammar - not some remote theoretical grammar, but the grammar of the language the students naturally use.

But that, as Americans might say, is another ball-game, and a controversial one. Let me end with two final quotations, both from poets, that take us back into the heart of the problem. Walter de la Mare caught the complex process of shaping thought in words by describing it as:

'- wooing from a soundless brain
The formless into words again.'

At rather greater length and in one rhetorical question, Louis Macneice mused:

'When books have all seized up like the books in graveyards
And reading and even speaking have been replaced
By other, less difficult, media, we wonder if you
Will find in flowers and fruit the same colour and taste
They held for us for whom they were framed in words,

87

And will your grass be green, your sky be blue,
Or will your birds be always wingless birds?' (36)

An imaginative and vital language across the curriculum policy might conceivably help preserve the power of flight in words.

REFERENCES

1. Barnes, D, J Britton & H Rosen: Language, the learner and the school. Rev. edn. Harmondsworth: Penguin, 1971 (First published 1969.)

2. Committee of Inquiry into Reading and the Use of English: A language for life (The Bullock Report). HMSO, 1975. p 529, Recommendation 139.

3. ibid. p 7, line 10.

4. Book review in Language, vol 33 no. 4, September 1968.

5. Chomsky, N: The utility of linguistic theory to the language teacher. In: J P B Allen and S P Corder: Readings for applied linguistics. Oxford University Press, 1973. p 235-37.

6. Bullock Report (see no. 2) p 50, 4.10.

7. Britton, J N: Language and learning. Allen Lane The Penguin Press, 1970.

8. Gusdorf, G: Speaking. Evanston, IL: Northwestern University Press, 1965. Quoted by Britton in: English in the curriculum. In: The space between...: English and foreign languages at school. Centre for Information on Language Teaching and Research, 1974. (CILT Reports and Papers 10.) p 37.

9. Russell, B: An enquiry into meaning and truth. Allen & Unwin, 1940. p 148.

10. Berger, P: The social reality of religion. Faber & Faber, 1969. p 21.

11. Langer, S K: Philosophy in a new key. Harvard University Press, 1942. p 41.

12. Berger, P and B Berger: Sociology, a biographical approach. Basic Books, 1972. p 73.

13. Bruner, J and others: A study of thinking. Wily, 1956. p 311.

14. Gatherer, W A: Language and education. In: Language across the curriculum; (by) Michael Marland. Heinemann Educational, 1977. p 43.

15. Bullock Report (see no. 2). p 192, 12.10.

16. Watson, J B: Psychology from the standpoint of a behaviourist. New York: St Martin's Press, 1979.

17. Mead, G H: Mind, self and society. University of Chicago Press, 1952. p 47.

18. Vygotsky, L S V: An experimental study of concept formation. In: Language in thinking; ed P Adams. Penguin, 1972. p 280-81.

19. Carroll, J B: Words, meanings and concepts. Harvard Educational Review, 1968 (34). p 178.

20. Johnson-Laird, P N and Wason, P C, eds: Thinking: readings in cognitive science. Cambridge University Press, 1977. p 169.

21. Catford, J C: English as a foreign language. In: Communication Research Centre: The teaching of English. Secker & Warburg, 1959. p 182.

22. Jones, D M: Implications of linguistics for the teaching of reading. In: J F Savage: Linguistics for teachers. Chicago: Science Research Associates, 1973. p 300.

23. Catford, J C, ibid. p 182.

24. Quirk, R: Linguistics. The year's work in English studies, vol 36, 1955. p 37.

25. Berger, P, ibid. p 201.

26. Froome, S: Note of dissent. In: The Bullock Report (see no. 2). p 558.

27. Goethe, W: Faust I. 1900ff, translated by G M Priest. Quoted in R Quirk: The English language and images of matter. Oxford University Press, 1972. Preface, p vii.

28. Steiner, G: Extra-territorial. Faber, 1968. p 96.

29. Newman, J B: Doublespeak, doubletalk and the functions of language. Quarterly Journal of Speech, vol 62 no. 1, February 1976, Forum. p 80.

30. Cazden, C: <u>Child language and education</u>. Holt, Rinehart & Winston, 1972. p 246.

31. Quoted in Stubbs, M: <u>Language, schools and classrooms</u>. Methuen, 1976. p 33.

32. Bullock Report (see no. 2). p 343, 23.24.

33. Robinson, W P: <u>Language and social behaviour</u>. Penguin, 1972. p 24.

34. Bullock Report (see no. 2). p 342, 23.23.

35. Shaughnessy, M P: <u>Errors and expectations</u>. New York: Oxford University Press, 1977.

36. Macneice, L: <u>To posterity</u>; collected poems. Faber & Faber, 1966. p 443.

LANGUAGE TEACHERS SPEAK WITH FORKED TONGUE

B C King

The aim of this paper is to examine dissimilarities and similarities in mother tongue and foreign language acquisition, development and teaching. It is essential that dissimilarities be identified, in order to obviate erroneous assumptions, thereby clearing the ground for the identification of real and fruitful points of contact for L1 and L2 teachers in formulating a language policy.

WHY A LANGUAGE POLICY?

In 1967 Harold Rosen wrote in a paper submitted on behalf of the London Association for the Teaching of English: 'We believe that many teachers are now prepared to go far beyond the older view that language was someone else's business, or, perhaps, that they were the guardians of linguistic proprieties. They are now prepared to consider what needs to be done to improve our procedures in schools in such a way that language becomes a facilitating force in learning rather than a barrier bristling with formidable difficulties' (1). This was perhaps not a statement of a new principle, even in 1967, but it serves to illustrate clearly the view which English teachers of today take of language.

This view of language as being vital in the learning process, but just as likely to hinder that process if care is not exercised is taken up and reinforced throughout the Bullock Report (2), in which 'a community and continuity of endeavour' with regard to language is called for from all teachers. 'In the secondary school, all subject teachers need to be aware of: (i) the linguistic processes by which their pupils acquire information and understanding, and the implications for the teacher's own use of language; ... To bring about this understanding every secondary school should develop a policy for language across the curriculum' (3).

The central message in the Bullock Report is perhaps embodied in the statement: 'it is a confusion of everyday thought that we tend to regard 'knowledge' as something that exists independently of someone who knows. 'What is known' must in fact be brought alive afresh within every 'knower' by his own efforts' (4). The last four words of this extract are particularly telling: while children may gain access to 'knowledge' or information via the receptive language modes of listening (to the teacher) and reading (a book), that knowledge may most efficiently be appropriated by them and assimilated via the productive language modes of speaking and writing.

These arguments are in themselves sufficiently powerful to persuade us that teachers of all subjects need to strive to reach a consensus on the role which language plays in learning. But there is a further step which will convince us even more. Michael Marland has written: 'If a school devotes thought and time to assisting language development, learning in all areas will be helped; if attention is given to language in the content and skill subjects, language development will be assisted powerfully by the context and purpose of those subjects... If ... the opportunities for pupils to explore ideas through language in the curriculum are developed, language will grow with the learning' (5).

Thus language assumes a vital importance in education. We learn through language, and what we learn promotes effective language development, which in turn fosters further learning, and so on. We have what Michael Marland calls 'a virtuous circle'. It is this evidence which prompts the National Association for the Teaching of English to write: 'A policy about language and learning, therefore, means that because it is through language that we learn, teachers must pay attention to the language that surrounds them and their pupils in school - the 'language-life' of the school. In other words, paying attention to language means paying attention to learning' (6).

Despite the overwhelming nature of all the evidence, there is considerable reason to doubt whether many schools are yet attempting to act on it: ten years after Harold Rosen's powerful arguments we read: 'Anyone can prove to himself by following a group of pupils through a day in a secondary school that their language experiences are largely a matter of chance... Secondary teachers need to be sensitive to the demands made on their pupils by the language of their special disciplines' (7).

If a 'community and continuity of endeavour' is to be achieved in a school by all teachers, representing a wide and varied spectrum of specialised subjects, full discussions between all departments will be necessary, with the aim of reaching an informed consensus as to what the role of language is in the child's social, emotional and academic development, and the ways in which all concerned may co-operate and contribute to the agreed ends. A full consensus may not be reached, since the nature of the subjects concerned is so disparate. Even if a written policy is not achieved, however, a common awareness of central concerns and needs should have been forged. It is not necessarily a final written document which is important when a staff agrees to work towards creating a language policy. However, though it may be said that the process is worth more than an end-product in terms of a written document, interim documents are important if a dialogue is to continue. The lack of such documents met by this working party is therefore not an encouraging sign.

CO-OPERATION BETWEEN MOTHER TONGUE AND FOREIGN LANGUAGE TEACHERS

Since the elaboration of a language policy requires close co-operation and understanding between teachers of all subjects, and since foreign language and mother tongue teachers are both apparently concerned with the same issue, language, then it would seem inevitable that modern linguists and mother tongue teachers should seek to establish close co-operation, and discuss areas of common interest in language. However, instead of just assuming that co-operation between the two departments on language is desirable, it is worthwhile seeing whether needs for co-operation can be established.

Professor Hawkins writes of the need 'to fill the vacuum which at present separates the teaching of the mother tongue from the foreign language' (8) and refers to the lack of contact between the teachers of these two subject areas, 'each of whom uses a grammatical terminology which may lead to the pupil being asked to attach different concepts to the same linguistic label' (9). Though this statement may lay undue emphasis on grammatical terminology as the main need for contact, it serves to point up the dangers inherent in a lack of co-operation between L1 and L2 teachers.

The author's own experience working with foreign language and English teachers bears out Professor Hawkins' description of a lack of contact between teachers of the two subjects. English teachers have often held discussions with (say) science, craft or humanities teachers, and invariably with teachers in the remedial department, but to find a foreign language department and an English department which have had more than superficial, informal chats is a rarity indeed.

And yet teachers of both subjects are indeed concerned with language, whatever their understanding of the term, and both, by virtue of being language teachers 'are concerned with social attitudes and with developing tolerance and understanding of cultural differences' (10), and they are both concerned with 'the need to equip children with communicative competence socially, and at the same time the need to develop their individual cultural awareness' (11). Since they have such central concerns in common, is it then acceptable that, as is very largely the case, they should be so unaware of each other's aims and concerns in a linguistic education? Let us at this point examine and clarify these aims and conerns.

THE AIMS OF ENGLISH AND FOREIGN LANGUAGE TEACHING

Britton has said: 'I think it is fair to say that as English teachers we have tended to regard teachers of a foreign language as having less concern with the cause we are promoting than have the teachers of most other subjects in the curriculum' (12). What then is this 'cause' which English teachers are concerned to promote? Obviously there will be a wide spectrum of aims amongst English teachers, and it is always risky to assume that recent developments in theoretical thinking will be reflected in classroom practice. In fact there is always a considerable delay before such developments become generalised in the classroom, and even then there is always a mixed economy, in which the old and the new exist side by side.

However, one could say that, in broad terms, the English teacher aims to enable the child to use language to mediate his experience as effectively as possible in the affective and cognitive domains. Since it is principally by means of his language that the child does this, then the development of language in these terms is the English teacher's principal concern. 'The field from which this subject-matter can be drawn is a vast one. It can include anything in the form of language, and anything to which a response in language is possible' (13). More recently some English teachers have led the field in the move to make teachers of all subjects more aware of their own responsibility for language as the principal means by which children acquire and assimilate knowledge in their subjects. However, looking at those areas which are the responsibility of English teachers, 'their objectives need to be seen in language terms. 'English' is a service agent, but not in the limited sense that it alone is responsible for pupils' spelling, punctuation, and sentence construction. It is for the English department to help pupils to investigate language explicitly in its various forms, and with support from other departments. The English teacher will so contrive matters that his pupils will extend their understanding and control of varieties of language while reading and writing about experience and subjects which interest them' (14).

The foreign language teacher has been described as seeing his subject as 'one of the essentially emancipating elements in the curriculum, without which the individual remains imprisoned in the environment in which he is raised or dependent on others to give him an account of the polyglot world' (15). He aims to help the child achieve the highest proficency of which he is capable in the foreign language in the four language modes. According to the ability of the child, and the length of the course followed, this aim will be limited more or less by the contexts in which the language is presented, the balance between the four modes, and the degree of accuracy expected in the productive modes. Further, the foreign language teacher hopes to foster a sympathetic appreciation of the people who speak the target language, and to give some understanding of the workings of language.

DIFFERENCES IN MOTHER TONGUE AND FOREIGN LANGUAGE LEARNING AND TEACHING

There seem to be few points of contact in the aims described above, in which one subject views the mother tongue largely as a means, and the other views the acquisition of skills in the foreign language largely as the end. The view expressed in a recent NCLE paper is most apposite:

'...there is indeed a fundamental similarity between L1 and L2 learning but ... as soon as we look at language learning in a classroom, there are important differences that have to be taken into account, some of them inescapable, some of them avoidable' (16).

It is best to acknowledge and admit the differences, occasioned in the main by the obvious but fundamental fact that the mother tongue is acquired in natural contexts, and the foreign language is learned 'in a classroom'. Initially English and foreign languages in the classroom shared similar aims and techniques, because of their common heritage from the teaching of the classics. As each forged its own claim to be a subject in its own right, however, so each developed along different paths.

Outlined below are important differences between L1 and L2 learning which must be taken into account. By acknowledging these differences the field can be cleared for finding more fruitful points of contact, and potentially dangerous and erroneous assumptions about similarities may be avoided.

As already stated most subjects in the curriculum must rely on English as the principal means by which the child understands subject content. In the process, the child's existing language is developed. In foreign language teaching the understanding and use of the foreign language are largely the goal. The way to proficiency in the foreign language is by using the foreign language and, while some explanations in English may be necessary, graded and insistent practice in the foreign language is the means to the end.

The most obvious external mark of the difference between the acquisition of L1 and L2 is that of speed of acquisition. The child acquires his L1 in an amazingly short time.

'It is, everyone agrees, a colossal task that the child accomplishes when he learns to speak, and the fact that he does so in so short a period of time challenges explanation' (17).

Britton offers his own explanation by arguing that it is the way in which the acquisition of L1 and the need to make sense of experience enmesh 'that explains how a child is able to perform his astonishing feat of learning' (18), and quotes Cassirer to substantiate his argument: 'Eagerness and enthusiasm to talk do not originate in a mere desire for learning and using names: they mark the desire for the detection and conquest of an objective world' (19).

Thus the child learns to <u>function</u> in his L1 - a task of such importance that 'no other understanding so abundantly proves its value in <u>making sense</u> to its user' (20). It would be idle to claim that L2 acquisition in the classroom can perform the same function: it is approached at a time when the child is already a long way along the road towards conquering the world via his own mother tongue. The L2 therefore must suffer in comparison in terms of immediacy and relevance, though the fascinating projects in <u>section bilingue</u> work may well show an important way in which language and learning can enmesh in L2 acquisition, echoing closely the processes of L1 acquisition. In these experiments children are taught a subject or subjects (eg geography and/or history) entirely in the foreign language, and are examined at the end of their course in the foreign language. The interaction of language and concepts in such classrooms is extremely interesting to note.

The child already has considerable command of his own language even when he first comes to school, whereas the foreign language teacher has to teach him the basic patterns of the L2 from scratch. Thus the L1 teacher's concern is essentially divergent, as he seeks to extend the child's control and uses of his mother tongue, and his appreciation of the variables of audience, function and self-image. The L2 teacher's role is essentially convergent, as he strives to teach the child basic standard language patterns. It is difficult to see how in the real world at the real chalk face L2 teachers might put into effect the plea for the development of different registers in L2, 'even at early stages', put forward in the following statement: 'The classroom needs to present a greater variety of (L2) language so that the learner's flexibility can be developed, rather than a single variety of classroom language' (21).

English teachers will therefore tend to have fuller expectations of the work of the child than the foreign language teacher, who sees the task in terms of the artefact and its precision, rather than a balance between the artefact and the content - how it illuminates the child's persona. Poor English teaching does this too. Thus, in terms of audience, the foreign language teacher is almost invariably 'teacher as examiner' and rarely 'teacher as trusted adult' or 'teacher in dialogue of equals'. In oral language also the foreign language teacher's attention is almost entirely directed to the artefact, as he listens for error, rather than to the content or meaning.

Thus it seems that L2 teachers on the whole concentrate on only one of the range of language functions which are the province of the English teacher. Sapir has said that 'the primary function of language is generally said to be communication' but continues by refuting this: 'it is best to admit that language is primarily a vocal actualisation of the tendency to see realities symbolically ... an actualisation in terms of vocal expression of the tendency to master reality not by direct and ad hoc handling of this element but by the reduction of experience to familiar form' (22). L1 teachers willingly accept their responsibility to foster growth in all the language functions described by (say) Tough and Halliday, while L2 teachers must perforce concentrate on commentation, and the formal characteristics of the code used, rather than on the content of communication. This contention is borne out by the fact that while communication is of course an important function in L1 for the child, he communicates in it not only with others, but also with himself. It is not normally expected when the child needs to explore issues and questions internally, that he will do so in his L2. Further, it is generally accepted that 'expressive' language is the language of exploration.

Since 'expressive' is a term used to describe a form of language which is close to the speaker or writer, and which reveals him to his audience, then it is difficult to see how the L2, necessarily distanced from the user, may fulfil this function.

It is apparent that there is an implicit assumption on the part of both that neither has any point of contact with the other's concerns. Indeed there is sometimes a feeling of mistrust, or even an impression that Ll and L2 teachers' aims are in some way inimical to each other. This is of course unfortunate enough for the teachers concerned, but the effects may well be more than merely unfortunate for the children. The preoccupations of L2 teachers tend by training to be with the technical control of language, with the artefact, whereas Ll teachers are generally more concerned with children as language users than with the 'propriety' of language forms they employ. Thus the view of language purveyed by the Ll teacher in his Ll and L2 Classroom language interactions with children and in his marking will tend to be that described by Harold Rosen as 'the barrier bristling with formidable difficulties' (23), or by James Britton as 'one more language to be wrong in' (24). On the other hand, the English teacher tends to accept children's language and to look positively for growth, since his concern is to respect a child's language and to foster in him a variety of registers in addition to his own language, which he views as part of the child and his background. Emanating from teachers whose central concerns are explicitly language, such distinct views of language must confuse the child's own view of language, while separating clearly in his mind foreign languages and English in school. 'Every teacher conveys attitudes to language by his use of it, and by the use of language that he asks or expects from others. Teachers contribute to a number of the ways which make young people what they are, and what they are to become' (25). Children are inevitably required to make their own synthesis of what may be two quite different approaches to 'language', with no help from teachers.

It is possible to enumerate more differences between Ll and L2 acquisition, such as time exposure, and the strictly limited contexts in which the learner meets the L2, compared with the Ll, but enough fundamental differences have been exposed here to show that it would be misleading, and even inimical to successful teaching of Ll and L2, to force common ground in the areas above. It is best to admit that such fundamental differences exist, and to recognise them clearly and honestly, as both subjects have suffered in the past from the uncritical adoption of assumptions over similarities in aims, objectives and methods.

Nonetheless, as implied in the statement: 'if... he (the teacher) believes that language learning is language learning wherever it occurs, as we would claim the evidence suggests...' (26), there are important areas in which L1 and L2 teachers could and should co-operate.

Firstly, there are the obvious features common to language teaching: the working out of a common terminology, attitudes to the teaching of spelling, marking policies (and in particular strategies for making marking part of the process as opposed to the end-product), presentation of work, the timing and manner of the introduction of language concepts, and so on. Agreements on these matters would certainly help to reduce the risk of the child having to reconcile differences in terminology, description, etc applied to the same concepts in two languages, though differences amongst languages must not be ignored, since much harm has been done in the past by teaching grammar as a separate service subject for English, Latin, French, German, et al.

When considering language it is necessary to be clear about terms of reference. Many important developments have taken place recently in our understanding of language, its uses and its nature, and teachers of the mother tongue and foreign languages need to acquire a clear common understanding of those developments. What, for instance, is meant by the term 'grammar'? L1 and L2 teachers each have important insights into language, and these insights tend to be special to each discipline. Thus, while fostering a common and updated view of language amongst teachers of the two subjects, co-operation and discussion would certainly be mutually beneficial from the very sharing of different specialist insights, as well as providing a powerful influence on teachers of other subjects, thereby making a language policy easier to attain.

As has been suggested already, L1 and L2 teachers' concerns have diverged sharply from their earlier common classical heritage. The foreign language teacher tends by training to be concerned with control of language - 'establishing control of syntax' (27), while the English teacher is less concerned with the language proprieties, and more with children as language users: 'Language matters, but people as language users matter especially' (28). These are both valid and important stances in language, contributing importantly to the child's linguistic education, but the general unawareness on the part of English and foreign language teachers of each other's preoccupations can lead to misunderstandings and a linguistic education for the child which 'speaks with forked tongue'. It is important that L1 and L2 teachers should exchange schemes of work, discuss each other's preoccupations, and understand the limitations imposed on each other by the classroom. Even if they do not as a result embark on co-operative schemes, an understanding of and a sympathy for each other's aims would greatly reduce the potential schizophrenia of the child's language programme, and L1 and L2 teachers would be enabled to support each other's aims and ethos. Many pupils do not try to reconcile the illogicalities which they are presented with, and while L2 usually suffers thereby, L1 may well also benefit from an integrated approach.

Such support for each other would also certainly affect the teachers own strategies, be it never so slightly, in their own subject teaching, thereby softening the sometimes sharply etched divisions between L1 and L2 lessons.

In addition to such rather intangible benefits, the exchange and discussion of schemes of work would help to avoid the more obvious needless repetition of content. The author has seen schemes of work in one three-tier area where the concept 'verb' was to be introduced three times to the same children, once at 10+ in French, once at 11+ in English, and again at 13+ in the upper school in French.

L1 and L2 teachers have specialist techniques which they could exchange with mutual benefit. L2 teachers have long-established techniques, born of long-established necessity, in (say) fostering comprehension skills, or in the teaching of technical control, whch would be of use to L1 teachers, while the latter commonly use techniques such as (say) group cloze and group prediction which would be of enormous benefit to the L2 teacher.

The development of functional-notional L2 language courses discussed earlier appears to offer a growth point for co-operation between English and foreign language departments. From the early grammatically based L2 courses, a transition to situational courses and now funtional-notional courses traces a gradual movement in foreign language teaching and learning towards mother tongue acquisition and development processes. Much of the theory underlying this development is difficult to understand fully, and the translation of the theory into practical foreign language courses demands a clear understanding of the principles. James Britton in the Times Educational Supplement quotes Rosen's description of a clear split in philosophies which he detects amongst English teachers, dividing those who believe in a need for structure and linear development, and those who deny the existence and appropriateness of such structure: ... in matters of language and the teaching of English in particular the battle-lines have been drawn ... the fiercest debates are between those who believe in carefully constructed linear programmes, buttressed by claims for sequence, system and structure, and those who believe that development in language can only be achieved by working in a much more flexible and open-ended way' (29). A situation is arising, therefore, where L1 and L2 teachers may well need to get together both to clear their thoughts on developments within their own departments, and also between their departments.

The area of teaching most susceptible of co-operation has of course always been the study of literature at advanced levels. In this area both L1 and L2 teachers clearly have the same aims and concerns. Examples of co-operation in the development of complementary courses are regrettably few, however, and there are great advantages to be gained from closer consultation and planning in every establishment where literature is studied in English and foreign language departments.

As a last instance of opportunities for co-operation, developments in faculty timetabling are worth consideration. Where a block of (say, 10 lessons is allocated to L1 and L2 with teachers from both departments available, and the splitting up of this time is left to the heads of department to decide, together with their colleagues, then there are possibilities for positive co-operation in offering elastic combinations of time, grouping and teaching styles in L1 and L2 for varying amounts of time. Co-operation can only be positive and fruitful in this, however, if each department is quite clear about the other's aims and needs. Much useful discussion can be built into the very fabric of the work of both departments as the needs change throughout the teaching programme, and understanding grows organically from the continuous planning process.

Above all it seems that discussion between L1 and L2 teachers towards establishing co-operation in language policies would lead both to relax strongly held specialist allegiances. The question needs to be asked, 'Am I a French teacher/a German teacher/an English teacher, or am I a provider of a linguistic education?' The clear differences in aims and stance described earlier in this paper show that a shifting of ground, a making of concessions to the other subject area would be necessary for real co-operation to ensue. The L1 teacher, for instance, who feels that translation work from L2 into L1 might interfere with his specialist aims may have to compromise those aims, since there is no doubt that, while translation from L2 to L1 may possibly not help the development of L2, the discussion and selection of translations appropriate to the register of the original L2 passage is certainly likely to 'help pupils to investigate language explicitly in its various forms' (30) and 'extend their understanding and control of varieties of language' (31). This is not to say that English teachers should take on again the teaching of grammar for the sake of the foreign language department. That is patently nonsense. It is however a statement of the inescapable conclusion that L1 and L2 co-operation towards a language policy will necessitate the compromising of strictly specialist concerns. If the teachers' answer to the question posed above is, in all honesty, 'I am a French teacher', or 'I am an English teacher', then there will not be much hope of establishing common areas in a language policy with a brief much beyond surface features. Is such a decision desirable? If so, are teachers ready to make it? La question s'impose....

'LANGUAGE' AS A SUBJECT

This area of potential co-operation has been allotted a special section, as it deserves close consideration. Many sources have described such a subject recently, amongst them Professor Hawkins: 'Firstly a new subject called the 'study of language' should be introduced into the secondary school' (32).

Harold Rosen and Leslie Stratt write: '...an interesting and exciting new study of language is beginning to emerge in English ...' (33).

HM Inspectorate say: 'If this broader concern with language is accepted, there may be a case for Including in the curriculum some enquiry into how human beings acquire and develop language... The subject could be interesting in its own right' (34).

In the main such proposals are based on carefully reasoned educational considerations. Curriculum developments can, however, be too easily accepted unquestioningly as a short-term stop-gap, or as an exciting innovation. It would be inadvisable to introduce the study of language as a subject purely because it affords opportunities for immediate co-operation between teachers of L1 and L2. It would further be counter-productive to introduce such a subject without a realistic and informed understanding of its essential nature by staff concerned. Detailed long-term planning and the careful provision of appropriate resources would be essential.

What would be the relevance of such a subject to the central concerns of English and foreign languages? What also would be the timetabling implications for these subjects, and for the balance of the whole curriculum?

The first consideration to be borne in mind is that 'language' is a most complex subject, developing new insights almost daily. From this complexity two dangers arise. Firstly, are there enough teachers with a clear enough understanding of the subject to be able to offer courses which would not denature it, and which would be interesting? Secondly, would pre-puberty children be able to grasp the concepts involved, however practical the bias of the course? Would such a course be more appropriate in the 4th and 5th years of secondary education than in the 9 to 13 age range, as has been suggested?

With regard to the central concerns of the English department, there is certainly a danger in lifting the study of language out of context, in making it 'academic' as a subject in its own right. Once again it can be seen that course planners would have to be well versed in their subject, and able to offer a considerable quantity of varied and practical resources. There seem, as ever, to be important initial and in-service training implications in these proposals.

Lastly, consideration must be given to the way in which such a subject might be introduced into the curriculum. Should it be offered in addition to the time allocated to L1 and L2, or should it take time from them? HM Inspectorate report that:

'There is no doubt that a reasonable allocation of time is essential for successful (foreign) language learning. Though the daily lesson, once traditional, may be hard to fit into a crowded curriculum, it is generally considered by modern language teachers that the minimum time-allocation should be four lessons of 40 minutes every week' (35).

And they continue:

'On this criterion only half the groups in the first and fourth years in secondary schools were allowed sufficient time, and only about 60 per cent of those in the fifth year. The second and third years were even less generously provided for; in the third year fewer than 40 per cent had adequate provision' (36).

It is a maxim of curriculum development that he who suggests the introduction of a new subject must also suggest what should be excluded to give it room. Since provision for L2 teaching, as reported by HM Inspectorate, is already generally under par, it is difficult to defend the introduction of 'language' as a subject at the expense of L2 provision.

Should it then be introduced as a separate subject, with separate timetable provision? If L1 and L2 teachers are to be involved, then staffing considerations must be taken into account (at a time when the effect of falling rolls is already being felt). Further, implications for the balance of the child's curriculum need to be borne in mind: would it be defensible for a child to study (say) English Language, English Literature, French, German and Language in the 11-16 phase?

The nature of the various suggested 'language-as-a-subject' courses differs considerably. For a detailed programme, essentially different from (say) Professor Hawkins' proposals, see A J Tinkel's paper.

POSTCRIPT: HOW TO GET RID OF BADGERS

A headmaster told an adviser recently that extra French teaching was needed in his school, and said that he wanted the head of English to undertake this. On seeing the adviser's look of disquiet, he said hastily, 'It's all right - it's a Faculty, with English and Foreign Languages'. Noticing that the adviser did not seem reassured, he added 'It's all right. In my experience when English teachers take French groups, they usually just do more English anyway...'.

There was once a man who was plagued by badgers. He had dogs and cats and, keeping them together in one pen, he called them 'Hunters'. Not having enough dogs to pursue the badgers, he decided to send a cat after them. On noting the disquiet on the face of his land management adviser, he said 'It's all right - they're all 'Hunters'.' His adviser's disquiet was obviously not assuaged, so he added 'It's all right. In my experience when cats are sent after badgers, they usually come back with mice anyway'.

Oh Brave New World that hath such faculties in it!

REFERENCES

1. Barnes, D J Britton & H Rosen: Language, the learner and the school. Harmondsworth: Penguin, 1969. (Penguin Papers in Education.)

2. Committee of Inquiry into Reading and the Use of English: A language for life (The Bullock Report). HMSO, 1975.

3. ibid., conclusions and Recommendations 138 and 139.

4. ibid., Chapter 4, paragraph 9.

5. Marland, Michael: Language across the curriculum. Heinemann Educational, 1977.

6. Torbe, Mike: Language across the curriculum: guidelines for schools. National Association for the Teaching of English in association with Ward Lock Educational, 1967.

7. Language in the whole curriculum: 'English' and a linguistic education 11-16. HM Inspectorate of Schools, October 1976. (Unpublished draft of Language. In: Curriulum 11-16: working papers by HM Inspectorate..... Department of Education and Science, 1977 (1978.)

8. Hawkins, E W: The linguistic needs of pupils. In: Foreign languages in education. Centre for Information on Language Teaching and Research, 1979. (NCLE Papers and Reports 1.)

9. ibid.

10. Perren, G E, in: The space between...: English and foreign languages at school. Centre for Information on Language Teaching and Research, 1974. (CILT Reports and Papers 10.)

11. ibid.

12. Britton, James, in: The space between... (see no. 10).

13. Language in the whole curriculum: 'English' and a linguistic education 11-16. (See no. 7.)

14. ibid.

15. James, C V: Foreign languages in the school curriculum. In: Foreign languages in education. (See no. 8.)

16. Cook, V J, J Long and S McDonough: First and second language learning. In: The mother tongue and other languages in education. Centre for Information on Language Teaching and Research, 1979. (NCLE Papers and Reports 2.)

17. Britton, James: Language and learning. Allen Lane The Penguin Press, 1970.

18. ibid.

19. Cassirer, E: An essay on man. Yale University Press, 1944.

20. Britton, J, op. cit.

21. Cook, Long and McDonough, op. cit.

22. Sapir, E: Culture, language and personality. University of California Press, 1961.

23. Barnes, Britton and Rosen, op. cit.

24. Britton, James: English in the curriculum. In: The space between...: English and foreign languages at school. Centre for Information on Language Teaching and Research, 1974. (CILT Reports and Papers 10.)

25. Language in the whole curriculum: 'English' and a linguistic education 11-16. (See no. 7.)

26. Cook, Long and McDonough, op. cit.

27. Perren, G E in The space between... (see no. 10).

28. Language in the whole curriculum: 'English' and a linguistic education 11-16. (See no. 7.)

29. Harold Rosen quoted by James Britton, Times Educational Supplement, 24.11.78. James Britton's article appears at the foreword to Teaching for literacy: reflections on the Bullock Report, ed Frances Davis and Robert Parker. Ward Lock Educational, 1978.

30. Language in the whole curriculum: 'English' and a linguistic education 11-16. (See no. 7.).

31. ibid.

32. Hawkins, E, in: The space between... (see no. 10.)

33. Rosen, Harold and Leslie Stratta: English as a mother tongue. In: The mother tongue and other languages in education. (See no. 16.)

34. Language in the whole curriculum: 'English' and a linguistic education 11-16. (See no. 7.)

35. HM Inspectorate of Schools: Modern language in comprehensive schools. HMSO, 1977. (HMI Series: Matters for Discussion 3.)

36. ibid.

THE RELATIONSHIP BETWEEN THE STUDY OF LANGUAGE AND THE TEACHING OF LANGUAGES

A J Tinkel

It is not a recent idea that the study of language should become a secondary school subject, but it has been given added impetus in the last few years by the suggestion that such a course links mother tongue and foreign language teaching. Hawkins (1) writes, for example, that 'Study of language in the curriculum could be the place where mother tongue acquisition makes contact with foreign language and with the language of immigrants' (page 64). Discussions on language policies in schools, arising out of the Bullock Report, have given further prominence to the idea.

The Bullock Report (2) emphasised the close interaction between language and learning right across the curriculum. It concluded that, in the secondary school, all subject teachers need to be aware of:

'(i)   the linguistic processes by which their pupils acquire information and understanding, and the implications for the teacher's own use of language

(ii)   the reading demands of their own subjects, and ways in which the pupils can be helped to meet them.'

(Conclusions and Recommendations 138)

The Report's recommendation for fostering this awareness in all teachers was that (3):

'...every secondary school should develop a policy for language across the curriculum.'

(Conclusions and Recommendations 139)

In the papers by B C King (Language teachers speak with forked tongue) and Derrick Sharp (Language policies in schools: a critical examination) teachers of foreign languages emerge as the ones least interested in talking to their colleagues and least aware of the need and purpose of a school language policy. Could the introduction of the study of language into the curriculum offer a way of breaking down the isolation of foreign language teachers and lead them to think more about their role in the total education of their pupils? Could it also be a fruitful development for mother tongue teaching?

Discussion of the study of language as a secondary school subject should not only deal with the pros and cons of such an extension of the curriculum, but also bear closely in mind the effects its introduction would have on the areas of the curriculum most connected with it - mother tongue and foreign language teaching. Language study links these two areas of language activity in the secondary school and, in the current emphasis on language policies across the curriculum, gives an added realism to arguments for including the study of language in the secondary school curriculum in its own right.

If the idea of language study being incorporated in the curriculum is to be accepted, these three questions must be fully explored and receive satisfactory answers:

(1)   What would a course of language study look like in practice, what would be its content and how would it be presented to the pupils?

(2)   What would be the educational justification for such a course?

(3)   How would it relate to mother tongue and foreign language teaching?

This paper will only ask these questions in the context of the 11 to 16 year old range of the secondary school. It is not concerned with language study in the sixth form, where there would be different answers to these questions.

WHAT KIND OF COURSE?

There are two principal ways in which the study of language can be approached at the 11 to 16 year old level. The choice between them must be made in the context of two further considerations: firstly that the pupils already know their mother tongue, and secondly that any course must be capable of adjustment to fit the ability and age range of the pupils.

Language study can be presented as a body of theoretical concepts to be acquired. These would be basic concepts of linguistics with which the pupil would analyse his mother tongue. For instance, the concept of the morpheme is presented to the pupil and then he is told to look for examples. His starting point could be a definition such as: 'A morpheme is a minimum unit of meaning equivalent to or smaller than a word, but not greater than a word'. His subsequent search for examples will force him to qualify and refine the definition. For example he will have to distinguish between bound morphemes, like 're-' in 'rewrite', and free morphemes, like 'back' in 'background'. Another instance of this approach to language study is to present the concept of a transitive verb with a definition such as: 'A transitive verb is a verb that is followed by a direct object'. The pupil then looks for examples of transitive verbs to show his understanding of the definition.

107

This approach to the study of language presents concepts in abstract terms. Learning depends on how well the pupil can handle the definitions and there will be many pupils either unable to apply an abstract definition to actual examples or just uninterested in doing so, because they can see no point in it. In addition, when the definition requires qualification and refinement in the face of less clear-cut examples, all but the most gifted pupils will be confused. It is hard to establish educational justifications for a language study course based on such an approach, to convince teachers that it would contribute to the mental development of pupils right across the ability range and to construct a course that would hold the interest of the majority of pupils.

The second way of presenting language study to 11 to 16 year olds is an examination of the mother tongue to discover patterns that underlie it. This examination would be informed by linguistics to lead the pupil towards an awareness of the questions that that discipline addresses itself to and the way it tries to answer them. For instance, the pupil is shown that the words of the language he uses can often be broken down into smaller units of meaning. This can be done first with free morphemes that combine, as in 'suitcase' or 'armchair'. Then the principle is extended to words made up of free and bound morphemes and so on. As the principle becomes clear, the term morpheme is attached to it. The same approach in the case of transitive verbs puts straightforward examples in front of the pupils and when they have begun to grasp the principle of transitivity in the examples, they are introduced to the name and to less clear-cut variations.

The approach to language study just outlined is centred on the pupil's knowledge of his mother tongue. The pupil is finding out how his own language functions in the first instance, as opposed to trying to grasp a series of terms and procedures for analysing language. A course based on this approach would be an examination of the pupil's control of the data, constructed according to the basic concepts of linguistics. It could vary from concentration on the pupil's immediate language environment to theoretical discussion of patterns discovered in language, but there would be a constant principle, namely that the pupil is led to examine his language for himself and thereby to gain insights about how his mother tongue functions.

The thinking behind this approach is similar to that of <u>Language in use</u> (4). 'Pupils bring to the classroom a native speaker's knowledge of, and intuition about, language and its place in human society. In this sense, the task of the English teacher is not to impart a body of knowledge, but to work upon, develop, refine, and clarify the knowledge and intuitions that his pupils already possess'. (page 11) The teacher is not presenting a body of knowledge for the pupil to absorb, since the pupil already knows his mother tongue. What the teacher is seen as doing - both in <u>Language in use</u> and in the second approach to language study being discussed here - is guiding the pupil to a great awareness of how his mother tongue and language as a whole function.

The term 'guiding' is seen in the same way as the Bullock Report's (5) comment that it is as ridiculous to suppose that teaching begins and ends with 'instruction' as it is to suppose that 'learning by discovery' means leaving children to their own resources. The teacher plots the course and arranges the tasks for the pupils to work their way towards the discoveries he has in mind for them. This second approach to language study uses the pupil's knowledge as its start and constant reference point. The structure of the course - how the teacher selects and orders that knowledge to enable the pupil to explore and gain insights for himself - is derived from basic concepts of linguistics. Such a structure must be systematic and comprehensive, not only so that the pupil is given a balanced introduction, but also so that he develops the feeling of confidence and security in the course that random examinations of his mother tongue would not give him. However the pupil approaches and discovers these basic concepts through having his attention focused on the relevant parts of his own knowledge.

The second approach to language study considered above is the one that promises to be more fruitful and relevant for pupils. Therefore it is this approach that will be considered in this paper from now on. It is an approach that could have a narrow or a broad emphasis. By 'narrow' is meant a concentration on the patterns of sound, structure, meaning and language variety of the pupil's mother tongue. Such an emphasis would complement current work in mother tongue teaching which aims to enable the pupil to use his language to express his personal relations and individual stance vis-a-vis the world.

The views of HM Inspectorate on mother tongue teaching embrace this suggested juxtaposition (6). 'In common with other forms of behaviour, language behaviour depends on an appreciation of the constraints that are operating at the time, and of the ways in which an individual can move within them. Paradoxically the deeper his understanding of the way conventions work, the more free the individual is to achieve his own purpose, to use the language appropriately as an individual but also with reference to the whole context.' (page 21) A 'narrow' emphasis in language study would therefore fit appropriately in a framework of English studies that concentrated on the pupil's personal use of his mother tongue and provide a systematic linguistically-based method of making him more aware of it.

Appendix A contains outline suggestions for the syllabus content of such a 'narrow' language study course. They are meant to be a basis for discussion and argument, not definitive. Two variations of the content are envisaged for two different kinds of pupil. A pupil following alternative A is seen as interested in diachronic language study, in the examination of abstract systems to explain language and in exercises to illustrate a principle of language study. He is the pupil whose interest in language prompts him to search for reasons to explain its nature and content. Alternative B is for the pupil whose interest is more likely to be restricted to the phenomenon of language itself. He is interested in language topics that impinge on him immediately and which contain their own relevance. For example he is more likely to respond to an examination of how his speech mechanism works or how the language he uses differs from other dialects of English, than he is in examining the great vowel shift or constructing a computer programme that illustrates the unbounded nature of a natural language.

Language topics which are proposed jointly for both alternatives would be given a different treatment depending on the kind of pupil being taught. Indeed this broad division of pupils into two types is a broad recognition of the fact that a language study syllabus, just like any other syllabus, must be adjusted to the pupils, if the best progress is to be made. It is wrong to aim to fit all pupils to a uniform syllabus. This does not affect the principle advocated above that language study should be based upon and revolve around the pupil's knowledge of his mother tongue. Some pupils more than others will develop their interest beyond their immediate language surroundings and the teacher should select and present the syllabus with this in mind.

Appendix A lists the proposed content of both alternatives under sub-headings of twelve areas of language study. The introduction of each topic under these sub-headings is related to years 1 to 5 of the 11 to 16 age range.

A 'broad' emphasis would still be centred on the pupil's command of his mother tongue, but would range more widely into, for example, language acquisition, non-linguistic communication, animal communication and instrumental phonetics. A course with a 'broad' emphasis would lead naturally into most other subject areas. Appendix B presents a model of such potential connections. It is not detailed or exhaustive. It is designed to show the central position that a 'broad' language study course would inevitably occupy in the curriculum. A course with such a wide perspective would not fit easily into English studies alone and it would therefore make more sense if it were seen as standing on its own as Language study. It would, however, still need to be based on linguistic principles and approached in a systematic manner. It would also still need to be based on the pupil's own knowledge of his linguistic ability.

EDUCATIONAL ARGUMENTS FOR THE STUDY OF LANGUAGE

These arguments are not presented in any order of merit or importance. Some may be more applicable to the 'narrow' emphasis; others may make more sense in the context of the 'broad' emphasis. No attempt has been made to categorise them according to these two approaches to course content. Finally, the arguments refer only to a pupil-centred data-orientated approach.

It has been argued that language study could complement current mother tongue teaching aims. If it is accepted that pattern and use are not two divorced areas of language, but inextricably involved with each other, then examining the phonological, syntactic and all other patterns of a language has as much place in mother tongue teaching as development of the pupil's own language used. Further, the reference by HMI to 'constraints' (already quoted (6)) must refer to all kinds of constraint in the pattern systems of the mother tongue if the statement is to be valid, not just to selected ones. If the methodology of the proposed language study coincides with the approach already adopted in mother tongue teaching - and the claim here is not only that it does coincide with the language area and approach identified by Britton (7), for example, as particularly the concern of the English lesson, but furthermore that it is the only feasible way of approaching language study in the 11 to 16 age group - then there would seem to be no pedagogical reason to exclude the element of language examination proposed here, without which the pupil's language education would be incomplete. Rosen and Stratta (8) write that: 'it remains a problem to find a way of linking the study of language not only with active learning but also with the productive uses of language. It may be that language study will remain in its own niche with only tenuous links with the rest of English. Yet if the old attractive goal of a unified teaching of English is to be reached, ways will have to be found of making the study of English part of the process of becoming a more proficient user of the mother tongue.' (page 35) The suggestions presented here may offer a way of meeting the challenge of Rosen and Stratta.

Gatherer writes (9) that: 'The place of grammar in the classroom has been diminished in the last half century because the traditional pedagogical grammar was thought to be deficient, but also because teachers lost faith in grammar work as a source of training in the use of language. Modern English teaching begins with the belief that you best learn English through using it, and our concentration on the productive involvement of children in practical language-using situations is unquestionably justified.' (page 62) He goes as far as to say that: 'The importance of such practice is so great that efficient teachers rightly resist any activity which may compete for the time required, especially when they cannot fully accept that the activity is genuinely useful.' (page 62) At the same time he points out (page 63) that 'There is a good case for the acquisition of grammatical knowledge by all teachers, so that they can convey to their pupils the linguistic insights which improve efficiency in the use of language at all stages and for all purposes.'

It is the argument of this paper that it would be possible to construct a systematic course, based on linguistic principles, that led the pupil to discover linguistic insights for himself in his own use of language. Gatherer does, in fact, envisage grammar in the English lesson. He states that (page 63) English teachers '... should be able, when they see the need, to give their pupils illustrated explanations to show the value of particular applications of rules and conventions - thus they should be capable of giving lessons on grammar in order to explicate a point of style, or to show how common errors can be understood and avoided, or to give the pupils guidance as to how they can construct more effective sentences. All of these activities are better thought of as rhetoric, the art of composition; but they require grammatical analysis to be properly appreciated.' Since grammar and, with it, grammatical terminology are going to make their appearance in the English lesson, it would be preferable if they were systematically presented in a manner that harmonises with the aims of current English teaching.

It is generally accepted that traditional grammar teaching did not improve performance in the use of English. Nevertheless there is a feeling that a better understanding of the functioning of the mother tongue has a beneficial effect on the use of it. This feeling is voiced in the quotation from HM Inspectorate's working papers on the Curriculum 11-16 (page 21). Gatherer (9) talks of conveying to pupils '...the linguistic insights which improve efficiency in the use of language.' (page 63) The authors of Language in use (10) state in their introduction to the course book that '...a basic premise of the volume is that the development of awareness in the pupil will have a positive effect upon his competence, although this effect is likely to be indirect and may not show up immediately.' (page 10)

It may therefore be that language study can have a beneficial effect on performance, but that the key lies in the method of presenting it and not in the actual study itself. The authors of Language in use (11) present this point, when arguing that there is a crucial relationship between awareness and competence. 'The long argument over the teaching of 'grammar' in schools really concentrated upon the effects of a certain kind of explicit knowledge of the language, such as classification of words and parsing, on pupils' use of language. When teachers discovered that there seemed to be no observable effect of the one upon the other, they rejected teaching about the language because they could see no justification for it. It was unfortunate that the study of language came to be identified with a rudimentary and inadequate type of knowledge about language, and that its validity was judged solely upon its power to increase competence.' (page 10)

The authors of Language in use (11) considered that their course book did not (12) '...ask for any special reading or preparation on the part of the teacher.' (page 8) This is not an opinion that would have much support now. Indeed since the emphasis in the Bullock Report on learning taking place through language right across the curriculum, it is held to be important for teachers of any subject, let alone the mother tongue, to have a course in language study as part of their initial training. Britton puts it in this way (13): '...(children) learn the mother tongue by using it to serve their own purposes; what they have achieved with its aid by the time they are five is a substantial grasp on what life is all about. It seems to me essential, therefore, that the years of schooling, in all areas of the curriculum, should continue that process, extend and intensify it. This is to see the mother tongue as a means to successful learning operations, and to value what is learned through language beyond anything that may be described as achievement in language. There is no paradox in suggesting that the task of assisting children to achieve more by means of language will demand considerable linguistic and pedagogical expertise on the part of all teachers,...' (page 35). Mittins claims that it is obvious that (14) '...all teachers of English, and certainly English specialists, should be conversant with those aspects of language study, of linguistics, that have relevance to the educational process.' (page 97) Teachers, and particularly teachers of English, are becoming more aware of language study in some form, both through their training and through arguments about its relevance to the language and learning of their pupils.

A course of language study would give an opportunity for a common terminology for talk about language to be established in a school. As such, the course would provide a base and a departure point in the curriculum on which to develop the language policy of a school. One instance of this would be systematic presentation to pupils in a language study course of grammatical, ie syntactic, terms and the concepts behind them. Such a presentation would be of relevance to all other teachers in discussing with pupils how to use language, but none more so than foreign language teachers. It was foreign language teachers that Hawkins had in mind particularly when he referred to the possibility of different teachers using 'a grammatical terminology which may lead to the pupil being asked to attach different concepts to the same linguistic label.' (15)

If a language study course were taught by teachers of other specialisms rather than mother tongue specialists, it would help to make the point that all teachers are teachers of language when they use language to teach. Only if teachers realise and accept this fact can they develop a coherent view of how they should use language with their pupils.

Godfrey and Hawkins (16), in discussing the training of foreign language teachers, recommend that they be equipped to teach younger secondary school pupils both their foreign language and their mother tongue for two reasons. The first stems from the crucial difference between mother tongue and foreign language teaching and its consequences in the classroom. 'The language teacher is at a disadvantage in establishing confident relationships with his pupils because he must so far as possible avoid using English in the foreign language classroom. Pupils' responses are inevitably stilted and this affects the kinds of teacher-pupil relationships that are possible and pupils' liking for and persistence with the subject.' Secondly, (16), 'The foreign language teacher who also teaches English to his pupils can help them in many ways to understand how the two languages interact. The teacher can also better appreciate the individual pupil's linguistic problems and see his or her performance in the foreign language classroom in better perspective.' (pages 75-6) A language study course would be suitable for putting such a proposal into effect and, if it were put into effect, it would make a contribution to involving the foreign language teacher more in the formation of language policies and to making him think beyond the borders of his specialism.

In their second reason for arguing that foreign language teachers should also be mother tongue teachers in the lower part of the secondary school, Godfrey and Hawkins state that the foreign language teacher could show the pupils how the languages involved interacted. If this principle is expanded, it would provide an opening in the curriculum, not only for an unemotional comparison of social and regional dialects of English, but also for the mother tongues of immigrants to be given recognition and sympathetic treatment. The possibility of using a course in language study to help solve this pressing and neglected problem is mentioned by Perren (17) who states that: 'Such a course would aim to promote an awareness of differences in language behaviour and should consciously aim to increase sympathy towards speakers of other dialects and languages with a different background or culture. Taking as a starting point the children's own experience of language (ie their own initiation into a foreign language, their experience of immigrant pupils in and out of school, and their acquaintance with local dialects) it could well provide excellent opportunities for enriching their use of English, for increasing their understanding of all communication processes, for developing an awareness of the contribution of other groups to society, and for providing insight into the development of Europe - and indeed the influence of Europe on the rest of the world.' (pages 113-14) Comparison of constraint and function between the mother tongue and other languages, as well as comparisons between various mother tongue dialects, could provide a means of opening up the minds of pupils and increasing their tolerance of other groups in society. It could also lead to greater self-respect in members of minority linguistic or dialect groups, when they see their own use of language treated on a par with that of the majority.

The development of notional syllabuses and more generally the increasing emphasis in foreign language teaching on the practical, communicative aspect of language, offers the possibility of bringing the foreign language teacher's conception of language closer to that of the English mother tongue teacher. Wilkins writes (18): 'Language learning has concentrated much more on the use of language to report and describe than on doing things through language. This is because the learning of lexical labels...has been substituted for the learning of how the acts themselves are performed and because grammatical categories have too often been taken as categories of communication too...' 'The whole basis of a notional approach to language teaching derives from the conviction that what people want to do through language is more important than mastery of the language as an unapplied system.' (page 42) The emergence of this trend could produce a greater sympathy among foreign language teachers for the aims of mother tongue teaching. It would also mean less emphasis in foreign language teaching on grammatical analysis. Of course the pupils will still need to learn the new set of linguistic patterns before they can use them and it is this inescapable fact that particularly distinguishes foreign language teaching from mother tongue teaching and most other areas of the curriculum. However, notional syllabuses emphasise to the foreign language teacher a view of language as a means of communication, rather than as a system to be explored.

A language study course would include a systematic examination of speech sound and rhythms. Its aim would be to make the pupils more aware of different sounds and speech patterns, as part of the process of awakening them to the fact that they live in a multi-dialectal, polyglot world. It would also have a more general educational value of increasing the accuracy of their listening. As Hawkins says (19): 'Children need to learn to hear just as they need to learn to see.' (page 68) A language study course would also emphasise the arbitrariness of linguistic signs and help the pupil to make a distinction in his mind between the concept and the naming of the concept. Hawkins has termed this 'breaking out of the monolingual straitjacket - grasping the difference between 'that's water' and 'that's called water'. (Private submission to NCLE Working Party B)

A language study course in the secondary school would be the ideal area of the curriculum to teach potential parents and potential teachers about the process of language acquisition in babies. As Hawkins points out (20), 'Contrast the excellent school courses in hygiene, diet, domestic economy, biology with most parents' insensitiveness and lack of sophistication in listening to their infants' language. How many parents appreciate the role that dialogue with parents, grandparents and other adults can play in the child's early conceptual/linguistic experience?' (pages 61-2)

A language study course would fill what Rosen and Stratta (21) term a 'vacuum' (page 29) in the curriculum by systematically introducing pupils to a field of human study, which is currently only haphazardly catered for. Hawkins writes (22) that '...most aspects of human behaviour in groups have come to have an accepted place in the curriculum.... (They) do not have to make their claim to be studied in the curriculum. Their place is accepted and the only discussion is about the best methods and materials to use, how to assess the learning and how to train the teachers. Yet the essential aspect of group behaviour on which the rest depends, namely language, is not a curriculum subject. Language as an aspect of human behaviour is not methodically studied though some aspects may be incidentally, and haphazardly, broached in the course of acquiring and using the mother tongue or, more probably, in the foreign language lesson.' (page 61)

OBJECTIONS TO THE INTRODUCTION OF THE STUDY OF LANGUAGE

That the subject matter of such a course would be deadening and the concepts presented would be too difficult for all but the brightest.

This objection is a valid one if the course requires pupils to make detailed and analytical statements about language, to learn a body of facts about language. The approach outlined on the first half of this paper seeks to avoid this objection by working through the pupil's own command of his mother tongue to lead him to awareness of concepts to do with language.

That linguistics is not a settled discipline and therefore is not ready to have a secondary school course based upon it.

This objection involves a confusion between general principles of linguistic enquiry and explanatory models of language. There is debate in linguistics over the kind of model that would best explain the facts of language, but this debate takes place within generally accepted principles of enquiry. These principles date back at least to the teaching of de Saussure before World War I and it would be upon them that any language study course would be based, not on one particular model of language. Culler (23) states that de Saussure provided 'the influence of specific concepts which are strictly original to Saussure but which he helped to promote.... Many of the developments of modern linguistics can be described as investigations of the precise nature and import of these concepts. Considering them in turn, we can see that even when Saussure's original formulations have been found wanting he posed the questions which have animated modern linguistics.' (page 80)

That there are not enough teachers capable of teaching language study.

This is a serious obstacle, but not as serious as it was 15 years ago when the authors of the Lockwood Report (24) stated: 'We should also like to see the foundations laid of a study of some of the basic principles of linguistics, with English as the language of exemplification. Because there is little study of this subject in the universities, however, and because, as a consequence, few teachers are equippped to give instruction in it, we should not regard a specialised course of this type as immediately practicable.' (page 27) The subject has expanded greatly at university level and there are now enough potential teachers at sixth form level to make it feasible for GCE examination boards to be introducing language study options into their syllabuses at A level. The number of possible teachers will be greatly increased when teacher training establishments put into effect the recommendation of the Bullock Report that there should be a specific compulsory component devoted to the study of language in the training programme of all teachers.

That there are no suitable teaching materials available.

This is less of an obstacle than the lack of suitably trained teachers, if a data-orientated, pupil-centred approach is followed. If the aims and objectives of such a course were clearly laid out for the linguistically trained teacher, he should be able to organise his own teaching and compile his own material for parts of the course. For other parts, as for example comparison of phonological systems of different languages, he will require expert help. The preparation of a course book with resource material, rather than a textbook, would seem to be what is required.

That there is no room on the timetable.

What disappears from the timetable does depend to a certain extent on what is already there. Hawkins (25) suggests: '...some of the time currently given to English and to a foreign language, because I see the new subject being a link between these two, and being worked out and taught in collaboration by the teachers of English and of the European and ethnic minority languages.' (page 67) Estimating an average allocation of 25 per cent of periods to mother tongue and foreign language teaching (26), ie 10 in a 40-period week or 9 in a 35-period week, two periods of language study per week from this total of 10 or 9 would leave 8 or 7 to be shared by the foreign language and the mother tongue teaching. A more precise answer would depend on the particular curricular arrangements of the school, particularly in the case of a language study couse with a 'broad' emphasis. It would also depend on the level of ability of the pupils and the age group.

That there is a danger of a language study course becoming a drilling of 'correct' forms akin to traditional grammar teaching.

The answer of this lies in the proper grasp by the teachers of the aims and objectives of a language study course and the way they guide the pupils along the course.

RELATIONSHIP OF LANGUAGE STUDY TO MOTHER TONGUE AND FOREIGN LANGUAGE TEACHING

The aims and conditions of mother tongue and foreign language teaching have been surveyed in B C King's paper (Language teachers speak with forked tongue), which makes clear the differences between the two kinds of teaching as well as points of contact. The aims of mother tongue and foreign language teaching are summarised here briefly for the sake of completing the argument.

HM Inspectorate define the aims of mother tongue teaching as follows (27): 'The English department must help pupils to investigate language explicitly in its various forms, and with support from other departments, to keep alive pupils' interests in and response to language.' 'The subject-matter of 'English; will be the study and production of language in variety, and the discovery of similarity, difference and pattern.' (page 21) These aims include without difficulty the study of language through the mother tongue.

A methodological approach to language study that makes the pupil's control of the data its central principle will complement and be in tune with mother tongue teaching, which sees the pupil's use of language as a means for personal exploration and expression and for extending the range of language that he controls.

The immediate aim of foreign language teaching is some degree of mastery of the target language. Beyond that there are broad educational aims that are summarised as follows by the Scottish Central Committee for Modern Languages in their submission to the Munn Committee (28): 'To develop in children an understanding of, an interest in and a respect for the way of life in a society other than their own, thus adding to their understanding of themselves and of their own society.... It has both an affective and cognitive side - affective in its fostering of attitudes of tolerance and respect for others; cognitive in the intellectual demands it places on pupils to view reality from more than one (their own) point of view.' (page 10) 'To sensitise pupils to the nature and the functions of language.' (page 11) Both of these broad educational aims of foreign language teaching can also be applied to a language study course based on the mother tongue.

The foreign language teacher's conception of language is beginning to change towards seeing language in terms of communicative acts rather than in terms of grammatical categories. This change brings foreign language teachers closer to mother tongue teachers in the view of language they hold.

Language study can provide an area of the curriculum closely related in its educational aims both to mother tongue and to foreign language teaching. With the possibility of a greater affinity in their concepts of language, there is greater opportunity for a language study course to provide a terminology of language which is relevant and acceptable to both.

Mother tongue teaching and foreign language teaching handle different learning situations. With that difference borne in mind, language study can form a link between them.

REFERENCES

1. Hawkins, E W: Language as a curriculum study. In: The mother tongue and other languages in education. Centre for Information on Language Teaching and Research, 1979. (NCLE Papers and reports 2.)

2. Committee of Inquiry into Reading and the Use of English: A language for life (The Bullock Report). HMSO, 1975.

3. ibid.

4. Doughty, P, J Pearce and G Thornton: Language in use. Edward Arnold, 1971.

5. Committee of Inquiry into Reading and the Use of English, op. cit.

6. HM Inspectorate of Schools: Curriculum 11-16: working papers by HM Inspectorate.... Department of Education and Science, 1977 (1978).

7. Britton, J: English in the curriculum. In: The space between...: English and foreign languages at school. Centre for Information on Language Teaching and Research, 1974. (CILT Reports and Papers 10.)

8   Rosen, H and L Stratt: English as a mother tongue. In: The mother tongue and other languages in education.. Centre for Information on Language Teaching and research, 1979. (NCLE Papers and Reports 2.)

9. Gatherer, W A: Language and education. In: Language across the curriculum; (by) M Marland. Heinemann Educational, 1977.

10. Doughty, Pearce and Thornton, op. cit.

11. ibid.

12. ibid.

13. Britton, op. cit.

14. Spicer, A, W H Mittins and C E Dawson: The education and training of teachers. In: The mother tongue and other languages in education. Centre for Information on Language Teaching and Research, 1979. (NCLE Papers and Reports 2.)

15. Hawkins, E W: The linguistic needs of pupils. In: Foreign languages in education. Centre for Information on Language Teaching and Research, 1969. (NCLE Papers and Reports 1.)

16. Godfrey, R J and E W Hawkins: The education of teachers of foreign languages. In: Foreign languages in education. Centre for Information on Language Teaching and Research, 1979. (NCLE Papers and Reports 1.)

17. Perren, G E: Some meeting points. In: The space between...: English and foreign language at school. Centre for Information on Language Teaching and Research, 1974. (CILT Reports and Papers 10.)

18. Wilkins, D A: Notional syllabuses. Oxford University Press, 1976.

19. Hawkins, E W: Language as a curriculum study. (See no. 1.)

20. ibid.

21. Rosen and Stratt, op. cit.

22. Hawkins, E W: Language as a curriculum study. (See no. 1.)

23. Culler, J: Saussure. Fontana, 1976. (Modern Masters.)

24. The examining of English language; Eighth Report of the Secondary School Examination Council. HMSO, 1964.

25. Hawkins, E W: Languages as a curriculum study. (See no. 1.)

26. HM Inspectorate, op. cit, and C Burstall: Primary French in the balance. (NFER Publishing Co., 1974), p 204-5, for information on allocation of French periods in the first two years of the secondary school.

27. HM Inspectorate, op. cit.

28. Modern languages in the secondary curriculum - Scotland (submission to the Munn Committee). Scottish Central Committee for Modern Languages. (Paper NC 3 for the First Assembly of the National Congress on Languages in Education.)

APPENDIX A

Pages 121 and 122 contain outline suggestions of the syllabus content of a language study course in the 11 to 16 age range, with elements of the main areas of language study related to their proposed year of introduction. Suggestions in the upper half only of each year group line (Alternative A) contain a greater diachronic and theoretical emphasis.

Those in the lower half only of each year group line (Alternative B) have a more synchronic and immediately accessible emphasis.

Those that are presented as applying to both alternatives in a year group line will still require variations in the way they are introduced to the pupils. Topics are not meant to be restricted to the years in which they are introduced. They can be continued into subsequent years.

Year	Aim	Non-linguistic Communication	Signs	Animal Communication	First Language Acquisition	Language as sound	Phonetics
1 (11-12)	A	use of mime, gesture, speech sound without clear articulation, intonation & stress,	examination of e.g. traffic signs, labelling of e.g the school with signs for non-English speakers,				description of human speech mechanism, speech sounds, - phonetic script, intonation and stress and their relation to
	B						punctuation,
2 (12-13)	A	examination of gestures in different cultures,		examination of examples of animal communication e.g. bees,		deaf and dumb language, morse, semaphore, braille, examination of different writing systems and alphabets, comparison of spellings of same words in different languages,	
	B						
3 (13-14)	A			attempts to teach animals human language, examination of	study of child learning to talk, analysis of		
	B						
4 (14-15)	A	analysis of e.g charades to show principles involved,	arbitrary and non-arbitrary signs, their use in	problems involved,	taped examples,	history of writing,	transcription of English, marking of intonation intonation exercises,
	B			as 3rd year A	as for 3rd year A, but with less analysis,		
5 (15-16)	A	examination of limits of non-linguistic communication,	e.g. history (heraldry), geography (maps),				and stress
	B						

Year	Alt	Instrumental Phonetics	Phonology	Syntactic Elements	Syntactic Relations	Semantics	Language Change and Variety
1	A		sounds of English, sound variation of English dialects,	examination of basic elements of English sentence structure,	examination of English sentence structure and compound sentences,	comparison of American and British English meanings, English dialect expressions, rhyming slang,	language families different languages in British Isles, language borrowings, regional variety in English usage, social variety in English usage.
	B						
2	A					secret codes, synonyms, homonyms, onomatopoeia, compounds,	register, variation of personal use of English, degrees of familiarity,
	B						
3	A		sound systems of other languages, changes in sound of same word in different langs.	morpheme theory, syntactic sub-categories, deviation,	complex English sentence structure,	extra-sentential reference,	examination of synchronic variation based on TV, radio, advertising, etc,
	B						
4	A	experiments and theory of physics of sound,	figures of speech based on phonol. and intonation,	figures of speech based on use of syntactic elements,	figures of speech based on syntactic relations,	figures of speech based on relation of meaning to context,	change in English since Chaucer – phonological, syntactic, lexical
	B		exercises in changes of sound to affect meaning and use,	as 3rd Year A with emphasis on example,	as 3rd Year A	as 3rd Year A with emphasis on example,	
5	A	measurement of pupils' speech,	phoneme and allophone,		computer programs based on English structure,	exercises in paraphrase, precis and anomaly,	
	B						

Model of Connections between Language Study and Other Areas of an 11-16 Curriculum

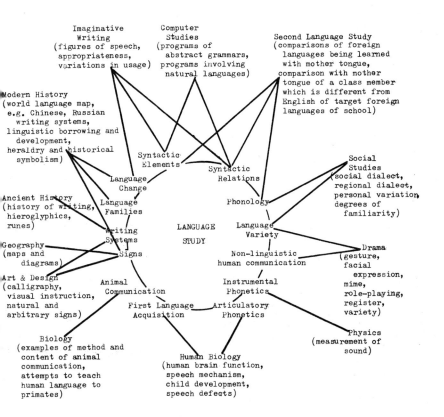

Imaginative Writing (figures of speech, appropriateness, variations in usage)

Computer Studies (programs of abstract grammars, programs involving natural languages)

Second Language Study (comparisons of foreign languages being learned with mother tongue, comparison with mother tongue of a class member which is different from English of target foreign languages of school)

Modern History (world language map, e.g. Chinese, Russian writing systems, linguistic borrowing and development, heraldry and historical symbolism)

Ancient History (history of writing, hieroglyphics, runes)

Geography (maps and diagrams)

Art & Design (calligraphy, visual instruction, natural and arbitrary signs)

Biology (examples of method and content of animal communication, attempts to teach human language to primates)

Syntactic Elements

Language Change

Language Families

Writing Systems

Signs

Animal Communication

First Language Acquisition

Human Biology (human brain function, speech mechanism, child development, speech defects)

LANGUAGE STUDY

Syntactic Relations

Phonology

Language Variety

Non-linguistic human communication

Instrumental Phonetics

Articulatory Phonetics

Social Studies (social dialect, regional dialect, personal variation, degrees of familiarity)

Drama (gesture, facial expression, mime, role-playing, register, variety)

Physics (measurement of sound)

LANGUAGE POLICIES IN SCHOOLS: A CRITICAL EXAMINATION

D Sharp

'... when we come into teaching we must recognise that we have entered a profession that is dependent on language: the curriculum depends on communication.' (Michael Marland)

INTRODUCTION

There is no attempt to be exhaustive in this study, which is an examination of material which could be gathered over a period of some nine months. There is no detailed reference to schools by name, because some asked that this should not happen, but the sources used are listed at the end of the paper. In addition there were many casual conversations with teachers and LEA officers which have contributed to the picture.

SCOPE

There is no attempt, either, to justify the Bullock Report recommendations or the many arguments which explain the importance of language across the curriculum. The paper will concentrate on examples from schools and local education authorities which have worked at the development of language policies and have provided written (or, in a few cases, oral) evidence. The concept of a school language policy has been examined in the companion paper by Dr W H Mittins, which should be read in conjunction with this one.

THE EVIDENCE

It has not been easy to collect examples of school language policies, apart from those published or advertised as readily available. Schools are understandably reluctant to release material intended for internal use, or perhaps at most for local or regional consultation, though gradually a fairly substantial body of evidence did build up.

There is in many cases considerable emphasis on the tentative nature of the work, and on the importance of the process, rather than formulation in writing, however ephemeral the particular document is intended to be.

'... some schools are beginning to discuss these matters (language for learning, language across the curriculum), and these discussions we feel must be valuable. We, however, think actual language policies should be approached with caution. All that we have observed in our work and have presented in this book suggests that no <u>single</u> operation will be effective.' (<u>Writing and learning across the curriculum 11-16</u>, Nancy Martin and others, Ward Lock Educational for Schools Council, 1976, page 169.)

Although the arguments against written policies are appreciated, because it in only too easy to think the task has been completed and 'enshrined' in a definitive document, the value of written records of discussions and decisions must not be ignored. They provide an accessible account of the all-important process on which to build and they are invaluable in a large school with dissemination problems. In any school they are of great service when a new member joins the staff and needs to be involved as soon as possible in the continuing development of language policy. These benefits are in addition to the valuable discipline of actually writing down a plan of action and the greater precision which this process encourages.

Important factors in the development of language policies are persistence and a refusal to be discouraged. It is a long-term process, even when the need for a school language policy has been appreciated, for confusion or doubt about the nature and aims of such a policy and about the meaning of the terms involved often remains. There are many examples of what may be called 'Stage 1' policies, records of excellent starts on some of the more obvious and immediate features (such as spelling and punctuation) which have gradually faded over a year or so without dealing more comprehensively with other important and more difficult aspects (such as technical/non-technical language). Reasons for this may include lack of expert guidance, the loss of a key member of staff, or simply ever-increasing pressures on time and energy.

There is also some evidence of a 'Bullock is dead' attitude to explain lack of action, sometimes genuinely, perhaps sometimes as a rationalisation. Because some of the Bullock recommendations need money for implementation, the suggestion is that the recommendations as a whole will be or have been abandoned. Admittedly, the appointment of specialist 'language consultants' to schools need money, though not as much as the establishment of language centres, but in most circumstances language policies may be developed and implemented with no, or very few, extra resources, often by redeploying existing staff, for example.

The 'Bullock is dead' attitude must be distinguished from a rejection of the concept of language across the curriculum for other reasons. Probably the most prevalent is a preference for the traditional idea of the mother tongue department servicing all the others, whereby language remains the concern of the English department alone. This preference may be reinforced by internal subject pressures on time and energy, and/or by mistrust of an exclusively English movement towards language across the curriculum.

VALUABLE FEATURES OF THE LANGUAGE POLICIES

Very many important features emerge from a study of the language policies. They cover a wide range, and what follows is a selection of those considered to be most important, most interesting or most stimulating, without any attempt to place them in rank order.

In general terms, the whole staff of a primary shool can operate as a unit, because they are usually more immediately sympathetic and aware of the issues, not least because most teach 'across the curriculum'. It is easier organisationally to develop and implement a language policy. Secondary schools, in contrast, normally need to work through a committee or working party; perhaps there may be several working parties, with varied compositions and tasks.

In large schools several different approaches have been tried. One started with a meeting for anyone interested and then called a meeting of representatives from the various curriculum areas. The work was broken down into manageable units after that. Another formed a staff committee of mixed subjects and levels of seniority which referred topics, such as reading levels and marking, for departmental discussion and report back, proceeding in this way for some considerable time. One school establishes a new working party each September, including only two members from the previous year's party for continuity. The aim is to involve more members of staff, and presumably in the long term some form of rota system will be used.

No one approach is better than the others. As with all aspects of this work, that method is best which suits the people involved and the circumstances. All agree that committees should concentrate initially on specific questions and make specific suggestions and recommendations. There is clearly a need to focus efforts, and to work from the study of practical problems to a grasp of the principles involved.

Ways of starting vary greatly.

The start may be purely exploratory, even sceptical, but it usually includes an examination of current practice in the school. An outside expert talking to the staff on the ideas behind the language for learning movement is normally not a profitable way in, because he may create misunderstandings and defensive antagonisms. One school carried out readability tests on all work-sheets and textbooks. Questionnaires are often used to stimulate discussion in framing them and to provide information for further discussion and exploration. (Examples may be found in Language policies in schools, (page 27) and Language across the curriculum: guidelines for schools, (page 21.)

Methods used to initiate language policy work also include a study of reading skills, an examination of the range of writing demands on a pupil (based on the 'diary' of one pupil for a day or a week), standards of presentation, and the taping of lessons in order to discuss the language aspects. More challenging opening gambits include oral work, assessment and criteria of language progress.

One school found that the teaching of study skills, including note-taking, was valuable in itself and as an approach to co-operation in language across the curriculum. The development of a unified marking scheme was another helpful approach. Another school decided that heads of departments should each produce a list of 20 words which are commonly wrongly spelt and that such lists should be used in the school detention. Consider the pros and cons of this as part of an opening campaign for a school language policy!

To what extent are striking techniques like the Fog Index of readability helpful in engaging colleagues' interest? May they be misleading, or even dangerous, by fostering incomplete notions about readability?

Case-studies of pupils' language experiences in school, usually in the form of 'diaries', are valuable not only initially, but continually, both to assess changing demands and to determine the effect of new policies.

Mixed-ability groupings create a special need for a language policy. They tend to highlight both the possibilities for development and the difficulties. Any good language policy will pay particular attention to the needs of the less able and will involve the remedial department, who have a vested interest in one aspect of language for learning (compare and contrast the English department).

Teachers must be willing to expose themselves to (constuctive) criticism by, for example, recording lessons for discussion with colleagues. Self-criticism is a vital first step, while reluctance to criticise self is a first and insurmountable barrier comparable in its effects to a refusal to tolerate 'interference' in subject aims and methods. How can a tradition of self-evaluation be encouraged amongst teachers? Critical analysis should extend to the general use of language in the school, as in assembly and on notice boards.

Many stress that there is value in the exchange of information about what goes on in curriculum areas other than one's own, both in its own right and as a first step in the formulation of a policy.

The staff library should include books on language across the curriculum, and also basic books on language. A policy must include increasing staff awareness and understanding of language in learning by reading, discussion and study of the total language environment of the school. This raises the often acute problem of who on the staff has the necessary expertise to initiate and lead study. Some universities, polytechnics and institutes of higher education do provide courses (some of them specific) which train 'language consultants' in the Bullock sense, but provision is far from adequate overall.

Several schools have found one-day in-service seminars for the whole staff of considerable help, both initially and later. Some prefer two half-days, spaced out. All stress the value of regular in-service work over a long period. Opinions are divided on the wisdom of inviting outside experts to such meetings, though those in favour think it is a matter for the second stage of development rather than the first. Similarly with published accounts of policies, which some find helpful but others regard as too restricting and prescriptive. These are matters of taste and interpretation, of course.

An agreed policy should represent intentions and should allow for individual approaches and interpretations within the agreed areas. Both short-term and long-term goals are needed, though we must remember the caveat on page 23 of <u>Language policies in schools</u>: 'A definitive language policy cannot usefully by regarded as an ultimate aim.' The process should be continuous and without a final end in sight, according to some, though others stress the need for a sense of progress and a clearly-laid-out path. Most agree on the importance of outcomes which can be seen to be realised within a term or a year.

The head's role is crucial. Even if not himself initiating policy, he needs to be fully in sympathy, strongly supportive and able to delegate. Certainly a senior member of staff should chair or organise, at least initially, to provide impetus, to confirm support and because there is value in knowing the attitudes and prejudices of the staff in order to develop successful tactics. Those organising the work must move slowly and carry as many colleagues with them as possible at each stage. A working party must be self-educating, and time is therefore essential.

Some schools find discussion papers from different subject areas helpful, but these often vary considerably in quality and insight, in some cases hindering by increasing tensions and interdepartmental rivalries. Others prefer to keep minutes of working party meetings as a basis for further discussion.

Science departments often take the lead, or are actively involved. Why? Perhaps because they are especially concerned about technical language, one important and easily recognised feature of language across the curriculum? Perhaps because science teachers see pupils struggling to apply new terms to new concepts in a particular register, or to grasp the significance of everyday terms used in specific, scientific contexts? Contrast the part played by modern languages as described later in this paper. Can we explain the difference in approach? Successful exploration of this question would illuminate the main areas of concern in this and the related papers.

The rival claims of 'lingustics' and 'language in education' are reflected in this field, with continuing problems of definition and lines of demarcation. 'Teachers do not generaly find linguistics helpful in this matter.' (Irene Robertson in an oral submission.) What does this mean?

What are the implications? How can linguistics be made more accessible and relevant to teachers? What kinds of linguistics are we thinking of?

Most schools feel the need for outside help and resources, though understandably on their own terms. Liaison between schools can lead to area activity, led by an adviser, though the role of the advisory service and teachers' centres varies greatly.

It is highly desirable to involve pupils as well as staff in any discussions. A simple example is for members of staff to explain their marking and assessment procedures to pupils and to be prepared to discuss them. One comment suggests that the preoccupations and aspirations of pupils have been largely unregarded in the consideration of language policies.

In a similar way parents should be involved as much as posible, usually at PTA meetings. Communication, understanding and involvement are crucial factors for all in language for learning.

THE ROLE OF THE ENGLISH DEPARTMENT

'In secondary schools, with only a few exceptions, consideration of language across the curriculum did appear to amount to little more than the preparation of papers by a few heads of the English Departments. In addition, when the implications for school policy and classroom practice of such papers were explored, it had soon become clear that the ideas ran counter to many people's social and educational convictions and that the ideas challenged the traditional ways of working in a secondary school.' (From the report of a talk by W R Jenkins HMI at a follow-up conference on 19 September 1978 on 'Two languages for life', organised by the Schools Council Committee for Wales.)

The Bullock Report seems to assume that the English department will have a special contribution to make to the language policy of a school. A study of what has happened to date raises two questions:

Is it true that all English departments are sophisticated or especially interested in language work?

Is it wise for the head of English to take the initiative, even if he is competent and is asked to do so?

Practice varies. The only general agreement is that members of the English department should have previously discussed language for learning within their own curriculum area.

Another typical response suggested that the English department has plenty to do within its own department. Members considered there was not enough talk or drama and too much emphasis on written language. They were too busy putting their own house in order. Here questions of priority often arise.

In the schools studied, English is seen, in some cases, as the supporting or servicing department. Others proceed with the development of a language policy but decide that the English department has a <u>special</u> function in this field.

In yet other schools the head of English does give a lead by, for example, chairing a working party or preparing a discussion document, and members of the department support him by regular attendance.

In contrast one school argues that <u>across the curriculum</u> should be reflected by the English department's not taking the lead in this way, while some schools reject the whole concept of language across the curriculum.

In primary schools the initiative usually rests with the head, although there may be a member of staff with responsibility for or special interest in language. Some of the internal organisational difficulties may well not exist, but equally there may be a great need for outside help.

As always the choice of approach depends on the people involved and the circumstances of the school, a constant theme in this paper.

THE CONTRIBUTION OF TEACHERS OF FOREIGN LANGUAGES

It would seem logical to suggest that teachers of foreign languages (like teachers of English) would have a special contribution to make. Yet they rate no mention in the Bullock Report.

There is very little interest shown by foreign language teachers, according to Irene Robertson. She suggests that many of them are only just beginning to consider language in terms other than the formal aspects. The language policies examined support Irene Robertson's view. One school reports that, apart from English, 'the most interested are likely to be the heads of mathematics, geography, physics and RE'. Another lists geography, history, science and English as most active, and a third mathematics, science, history, craft and English.

In two of the cases found in which modern languages had taken part, their contribution was at a low level and seemed concerned solely with superficial aspects of language. One would like to think that these were starting points, but there was no indication that this was so. The controversial aspects, such as syllabus structure, sequential teaching ('brick upon brick') and grammar, tend to dominate in contributions from teachers of foreign languages.

What seems to be needed is a clarification of the reasons for teaching a foreign language. These reasons may vary from language to language. It is not enough to assume academic motivation or communication on an L1 model.

The process of clarification in itself would provide a firmer basis for decisions about co-operation with English departments as part of a joint concern for language, or, as some prefer, with departments such as history, because the needs of mother tongue and foreign language learning and teaching are seen as entierly divorced from each other. Even if English and foreign languages were to be accorded no special relationship, the departments are more reluctant than many others to co-operate in language policies across the curriculum.

At present, the variations in theory and practice amongst teachers of foreign languages equal those amongst teachers of English.

AREA CO-OPERATION

This section is restricted to work in three authorites, with a contribution of detail from a fourth.

The value of co-operation between schools, both vertically and laterally, whether supported and guided by advisers or not, cannot be stressed too much. It leads to a profitable sharing of experience, fresh light on difficult issues, and mutual support and encouragement. It has been argued that it is especially useful to primary schools, but it might be suggested that it is just as helpful to secondary schools. Without doubt, co-operation at the ages of transfer (from infant to junior, junior to secondary, or first to middle, middle to high, etc) is of great value.

Authority A leaves the initiative with schools, who simply request to be put on a mailing list. Discussion papers are prepared and sent to schools on the list at intervals, the aim being to make them available in the staff room in order to promote discussion.

The papers are prepared by a committee, at conferences and by local groups as an important part of in-service work. Response from schools is sought, and reports of interesting work in hand are circulated to other schools if permission is given. This point is in keeping with the voluntary nature of the whole exercise.

There is a practical emphasis in the discussion papers which are colour-coded according to five sections on general, listening and talking, writing, reading, and topics and themes. One general paper lists nine strategies for the development of language policy, several with alternatives. Choices to be made by the school appear at every stage of the task. In effect each school may develop in a unique way. Balance of skills is stressed, and it is regarded as important not to exclude literature, especially in primary schools, from consideration of language. Reading needs attention across the curriculum, for not enough scrutiny has been made of the accessibility of information in textbooks, for instance.

Inter-school co-operation is also emphasised, particularly at the ages of transfer. The keynotes of this scheme are awareness, thinking and planning, without central control.

Authority B bases its scheme on a most detailed and comprehensive set of guidelines and a pupil's record card which goes with him from school to school. '...the major aim of the guidelines record card project is to promote coherent developmental language programmes in and across schools, while affirming the professional responsibility of the teacher and the school, and relating diagnosis and teaching firmly to the child.'

There is an extensive support service, best explained in the words of the senior adviser:

(a) We produced our language development guidelines and record card (5-14) over some two years, in a working party involving teachers of children across this age range.
(b) To fulfil county policy, we run 3 four-week full-time intensive courses in language development each year. The aim is that each primary and middle school should have a language consultant, equipped to promote an informed language policy in his/her school.
(c) We have 'done' about 150 out of the 250 schools now, and there is a long waiting list for the courses.
(d) The consultants who have done the course work get together in fortnightly area group meetings, discussing, supporting, and advising each other, forming links and resource co-operatives, and developing materials/projects for consultants and colleagues.
(e) Secondary heads of department have been urged to promote liaison meetings with contributory schools. We are monitoring and recording the progress and problems of three of these areas.
(f) The matrix of guidelines, record card, intensive courses, consultant working groups and liaison meetings is very effective. To remove any one of these ingredients would certainly spoil the cake, in our opinion. Of course we would not make our guidelines or record card mandatory, being anxious above all that fruitful dialogue should take place. Certainly the amount of talk and work between schools has increased enormously, and we are more than pleased where a group devises its own record card (as opposed to the LEA's), to be used by all schools involved. We have found that they feel a bit guilty about doing this, but we are naturally always delighted that such productive work and co-operation have taken place!'

Area C has a most thorough-going policy which attempts to involve all schools on a voluntary basis, and which relies to a large extent on an exchange of language policy documents amongst the schools involved. Only a part of the work can appear in writing, though, for the many discussions, meetings and classroom interactions cannot be fully reported, nor can the long, slow realisation of salient features by individuals. The importance of school-based work is stressed, with the essential support of a thoughtful in-service programme in the LEA as a whole. All is stimulated, co-ordinated and maintained by the curriculum development officer.

The crucial, central concept is that of 'seepage', as opposed to a direct, public thrust for all schools to formulate language policies. The indirect approach leads to gradual, 'insidious' learning and realisation of problems and solutions, so that the end product is more surely grasped and therefore more effective. It relies on the notion that teachers must continue to be learners and it sees pupils as partners in the process, for pupils' learning is the central concern. Pupils can have impressive insights into their own learning and their comments, perhaps at first disconcerting, may eventually prove most helpful.

Lengthy expositions of theory are not helpful. Descriptions of action being taken are more profitable, because they are more readily accepted and digested by teachers. It is not easy, though, for a teacher to look squarely at his or her own practice and (inevitably) change it. It is not a good idea, therefore, to start by looking at the language of teachers, a sensitive area. Apart from the starting points mentioned above, one stimulating and valuable approach suggested by one school was a joint study of ways in which the tape-recorder could be used in the different curriculum areas. In this study a modern languages department had made a notable contribution.

Other points which emerge from the accounts of work in this authority include the observation that a 'publication' causes more apparent stir in schools other than the one in which it was produced; that there is scope for teachers to write core material for their own children; that good questioning technique is vital; and that apparently mundane subjects, such as homework, can promote valuable discussions.

Altogether, the efforts in this LEA present a picture of lively, co-operative endeavour and sound progress towards language policies tailored to the needs of the schools. This success is combined with the duly modest realisation that 'answers' are bound to be interim and inconclusive, because the process is continuous.

The fourth example is a detail from Area D. It is called a 'Work pack for secondary school' and lists what is to accompany the pupil when he goes from primary to secondary school:

(a) A list of stories read to the children in the fourth year. This can include novels, individual short stories, or collections of stories.
(b) A list of stories read by the child in the fourth year. If a child read a lot in the third year and not in the fourth, it would be helpful to know that. If the child has read only material from the reading scheme, that should be indicated, without listing the material.
(c) A piece of writing chosen by the teacher as being a typical example of that child's writing, preferably a story.

(d) A piece of writing chosen by the child, which is the child's favourite piece of work done during the fourth year.
(e) The child's written comments about his or her work in reading, writing and talking. One way of organising this would be to invite answers to these questions:
    (1) What three books have you read this year that you enjoyed most?
    (2) What sort of thing do you like reading most?
    (3) What sort of thing do you dislike writing?
    (4) When you have read aloud, what sort of thing do you find easy and interesting?
    (5) What do you think you're good at and bad at when you read, write and talk?
(f) The teacher's comments about (e) on the same piece of paper.
(g) Notes on such things as substantial absences and serious illnesses, but only if they have affected the child's work.

OTHER RELATED WORK

The spread of interest in language across the curriculum amongst subject associations other than the National Association for the Teaching of English has been slow and uneven. There are some initiatives, though progress has been very limited indeed. Examples include:

Historical Association - conference on 'Language in history teaching' - February 1977.

Association of Teachers of Mathematics - an article entitled 'Language across the curriculum: mathematics' was published in Mathematics Teaching, no. 79, June 1977. It explored the possibilities, but the authors report no response or follow-up.

Association for Science Education - a working party has prepared for publication material from various sources on language across the curriculum. This will raise questions for discussion rather than make recommendations.

The Amateur Rowing Association places great emphasis on the role of language in its manual for training coaches. The approach is entirely practical and the advice is a distillation of the experience of rowing coaches over many years. But it could well provide the basis for a study of language for teaching and learning as a part of a school language policy.

Chemical Society - members are carrying out tests in schools on 'Difficult words in science'. They are particularly interested in words in common usage which have a specific meaning in a scientific context.

CONCLUSION

This study of language policies in schools clearly raises fundamental questions for discussion and pinpoints problem areas. The benefits of developing language policies in schools are not so easy to define, but they may be seen in the enthusiastic reports from schools which have worked in this way, and by reading the wealth of material listed in the sources used for this paper, including the bibliography (Sources, no. 27).

The evidence gathered indicated that it might be more profitable to investigate separately the special contribution to language policy which might be made by each group of teachers, rather than to concentrate on areas of co-operation. While teachers of English figure prominently, in various ways, in the devleopment of language policies in schools, modern linguists appear rarely and play a minor role, with notable exceptions.

This is to consider what happens in practice at present, however, rather than what might happen or what should happen. Our concern is to explore what ought to take place, and to discover ways of implementing desirable changes in current practice. If we adopt this approach, we take the findings of this paper as background information which shows the existing framework on which we may build, and we look at two areas in particular for further study.

The first is the common interest in language, whether or not it centres on the place of language study or language as a curriculum subject. A J Tinkel's paper raises many of the issues here, in what is a highly controversial area for all language teachers.

The second is the points of contact between the two groups of teachers as listed and examined in B C King's paper. At the same time we must not ignore the difference to which he refers or attempt to create common interest where none exists.

The most encouraging aspect is the fairly general agreement that collaboration between teachers of English and teachers of foreign languages is important.

SOURCES

1. Language policies in schools: some aspects and approaches. Schools Council Project: 'Writing across the curriculum 11-16'. Ward Lock Educational, 1977.

2. Language across the curriculum: the implementation of the Bullock Report in the secondary school; by Michael Marland. Heinemann Educational, 1977.

3. Language in the curriculum. Abbey Wood School.

4. Language across the Hele's Curriculum.

5. Discussion with Irene Robertson, Director of the Schools Council Project, 'Language across the curriculum' (report not yet available).

6. Language across the curriculum: guidelines for schools; by Mike Torbe. National Association for the Teaching of English in association with Ward Lock Educational, 1976.

7. Language for learning; eds Andrew Wilkinson and Graham Hammond. Exeter University School of Education, 1977.

8. Southlands School, Reading.

9. Durrants School, Croxley Green.

10. Language development guidelines; Somerset County Council Education Authority, 1978.

11. Towards a language policy. Derbyshire County Council Education Authority.

12. Woodway Park Primary Schools.

13. Language policies in action: language across the curriculum in secondary schools; ed Mike Torbe. Ward Lock Educational, 1980.

14. ALPINE - A Language Project in Norfolk Education.

15. Comments received from Schools Council Modern Languages Committee and English Committee.

16. Comments received from Professor Eric Hawkins.

17. 'The influence on language teaching of changing concepts of the role of the teacher in relation to the learner'; by Anne Lyne. Unpublished Main Education thesis, University of London, 1979.

18. Lawrence Oates Middle School, Leeds.

19. Paignton School and Community College.

20. Eastmoor High School, Wakefield.

21. Claires Court School, Maidenhead.

22. Archbishop Michael Ramsay School, Inner London.

23. Aylestone School.

24. Department of English, Sheffield City Polytechnic.

25. Discussion paper by Clive Grimwood, Hurlfield Campus, Sheffield.

26. Towards a language policy for the middle years of schooling - a discussion document. Norfolk County Council Education Authority.

27. Other works in the bibliography prepared by CILT for Working Party B - see page 138.

BIBLIOGRAPHY

Prepared by H N Lunt and J A Price of CILT

ANDREWS, Stephen: Out of step – a reappraisal of the relationship between the teaching of foreign languages and other subjects in the school curriculum. Audio-Visual Language Journal, vol 17 no. 1, Spring 1979, p 5-11.

BRITISH ASSOCIATION FOR APPLIED LINGUISTICS: Languages for life: papers from the BAAL seminar held at La Sainte Union College of Higher Education, Southampton, 13-15 December 1976. BAAL, 1977.

BRITTON, James, Myra Barrs and Tony Burgess: No, no, Jeanette! A reply to Jeanette Williams' critique of the Schools Council Writing Research Project. Language for Learning, vol 1 no. 1, February 1979, p 23-41.

CASHDAN, Asher, ed: Language, reading and learning. Oxford: Blackwell, 1979.

CENTRE FOR INFORMATION ON LANGUAGE TEACHING AND RESEARCH: The space between...: English and foreign languages at school; papers from a conference on Language in the Middle Years of Secondary Education held at the Manchester Teachers' Centre, 20-22 November 1973. CILT, 1974. (CILT Reports and Papers 10.)

COMMITTEE OF INQUIRY INTO READING AND THE USE OF ENGLISH: A language for life; report of the Committee of Inquiry appointed by the Secretary of State for Education and Science under the Chairmanship of Sir Alan Bullock FBA. HMSO, 1975.

COUNCIL OF EUROPE. Committee for General and Technical Education: Symposium on the connection between the teaching and learning of the mother tongue and the teaching and learning of other modern languages; Turku, Finland, 11-16 December 1972; papers by H Adamczewski, A Ellegard, E Hawkins, G Nickel, H Nurogam-Poutasuo, E Oksaar, P E Owen, D C Riddy, E Roulet, T Sandlund, H Schwenk.

DAVIS, Frances R A and Robert P Parker, eds: Teaching for literacy: reflections on the Bullock Report. Ward Lock Educational, 1978.

DAWSON, C E: Footnotes to Bullock (1) – Foreign languages and English: prospects for partnership. NALA: Journal of the National Association of Language Advisers, no. 9, 1978, p 36-38.

DEPARTMENT OF EDUCATION AND SCIENCE: Language study courses in colleges of education; a conference held in July 1973 at Coloma College, West Wickham. DES, 1973.

DIXON, John: Growth through English set in the perspective of the seventies. 3rd edn. Published for the National Association for the Teaching of English by Oxford University Press, 1975.

DOUGHTY, P: Language, 'English' and the curriculum. Edward Arnold, 1974.

DUNDAS-GRANT, Valerie: Footnotes to Bullock (2) - 'Language in the classroom': considerations for the foreign language teacher. NALA: Journal of the National Association of Language Advisers, no. 9, 1978, p 39-45.

GANNON, P: Post O-level English - the study of language. Trends in Education, 1976/4, December 1976, p 28-32.

GARNER, Eric: Beyond formalism: some thoughts on modern languages and the secondary school curriculum. Cambridge Journal of Education, vol 5 no. 3, 1975, p 131-47.

HM INSPECTORATE OF SCHOOLS: Curriculum 11-16: modern languages: a working paper...July 1978. Department of Education and Science, Information Division, 1978.

HM INSPECTORATE OF SCHOOLS: Curriculum 11-16: working papers by HM Inspectorate: a contribution to current debate. Department of Education and Science, 1977 (1978).

MACAULAY, R K S: Language, social class, and education: a Glasgow study. Edinburgh: Edinburgh University Press, 1977.

McLAUGHLIN, Patrick J: A whole school language policy. Teaching English, vol 10 no. 2, Spring 1977, p 10-15.

McNAIR, J: Modern languages in today's curriculum. Modern Languages, vol 58 no. 4, December 1977, p 167-74.

MARLAND, Michael: Language across the curriculum: the implementation of the Bullock Report in the secondary school. Heinemann Educational, 1977.

NATIONAL CONGRESS ON LANGUAGES IN EDUCATION: Foreign languages in education and The mother tongue and other languages in education; papers from Working Parties for the First Assembly, Durham, 1978; ed G E Perren. Centre for Information on Language Teaching and Research, 1979. (NCLE Papers and reports 1 and 2.)

NATIONAL UNION OF TEACHERS: A language for life: the NUT's commentary on the Bullock Report. NUT, 1976.

NOTTINGHAM UNIVERSITY. SCHOOL OF EDUCATION: Preparation for English teaching. A report to the Department of Education and Science on the completion of the Curriculum English Project (1972-75). Eds E Ashworth and S J Parker. School of Education, University of Nottingham, 1976.

ROSEN, Harold, ed: Language and literacy in our schools: some appraisals of the Bullock Report. University of London Institute of Education, 1975.

SCHOOLS COUNCIL. Language across the Curriculum Project: Project EN 11 05, at Rachel McMillan Teachers' Centre, London. Project director: Irene Robertson. No reports to date. (Address: 83 New Kent Road, London SE1 6RD. Telephone: 01-407 5429.) See Language and language teaching ... 1975-77, entry no. 2246, and Schools Council Project profiles.

SCHOOLS COUNCIL. Writing across the Curriculum 11-16 (Project): Language policies in schools; some aspects and approaches. Ward Lock Educational, 1977.

SCHOOLS COUNCIL. Writing across the Curriculum 11-16 (Project): Writing and learning across the curriculum; report by Nancy Martin, Pat D'Arcy, Bryan Newton, Robert parker. Ward Lock Educational, 1976.

SOMERSET COUNTY COUNCIL. Education Department: Language development guidelines. The Department, 1978.

TORBE, Mike: Language across the curriculum: guidelines for schools. National Association for the Teaching of English in association with Ward Lock Educational, 1976.

UNITED KINGDOM READING ASSOCIATION: Reading: implementing the Bullock Report; proceedings of the fourteenth annual course and conference of the UKRA, Avery Hill College, London, 1977. Eds Elizabeth Hunter-Grundin and Hans U Grundin. Ward Lock Educational, 1978.

WHITFIELD, R C: Modern languages - their distinctive contribution in the context of the whole curriculum. Modern Languages in Scotland, no. 6, January 1975, p 22-30.

WILKINSON, Andrew and Graham Hammond, eds: Language learning. Exeter University School of Education, 1977. (Occasional Publication.)

WILLIAMS, Jeanette T: Learning to write or writing to learn: a critical analysis and evaluation of the Schools Council project of written language of 11 to 18 year-olds and its development project, 'Writing across the curriculum'. Windsor: NFER Publishing Co., 1977.

Periodical:

Language for Learning. Edited by Andrew Wilkinson and Graham Hammond. Published by the language in Education Centre, University of Exeter School of Education. 3 issues p.a. Vol 1 no. 1, February 1979.

SECTION III: METHODOLOGIES AND MATERIALS FOR LANGUAGE TEACHING

Report of Working Part C

A comparison of the various methodologies and materials involved in the teaching of English as a Foreign Language, Modern Languages, and the Mother Tongue, and an examination of their relevance to each other.

REPORT OF A WORKING PARTY COMPRISING:

Professor J M Sinclair (University of Birmingham), Chairman
Dr A Davies (University of Edinburgh)
Mrs A Griffiths (Bell College, Saffron Walden) Secretary
Mrs J McDonough (University of Essex)
Mrs B Mason (Modern Languages Adviser, Dorset)
E Reid (Linguistic Minorities Project, University of London
                 Institute of Education)
G Taylor (Blandford Upper School, Dorset)

INTRODUCTION

The Working Party set out to examine the professional interest of four groups of language teachers, those involved in:

(a) English mother tongue teaching (EMT)
(b) Foreign language teaching (FLT)
(c) English for foreign students in the UK (EFL)
(d) English as a second language (for minority ethnic group students in the UK) (ESL)

Our starting point was in EFL, but we decided from the outset that our brief did not include the making of recommendations for that area, because most EFL takes place outside the mainstream of formal education in the UK and is not represnted among the constituent bodies of the NCLE. We have also not accounted for all the variety of language teaching in the UK. In particular, we are conscious of excluding the teaching of other mother tongues than English, both the Celtic languages and the non-indigenous languages that are now common in many schools.

Initial reading and discussion was based on The space between by G F Perren (CILT Reports and Papers 10, 1973) and on papers presented at the First Assembly and published as NCLE Papers and Reports 1: Foreign languages in education and 2: The mother tongue and other languages in education, CILT, 1979.

The Working Party found in its early stages that the different branches of the language teaching tradition in UK are fragmented. Few statements about language or the teaching of it would be accepted by all; concepts and terms, attitudes and priorities are notably different. Our first job was to establish a basis on which we could discuss current issues.

The conclusion of our discussions was a feeling that this fragmentation is unnecessary and almost unhealthy for the profession and for school pupils. Where we considered matters in more detail under the headings below, we found that the consideration of different experience, other points of view, and alternative methods was helpful and refreshing, as well as informative.

We decided to set out a broad comparative review of the four different approaches, pointing out in which directions they were heading, and what the current practice and problems were. Rather than develop several individual papers on aspects of the brief, we chose to concentrate on establishing a common dialogue, and allowing contrasts to emerge from that dialogue in as constructive a manner as possible.

We have found this dialogue useful, and our report has the basic aim of encouraging a continuation of it. The several areas of language teaching have developed apart for too long; teachers have been trained in separate traditions, and are often not aware of their colleagues' work, because they lack the common conceptual basis to understand each other. Yet nowadays many FLT teachers have a period abroad teaching EFL; they may return to a Modern Language department, or they may be attracted to ESL work in the inner cities. EMT teachers find themselves in teaching situations where ESL expertise would be an advantage; EFL teachers return to UK to teach EMT.

There is enough inbuilt dissimilarity among the circumstances of our four branches of language teaching to resist any uniformity, and the transfer of ideas, methods, materials, assessment procedures from one to another will normally involve adjustment. But the pupils in schools encounter us often one after another, and the more the branches can intercommunicate and become aware of each others' work, the more coherent will be the pattern presented to the pupils.

AIMS OF LANGUAGE TEACHING

There is therefore a need for all branches of language teaching to ensure that their aims are carefully defined and that the relationship between these aims and classroom practice is clear if confusion among practitioners and interested parties is to be avoided. Reference to aims will often clarify obscurities elsewhere.

All branches of language teaching need to recognise the importance of recent developments in understanding the nature and variety of language usage and of the communicative process, and should incorporate such understanding in the formulation of aims and classroom practice.

In EFL we find growing concern to write down aims carefully and develop from them objectives, targets, etc. This comes partly from commercial pressures (eg competition among English Language schools and publishers) and partly because much English Language teaching is now specially designed for a particular group of learners. Typically the aim in EFL is to provide the students with a proficiency in English (either general English or special English) appropriate to their needs. Students' needs vary from having enough English to enter full-time higher education in the UK to being able to make simple conversation with tourists at home. The aims in ESL relate closely to the need to equip pupils, who may be particularly likely to suffer discrimination in school and outside it, with the communicative means to benefit fully from their education as a whole and to participate as full citizens of a democracy.

It is important, in the converging work of EMT and ESL practitioners, that the particular concerns of bilingual children are not forgotten. The current separation and different traditions of EMT and ESL do not easily allow the linguistic growth of bilingual children to be monitored and fostered as an integral part of the language teaching. Among other considerations, it should be noted that ESL children do not start from a uniform base, and their starting points are different from the majority of EMT children. When these points are adequately catered for, the movement to bring together EMT and ESL methods and aims can proceed with full encouragement from the profession.

In EMT the aims are appropriately very broad, embracing all varieties of growth in oracy and literacy in and out of school. The aims of EMT incorporate those of EFL and ESL but are considerably wider. Such breadth does inevitably make for difficulty in specifying exact aims in a subject which includes as well as explicit focus on language analysis, also language as the springboard into areas of self discovery and personal growth. EMT is concerned with the person, with the culture and with the language which brings the two together including the operational skills needed by the pupil in his post-school roles. EMT specialists can be helpful in examining the relationship between EFL/ESL and other subject areas, particularly as they relate to identifying and satisfying the communicative needs of other subjects, since EMT specialists share a responsibility for language across the curriculum. At the same time EFL/ESL specialists can play a useful part in paying attention to the language demands of other subjects in the curriculum. The initial training of all language teachers should take into account the need that arises for them to provide expert advice on matters of language and communication and language and learning throughout the curriculum. At the same time we recognise that the route from the global aims of EMT to day to day classroom work is not always obvious. Furthermore, the aims of EMT are general enough for models and methods to vary widely.

It is difficult to generalise about the range of aims in EMT because the principles which have gradually been established since the sixties have come into practice in varying ways and in different proportions; so our EMT classrooms can show a variety of teaching which reflects the development of this sector of the educational debate over many years.

In FLT there are differing views of how to achieve the same aims. Access to attractive cultures overseas is a common denominator and this aim is often pursued largely through the written language and by putting a high value on accurate prose. On the other hand, the aim can also be approached through emphasis on operational use, demanding in turn proper faciltiies for practice and clear practical opportunites in the future. This growing interest in communicative proficency is in line with the present and future needs of UK citizens, who are now members of the EEC, and this can put a very practical focus on the aims. Such differing approaches are not incompatible, but they do require very careful planning to be integrated.

The level of generality of aim differs for the four groups. EMT probably has the most general type of aim, indicative of the range of demands EMT sets out to serve.

One result of this range is that the relationship between aims within EMT is more complex than in other areas. For example, the aim of personal growth can be interpreted in many ways.

As we have seen, the other branches of language learning overlap a good deal with EMT. The continuum of language learning contains at the one end beginners and at the other end students who have become, through their own social history or through their own efforts, virtual native speakers. The difficulties and strategies of EFL/ESL students overlap at the more proficient end of the continuum with EMT students and it is simplest to see the continuum as containing EFL/ESL and EMT. The methods and styles of EMT and EFL/ESL are remarkably different considering the overlap of aims and of difficulties. For example the acquisition of advanced writing skills is often approached with entirely different methods in two branches.

There is a general movement towards greater openness, clarity and explicitness in language teaching. Explanations are given in syllabuses, text-books and sometimes by the teacher to his/her class as to why an activity should be done, what it is designed to achieve and what its value is. This is in tune with a less authoritarian approach to education generally, and it argues confidence in the analytical base of the teaching. More easy to find in mature classes, this is a feature characteristic of recent EFL work and of the recent situation-bound approach in FLT. It occurs, ad hoc, in all teaching but not in a conscious organised way in EMT, ESL or the more traditional forms of FLT.

The need is great for teaching materials to be explicit to the teacher about every aspect of the design activities. Such variety is possible that teachers could very easily make honest mistakes. The inadequacy of teacher training highlights this need, as the recent DES survey on the BEd degree confirms. A useful byproduct would be more careful attention being given to details of materials construction. Again EFL work tends to be most detailed, having presumably fewer institutional constraints. Language teachers also need to explore the effects on student motivation of greater explicitness as regards individual activities and the design of whole courses.

A language teaching syllabus used to be of interest only to curriculum designers. There was little dispute about what should be taught and in what sequence. Now syllabus design can be a major variable and a source of controversy. EMT does not devise syllabuses in the same way as the others, and does not have an agreed, step-by-step list of items to be taught. The others have taken different attitudes; EFL and FLT used to have a structurally sequenced syllabus as a foundation stone but are trying to write new syllabuses sequenced on other criteria. ESL shares this development but finds an explicit syllabus difficult to achieve. In a period of change as regards syllabus design, it would be beneficial for all branches of language teaching to examine each others' attempts to design new syllabuses. This would at least have the effect of promoting understanding of each others' problems and might perhaps avoid conflicting approaches to language in schools. An example of conflicting approaches would be attitudes to the traditional correctness of spelling, punctuation, lay-out, etc. Syllabus changes can only be effected in conjunction with the provision of appropriate courses in initial and in-service teacher-training.

NEGOTIATION OF SYLLABUS

Since language use is a personal skill it is sometimes thought that explicitness should be carried a stage further and the whole syllabus be negotiated with the students. The idea of negotiation is that students participate in decisions concerning their learning; what kind of work they do, what sequencing is most effective, etc. The teacher can make use of this kind of feedback in his planning of the day to day work of the class.

Negotiation is, or should be, a central part of EMT, and suits a system where there is emphasis on student-centred learning. There are many constraints, from doubts about the value of such negotiation with very naive children to the demands of public examinations. Where FLT is thought of as a 'knowledge' subject, there could be little room to negotiate. In EFL the work known as 'personalised learning' is also gaining popularity.

PROFESSIONAL STANCE

A language is not only a subject of study in its own right; it is more often a medium of learning. A language is necessary for access to new intellectual experiences: in EMT the language of the EMT class is the medium of the other school subjects. The language teacher must have available an appropriate professional stance, especially in times of change. He must be able to relate to other teachers of language, teachers of other subjects, and professional advisers. He must be aware of pressures to change, and know his evaluation of them. If his initial training turns out to have been inadequate for his current role, he must have in-service training.

The emphasis on language across the curriculum in the Bullock Report has attracted support and interest among EMT teachers who sometimes help to bring together subject teachers to discuss common language problems. EMT teachers have been reluctant to take over these language problems in a service capacity, since they insist that language and content must be taught as a unity, and it would not in any case be desirable to leave the initiative to English Departments alone. Attempts to foster the study and development of language across the curriculum have not often succeeded since it is not easy to persuade busy subejct teachers that they should be concerned with language; nor is it always possible to establish a common language for discussion.

In EFL a major development has been the provision of a medium for some other subject. There is a current interest and in the provison of courses in English for Specific Purposes (ESP), including Academic Purposes; EFL has enjoyed a parallel development to the EMT language across the curriculum. EFL has however been eager to take responsibility for the language of other subjects, perhaps over eager since this has presented the problem of trying to teach language without content. The result has sometimes been to offer advanced science students a course in the English of very elementary science, which such students do no necessarily find acceptable. And EFL teachers of ESP themselves can be at a loss in not understanding very much of the content of the special subject. In the most happy situations there is of course a successful co-operation between EFL and subject teacher, an integration of subject and language. This is one way in which EFL has made a serious contribution to meeting its students' communicative needs. But if EMT has too firmly rejected a service role so EFL has not always avoided the false claims that acceptance of such a role can bring.

It is more difficult to see a way in which FLT can acquire utility value in the school situation. Prospects of visits and holidays are not enough. Bilingual countries can divide the curriculum between languages. But in a culture like ours, where the everyday language is also the world language, foreign languages have problems in demonstrating their utility value.

In the ESL area, the practical needs of the children dominate, and additional help is given, sometimes by EMT teachers and sometimes by subject teachers. A growing number of subject teachers are becoming aware of specific problems of communication associated with their discipline. All language teachers need to be able to give expert advice to non-language colleagues, but in many cases they cannot because they lack appropriate training and because subject teachers are unclear about the place of language in education. All the evidence points to a need for greater expertise on the part of teachers in the linguistic demands made on learners, as recommended in the report of the Bullock Report.

These remarks on Language in the subject areas are mainly applicable to the secondary school; in the primary school there is no alternative to a sharing of the responsibility for developing language skills among all staff.

The kind of training that a teacher of language requires is an understanding of the nature of language as a system of communication; as a social construction; as a personal attribute; and as a resource of skill to be acquired. There would be special interest in the uses of language in the educational process, and in the educational institutions.

MOTIVATION

The most common motivation for using language is the desire or need to communicate with other people or with oneself. Most language teaching uses this motivation to a greater or lesser extent in the classroom and often substitutes others - inherent intellectual interest, other ways of life, the joy of personal creation, perhaps. EFL is very often motivated by at least some of the considerations mentioned here in relation to foreign language teaching. In addition to this, there is, of course, strong motivation attached to learning a major international language, though this is more of a general prompter than something which carries the student forward day by day. More recently, in the energetic branch of EFL called English for Specific Purposes, there has developed a motiviation by association with some other vocational or professional course, for which English is an essential tool.

This need for English as a tool is equally obvious to students in ESL; since the students work and partly live in an English-speaking environment, there should be adequate motivation from a linguistic viewpoint; the learning problems largely lie elsewhere and have to do with questions of ethnic identity and conflict between school and home.

Motivation in EMT is a complicated business. The frequent rejection of formal grammar and the literary heritage is commonly explained for motivational as well as pragmatic reasons, and EMT teachers have accepted the heavy responsibility of making each class motivating in itself, using a wide range of language experiences, trying to tap inner drive towards expression and personal achievement. In this they have gone further than any other group and shown the importance of engaging the student in the learning.

In FLT, motivation is a very difficult problem, particularly starting with English as Mother Tongue. Because of the status of English as a world language, the lure of access material which is not available in one's own language is not there. The chance of using the new language in one's daily round is not there. The usefulness of a foreign language as a servicing tool in other vocations is only just beginning to gain credibility, though there are great possibilites in this direction. For the most part it is only some vague reference to wider cultural experience in the distant future that can be offered.

The profession is alive to this problem and is beginning to work out some new strands of motivation - for example the limited proficiency goals. These make use of a valuable secondary motivation - variety of immediacy of access - in order to stimulate students' interests.

There is some support for the view that motivation can be maintained by allowing as much individual choice as possible to a student, and various kinds of self-access and personalised schemes are under development, in line with a general attempt to free students from the need to keep pace with each other.

FLT offers the prospect of foreign travel, but not to all students; and it is widely held that speakers of English are accommodated easily in Western Europe. So the only motivating goal here is distant and difficult - access to the finer points of cultural perception. The maintenance of the Foreign Language Assistance Scheme is seen to be of paramount importance for teachers in training. For teachers in post, opportunities for professional development include teacher exchanges, contract teaching abroad, hospitality visits, school or town-twinning and in-service courses.

It may be that all language teachers exaggerate the importance of motivation in their work, forgetting that it is equally a problem for other school subjects. Motivation is difficult to handle empirically and seems most useful as a means of commenting on failure: these students failed because they were not motivated. It is a truism that students in good language departments are well-motivated, the department being a major factor in successful learning.

CREATIVITY AND COMMUNICATION

The principle of creativity is fundamental in modern linguistics, stemming from the intuition that we create and understand sentences we have not heard before, that we do not construct or interpret sentences by remembering and referring to whole sentences. On the formal side of language description it can be shown that no finite list of all the sentences in a language can be made since it is always possible to add to or change the sentences already listed. This is a broader concept than the linking of creativity with imaginative composition.

This stance was originally taken in direct opposition to the notion that language was largely accountable within behaviourist terms and developed into a strong attack on many established techniques in EFL, ESL,

FLT and even EMT. Drills, systematic exercises, anything habit-forming - all come under suspicion.

More recent emphasis in EFL and ESL on communicative goals stresses the operational command of a language rather than a static body of background knowledge. This position contrasts equally sharply with the habit-forming kind of teaching, because structural accuracy is felt to be secondary to effective deployment of the language. It seems to have a lot in common with the original notion of creativity, but puts it into an interactive setting.

There is no sense yet of an established position on the inter-relation of structural and communicative teaching. The latter now is fashionable in EFL and ESL and is likely to dominate the profession for some years. But many, if not all, experienced teachers are unwilling to abandon the systematic coverage of syntax and vocabulary that characterised their previous teaching.

Teachers are uncertain how to develop a methodology for communicative language teaching: they are concerned about how to organise selection and measurement, and how to present new material, what to do about classroom management, and how to handle errors. In EFL there are at least two distinct senses in which communicative language teaching is used. On the one hand there is the kind of teaching where structural considerations are not mentioned at all (eg games, some role play). On the other hand there is the kind of teaching which uses functional material with a carefully worked out structural input.

Foreign language teachers who are not themselves native speakers of the foreign language have a particular problem in developing communicative skills in which they themselves may lack total confidence. This is recognised as a serious difficulty, but efforts in training can and should be made to overcome it. FLT specialists will need frequent access to communities of native speakers of their chosen language, in order to maintain the level of operational competence demanded by a communicative approach.

It would be wrong to imply that all communicative teaching is creative and structural teaching is not. What is noticeable about students engaged in a real communication exercise is that they are driven to combine and recombine elements of the language in ways that could not be reliably induced by the structural method. It is in this way that students gain access to the creative principle in language.

Communicative teaching thrives in an environment of the target language, because it relies, in its purer forms, on developing the learner's ability to deal with an uncontrolled exposure to the language, and the more the better. It is thus more readily accessible to ESL than EFL, (even EFL in the UK), and least of all to FLT. The question is whether it is important enough to FLT for efforts to be made to promote its development. Experience in EFL suggests that this effort is worth making.

In EMT a different development has taken place and creativity is thought of as a much broader concept - the creativity of the language itself. In this view, too much emphasis on the structural features for the language can be seen as hindering the release of creativity, taking farther the point that formal correctness is only one part of the integrity of an individual's meaning.

The similarity in aims and general principles between the communicative teaching of EFL and the creativity teaching of EMT is very important indeed for the future. One of the main thrusts in EMT is the development of a linguistic view of the task which, it may be hoped, will elaborate the linguistic aspect of the creativity teaching of EMT.

CLASSROOM TALK

Most talk is between the teacher, as one participant, and the class, or one of its members, as the other. The teacher talks most or all of the time, and the students are confined to a responding role. A number of researchers (eg Barnes, Stubbs, Sinclair, Coulthard, Bowers, Mitchell) have looked at the discourse problems of EMT, EFL and FLT classes in some detail.

It is often claimed that a major opportunity is lost in language teaching by not exploiting the possibilities of the communicative potential of teacher to class, and student to student. This criticism has two facets:

(a) Actual communication in the real world of the school has a quality which is only partially captured in the classroom through activities such as simulations, role play, and formal practice of conversation. Such work is motivating and absorbing, and allows a wide range of discourse roles to be played fairly naturally. As in all teaching there will be selection by the teacher of roles and situations and this selection will have a restricting effect on the language deployed. Whether or not this is artificial will depend on the view its observer has of teaching.

(b) Group work, pair work and individual work can be developed in order, partly, to increase the participation of students in the talk. This is increasingly a feature of EMT, EFL and ESL teaching, and has long been advocated in other fields as well. It requires some provision of specialised teacher-training, materials and equipment.

Given these improvements, the communicative approach to language teaching should flourish.

It is unfortunate that teachers in training are not often offered the sort of methods that they will be encouraged to apply in their own teaching.

As providing models and experience of contemporary practice, training institutions have a very important role.

TESTING AND MEASURING PROGRESS

Developments in teaching have revealed considerable problems both in the measurement of progress (internal; for the student, the teacher and the syllabus), and in the public qualification of students (defining standards of achievement). It is not in our brief to consider examinations in detail, but only to note their 'wash-back' effect on teaching, thus reminding ourselves how important it is that the examinations should be valid, and subject to the same general approach to language as the teaching.

Nothing yet exists which is analagous to the ordered syllabus of traditional language teaching. Progress cannot wholly be measured with reference to the acquisition of distinctions, the extension of vocabulary, and the construction of sentences of increasing complexity. A number of attempts are currently being made to provide either a teaching or a testing syllabus, eg

(a) Threshold, popular in EFL in Europe: links functions with syntactic forms directly

(b) Needs analysis (eg Munby): analyses communication tasks and specifies work skills in EFL, but stops short of linguistic realisations

(c) FLT certificates of levels of proficiency, both global and discrete skills

(d) Specification in oracy programmes of varieties of English for recognition testing (Wilkinson and Stratta)

(e) EMT measures of progress both of sentence complexity (eg Harping, A Wilkinson) and of cognitive, affective and stylistic perspectives

(f) The work of the APU (Assessment of Performance Unit), which is expected to provide relevant new methods of assessment.

Some of these satisfy specialised requirements, but leave the general matter of measurement unresolved.

Another problem emerges particularly in oral work, although it has a reflex in writing. Skill in conversation, for example, rests upon ability to manage an interaction, and so the behaviour, reaction, etc of at least one other participant is a variable which affects performance and is extremely difficult to control. So at present conversational skill can only be tested by collecting tapes in the language laboratory for later analysis or in expensive face-to-face and one-to-one encounters, and by impressionistic grading. However, there is good evidence that careful

152

standardising can produce adequate reliability in impressionistic marking, and new development in group assessment may overcome some of the difficulties.

Written production can be tested by long-established methods, but these attract consistent criticism of the kind of exercises set, and of the poor reliability of the grading. Students are tested on material written only to be presented as tests. It is generally accepted that people use language differently if they are communicating through it, compared with the way they compose it for examination. Frequent attacks on 'the school essay' point to its aridity as a means of communication, but the real problem of testing writing is to provide valid written tasks which can be marked reliably. There is evidence similar to that for testing oral production that it is possible to standardise impressionistic marking. Two interesting developments in EFL testing of reading and listening have been the revival of dictation and the introduction of the cloze technique, both making claims about the importance (and possibility) of testing the addressee's predictive ability.

The consideration of measurement points up some fundamental differences between old and new methods and goals in language teaching. All varieties are affected. Although EMT was first in the field against structural orthodoxy, it has as many assessment problems as in the other areas - it is very obvious that the O-level papers have not kept up with developments in the teaching of EMT and ESL.

MIXED ABILITY

Mixed-ability grouping does not go well with a neatly graded syllabus but suits a style of teaching/learning where individual progress is monitored and group activity encouraged, as in EFL, ESL and EMT. It has not proved effective in FLT where classrooms are large, control over the target language in group activities very difficult and course materials not available: in this branch of language learning, mixed-ability teaching is normally discouraged after year one. The difficulties encountered in this kind of teaching do not, however, invalidate its potential usefulness. For example, the communicative approach suggests that learners acquire language efficiently by actually using it, and a mixed-ability class automatically produces communication demands, in whatever language or subject. If the class is well taught, the differences between pupils can turn into an advantage.

INTENSIVE TEACHING

This is not normally offered in FLT; EMT is automatically intensive because all the school subjects are extending the linguistic repertoire. In ESL work, it is often possible, particularly when a new student is being taught at a language centre. It is widely held in EFL to be a major factor in efficient language learning. The more intensive, the better, From this point of view it is probably the 'skill' rather than the 'knowledge' side of language that is being stressed, though, particularly with adult learners, the 'knowledge aspect' is regarded as important, and is not therefore omitted.

MATERIALS

In the context of discussions on methodology, the Working Party also concerned itself with a preliminary evaluation of samples of the materials used in each of the four language teaching areas represented by Working Party members. The work reported on here is incomplete, but the Working Party, considering it a project worth continuing and carrying out more systematically, has set out some of its recommendations to that effect.

The design of 'materials' (or perhaps, more generally, the design of tasks) needs to be based firmly on a view of language teaching pedagogy as a total dynamic process, and 'materials' cannot be isolated from decision at different levels concerning aims, needs, motivation and syllabus construction, as well as the role of the teacher and questions of classroom management. Thus it becomes increasingly clear that materials - in any of the areas of language teaching under discussion - which derive solely from the analysis of a corpus of language, sequenced in some way, are likely to be inadequate to their task, since they are then not the focus of a reasoned set of interrelated decisions.

Materials were evaluated in terms of their potential relevance to areas other than those for which they were designed. The bold arrows show the 'directions' in which this took place (eg an arrow from ESL to MTT indicates that MT materials were evaluated from an ESL point of view), the dotted arrows those in which it did not. The fact that there are some gaps in the evaluation process may indicate that overlap between those areas is less significant, or may currently be felt to be less significant, though this comment would need to be substantiated by further work.

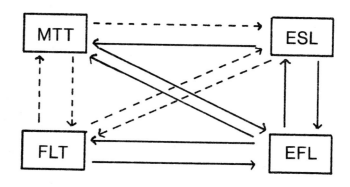

In order to comment on the appropriacy or otherwise of materials from a different area from one's own discipline, it is necessary to find a level of generalisation whereby evaluative categories are valid <u>across</u> materials. Such categories are therefore unlikely to include such considerations as age groups, choice of topics and precise context, and are more likely to include questions such as type of organisation and implied view(s) of language. (For a fuller list, see (b) below).

Generalisability is further made difficult by the fact that different practitioners naturally approach materials with different assumptions.

Further, since evaluations were carried out on the basis of a limited amount of data, depending on materials that were most readily available, it would be unwise to draw too many firm conclusions.

(A) SUMMARY OF FINDINGS

(1) MTT — EFL (1, 2, 3)

The more general functional material (1) was found to be interesting linguistically, but too limited in scope for use in MTT, mainly because it assumes little knowledge of culturally determined ways of expressing oneself in particular situations. Functions covered are also factual and 'transactional', and not sufficiently 'expressive/ poetic' for MTT purposes.

The material more oriented to Study Skills (particularly (2)) was felt to be potentially more useful, especially in the context of Language across the Curriculum, since it concentrates in some detail on the development of particular language skills (reading and writing).

(2) ESL — MTT (4)

There seems to be considerable overlap in this area, both in terms of thematic organisation and general methodology. The qualification was made that it might be necessary, with less advanced ESL students, to adopt a more structured approach.

(3) ESL — EFL (5)

In a sense this was felt to be a mirror image to the MTT material examined: the cultural and thematic content was considered unsuitable and inappropriate, but the well-ordered functional organisation of language items more interesting.

(4)   EFL___FLT (6)

There are clear parallels in the development of functional materials between EFL and ELT. It was felt, however, that such materials should give further consideration to the sequencing and grading of functional items, as well as to the possibility of treating the '4 skills' less traditionally and discretely.

Despite obvious overlap of aims and methodology, EFL recognises that FLT is bound by greater, or at least different, constraints, particularly with regard to student motivation and to the necessity of working within an examination syllabus.

(5)   EFL___MTT (7, 8, 9)

The wide range of materials available made generalisations difficult: some materials had a strong base in structure practice (7), whereas in others, such considerations were not taken into account at all.

On the plus side, the amount of imaginative input in the form of 'raw material' was impressive. More negatively, there was sometimes considerable emphasis on questioning and testing procedures, and insufficient attention was given to the teaching and learning of 'skills'. In some materials this goes hand in hand with only a limited view of what the concept of 'skill' might involve.

(6)   FLT___EFL (10, 11)

The most interesting aspects of these materials were felt to be twofold: the relatively developed nature of functional analysis as incorporated into the design of the materials, and the variety of methodological techniques, such as role-play.

(7)   EFL___ESL (12)

The overall impression is that the materials are closer to MTT in conception and execution than to any other area. They also contain a considerable amount of varied input, and suggest a number of activities appropriate to the age group for which they were written.

(B) CRITERIA FOR EVALUATION

A number of models for evaluation are available, and Working Party members did not adhere rigidly to any particular one, though they were aware of (i) below. If a more extensive investigation were to be undertaken it would probably be useful to work within a commonly agreed framework, such as the following:

(1) Stated aims of materials
Intended audience
Overall organisational principles
View(s) of language stated/implied
View(s) of learning stated/implied
Skill(s) covered
Topics/subject areas covered
Types of activity
Types of exercises
Principle(s) of sequencing and grading
Relation to any particular examination
Levels of internal consistency: relations between categories

(2) A Cunningsworth ('Evaluating Course Materials', in <u>Teacher Training</u>, Modern English Publications, 1979), lists a number of factors under 5 general headings:

Language
Methodology
Psychological factors
General (eg Supporting material available)
Conclusions and overall comments

C) MATERIALS EXAMINED

<u>Functions of English</u>, L Jones, CUP, 1977.
<u>Think and Link</u>, J Cooper, Arnold, 1977.
<u>Written Communication in English</u>, S Freeman, Longman, 1977.
<u>Look Out</u>, Mills and Taylor, Harrap, 1974.
<u>Say What you Mean in English</u>, J Andrews, Nelson, 1977.
<u>Destination France</u>, D R Ellis & M P Pearce, Harrap, 1979.
<u>The Art of English</u>, K Newson, Schofield and Sims, 1966.
<u>Write Again</u>, A Forsyth & C Gray, Oliver & Boyd, 1979.
<u>Contemporary English</u>, J Foster, Macmillan, 1977.
<u>Play your Part</u>, G Ramsey, Longman, 1978.
<u>Streamline English</u>, Hartley and Viney, OUP, 1978.
<u>Scope</u>, H Hester & J Levine, Schools Council, 1972.

D) MATERIALS AND PUBLICATION

There may be genuinely wide markets for materials beyond the specific concerns of specialised groups. This view is borne out by the investigation into materials across disciplines: it has already been noted that the establishment of common ground between language teaching areas has been an important aim of the Working Party, and clearly the question of materials design is no exception to this. It is worth reiterating some of the design factors - linked, of course, to the criteria for evaluation set out above - which appear to be of potentially wider applicability than just one area, since it is these kinds of considerations the publishers might like to contemplate as a basis for 'framework' materials.

(1)   Views of language, in general, especially

    (a)   structural

    (b)   notional-functional.

(2)   Interrelations between these views eg the implications of notional-functional criteria for functional selection; the question of the sequencing of functions.

(3)   General problems of sequencing and grading.

(4)   More refined views of 'skills' as a principle for course design in general - clearly related to both Study Skills, in EFL terms, and Language across the Curriculum.

(5)   More specifically, the nature of skills and their potential pedagogical breakdown and sequencing into 'macro-skills'.

(6)   The nature of 'situational' materials.

(7)   Relations between different levels of materials according to primary and secondary features, eg if 'skill' is the fundamental organising principle, what implications are there for the analysis of language?

(8)   Views of the language learning process and their incorporation into materials.

(9)   Types of classroom activity.

This list can be both expanded and formalised, but is set out here as a basis for discussion.

The Working Party is aware that responsibility for the elaboration of general design factors of this kind cannot be expected to lie solely with publishers. Ultimately, impetus must come from the profession, which itself urgently needs to be aware of the common ground linking its many branches.

Acknowledgements

The Working Party would like to express gratitude for the professional advice and help received from colleagues, and for the generous financial support provided by the Centre for British Teachers and the Bell Educational Trust.

158

TEACHING ENGLISH AS A FOREIGN LANGUAGE

J McDonough

INTRODUCTION

'EFL' here refers principally to the teaching and learning of English as a Foreign Language in the UK, and these notes are mainly concerned with overseas adult students in higher and further education, or in language schools in the private sector. It can nevertheless be seen in the report itself that there is a level of generalisation at which trends and questions in the EFL field (as delineated here) overlap significantly with MTT, ESL and FLT, dealt with elsewhere. It is worth pointing out that EFL in the UK is closer in many ways to ESL and MTT, whereas overseas in general terms it has more in common with FLT.

For convenience and clarity, these notes follow the sequence of categories as set out in the main Report.

AIMS

The 'growing concern' to specify aims more precisely is to a large extent a direct result of the increasing number of specially tailored programmes (ESP) throughout the world, and not only in the UK. (There is further pressure from the 'paying customer', whether in private language schools or in tertiary education, and whether following an ESP course or a more 'general' EFL programme, who quite reasonably expects the aims and objectives of his course to be stringently thought out.) The ESP student typically has only a limited amount of time for learning, and is anxious to perceive relevance to his needs and interests.

The concept of English as a 'service', where the language is examined in relation to its use in other areas of knowledge and experience for the student who is not an English specialist (rather than being a 'subject' in its own right) is of major importance in EFL. There is a fundamental orientation towards a 'learner-centred' syllabus with a prior analysis of needs, rather than towards a situation where a syllabus type is selected a priori, and subsequently imposed on the learner. (See, for example, Mackay, 1978; Jordan, 1977; Mackenzie, 1977.)

The analysis of needs, and the concomitant specification of aims, is obviously not a straightforward task. For instance, the definition of 'needs'; the distinction between 'real' and 'felt' needs; the setting up of models to process needs; and the practical constraints on an idealised 'needs profile'; are all currently under discussion. (See, for example, James, 1974; Richterich, 1975; Munby, 1978.) As well as quasi-theoretical questions of this kind, EFL too is concerned with the route from aims to other levels in the course, down through the writing of the syllabus, the design of materials, and the management of classroom work. There certainly has to be further discussion among practitioners on the relative desirability (and not only for ESP courses) of direct routes (eg if English is only needed as a library language, then the course should consist entirely of reading) and more indirect routes, which tend to take a wider spectrum of skills into consideration.

EXPLICITNESS

It was implied in the preceding section that pressure to be explicit about the nature and aims of the syllabus is on the increase. There is an important sense in which the teacher is the focus of the pressure, which could even be described as multi-directional: the teacher increasingly expects the syllabus and materials with which he has to work to be explicit about their aims and the context(s) in which they are intended to be used, and his students in turn will expect their teacher to pass on this explicitness to them, given their general level of maturity and degree of cognitive development. Furthermore, there is often added institutional pressure on the teacher to be explicit about his programme: in fact, it is worth adding here that the EFL teacher is frequently course designer and materials writer as well, and is not always simply at the end of a long chain of decisions over which he has little control. A final point in this section is that types of syllabus currently being developed in principle lend themselves more readily to clarity of exposition in this sense, being based ab initio on greater specificity.

NEGOTIATION OF SYLLABUS

In EFL, especially where mature learners are concerned, this question is in many way an extension of the degree of explicitness within a syllabus. Just two aspects can be mentioned here. Firstly, it is often the case that groups of motivated learners, highly conscious of their reasons for learning, engage in helping to set up the details and decide the emphases of their own programme within a specified framework; after all, they are probably just as aware as their teachers, from a different perspective, of the linguistic demands of their own subjects. Secondly, many practitioners are strongly in favour of 'self-access' materials, where students are able, with guidance, to work through a highly individualised programme. (See, for example, ETIC Occasional Paper, 1978.)

PROFESSIONAL STANCE

It is particularly when English is viewed as utilitarian, ie in ESP situations, whether in the UK or overseas, rather than as a specialism in its own right, that the role and status of the teacher is highlighted and indeed questioned, not least by himself. (The non-utilitarian 'school subject' aspect clearly has parallels with FLT in this country.) The humanities-trained teacher finding himself in an ESP job often perceives this situation as both threatening and restricting, since it initially seems to represent the breaking down of what he sees as the boundaries of his subject. These boundaries typically enclose the study of literature: Strevens (1971) put the case against the supremacy of literary study quite strongly, and it is a view which has wide acceptance. ESP can be claimed, on the contrary, to offer a challenging opening-up of professional horizons, and indeed to provide insights into syllabus design which can throw new light onto literary study. It also necessitates a redefinition of a teacher's role vis-a-vis his students: the language class can no longer be seen as a one-way information flow. (See, for instance, Webb, 1976.)

MOTIVATION

'Motivation' in EFL is closely bound up with the analysis of needs and the specification of the aims of a syllabus, and in general with the trend towards making the learner the focal point in setting up EFL programmes. That students on ESP-type courses, and/or learning English in an English-speaking environment, are likely to be motivated, is not unduly surprising. Nevertheless, the fact that there is a spectrum ranging from very high motivation to strong resistance to learning English, is sometimes overlooked. The latter attitude is not uncommon amongst tertiary level students who are in the UK to study their own specialism and who often actively resent the requirement to attend English language classes. This is, perhaps, not very far removed from the school 'captive audience' situation.

CREATIVITY AND COMMUNICATION

Despite the influence of fashion, the choice of syllabus types in EFL is still in a state of flux. The 'traditional' structural syllabus is still probably the most widespread, not least because the principles are so well-established and the details carefully worked out. However, it is undeniable that notional-functional (or 'communicative') syllabuses (as set out, for example, by Wilkins, 1976) are gaining ground, and as they do so, productive discussion is taking place as to the kinds of teaching situations in which they are most relevant. (For example, Johnson, 1978.) Despite the occasionally unfortunate 'bandwagon' effect, thought is also being given to such 'problem' areas in the construction of this type of syllabus as the relation between form and function and questions of sequencing and grading.

The communicative syllabus is also accepted as being appropriate to much ESP. Widdowson (1978) for instance, claims that we are being less than fair to our learners if we seek to teach them only a list of the structural items most commonly found in scientific writing in English. It is very likely that learners in an ESP context will have some knowledge of the methodology of science as expressed in their own language. They will know, for example, that science proceeds by the use of such concepts as definition, classification, hypothesis-formation, all of which have a number of structural realisations. It would therefore be more realistic and economical, he claims, to make such categories the defining feature of syllabuses. (Quoted from McDonough, 1978.) (Some examples of 'general' and 'ESP' teaching materials based on these principles are listed in the bibliography.)

Closely related to communicative teaching is work in the area of 'study skills' (cf. Candlin et al, 1978), in which the starting point is an analysis of study situations, and which is interestingly related to the MTT debate on 'language across the curriculum'. A programme based in the first instance on study activites (eg making notes; understanding non-verbal data; writing essays and reports; reading for reference; answering examination questions, etc) also calls into question the traditional and rather artificial division between the 'four skills', since the skill boundaries quite clearly overlap.

CLASSROOM TALK

Despite positive developments in the design of communcative syllabuses and materials, the input can still be highly controlled, so it does not necessarily follow that the ratio of teacher talk to pupil talk has changed significantly. Many EFL teachers share the general concern about the amount of teacher talk and, being aware that the learner has more to offer than a certain degree of knowledge of language structure, are trying to develop work in small groups and pairs; in role-play; in discussion; to increase the amount of active participation on the part of the student. (Reference can be made here, for example, to Modern English Teacher, vol 5, no. 1; vol 7, no. 1; and to ELT Documents, 1977.)

TESTING AND MEASURING

As far as EFL in the UK is concerned, language examinations in the accepted school sense are more or less insignificant. Two points might be made here, however. Particularly in the private sector, some students study English in order to take one of the Cambridge examinations, but this is something which usually arises from their own motivation, and which is only indirectly imposed by external necessity. For students entering tertiary education there is a proficiency requirement of some kind, but this is a complex area with no closely defined criteria, and the whole question is currently under review.

In EFL, however, particularly in ESP, the choice is not always present. The in-term 'service course', for example, is typically both mixed proficiency and mixed subject. In such cases, making a virtue out of a necessity can be a challenge, provided it is accepted that the learner has more to offer than a knowledge (or otherwise) of language structure.

INTENSIVE TEACHING

Outside the overseas school system, in the context under review in this paper, a great variety prevails. Within university EFL programmes, there are three main types of course from the point of view of 'immersion':

(a) The pre-session course, which lasts anything from three weeks to three months, is usually intensive, and usually contains 'language practice', 'social English' and 'study skills' components.

(b) The in-term service English class, which typically runs over one or two terms, is often modular, and students attend for only a small number of hours per week.

(c) In some institutions, longer full-time courses, usually of one academic year, are taking place for certain groups of learners. Such courses almost always have a study skills orientation.

Within the private sector, course types (a) and (c) above are not uncommon. The general tendency is for intensive courses of varying length and with varying specifications. It is unwise to state that one method is to be preferred to any other: it depends crucially on the learner or group of learners for whom the programme is being designed, and of course on the practical constraints that are likely to bear on that programme. Nevertheless, the consensus of opinion is that intensive, or at least semi-intensive courses are probably more successful and efficient from the points of view of both teachers and students: it is in general easier to prepare a more integrated and internally consistent programme, and such courses are less likely to carry with them the frustrations felt on both sides of simply not having enough time available.

CONCLUSION

Developments in EFL methodology and materials at the moment are somewhat in a state of flux, and many details arising from the implications mentioned above have not yet been resolved. Perhaps the most interesting thing, in fact, is that a number of basic questions are being thrown up, and deep-seated assumptions held up for scrutiny. Among all the factors discussed, one must highlight a few as being the most significant currently in EFL: the relations between language teaching and other disciplines, both in terms of language analysis and pedagogical procedure; the different types of syllabus that might arise from this; and the rather different types of learner now taking English courses.

FOREIGN LANGUAGE TEACHING

B Mason

AIMS

The study of submissions made by professional associations to Working Party 1 of the National Congress, together with a survey of 'Schemes of Work' in Modern Languages Departments in schools demonstrate clearly that the aims of modern language teaching and the justification for its inclusion in the school curriculum have multiplied rather than changed over the past 50 years.

It is rather the methods and materials which, following the dictates of psychologists, sociologists and linguisticians have reflected the never-ending 'revolution' in foreign language teaching. The ultimate aims of modern languages teachers have never varied substantially but the 'approach' has.

Still present as articles of faith are such statements as 'culturally broadening ... educationally humanising and help to train the mind' (HMC Report, 1976), and 'an instrument of education and culture which should be available to all' (Council of Europe). To these have been added 'the opening of doors ... ensuring that the child is not inescapably chained within the limits of his environment' (Dunbar 1977) '.. to enable the learners to use the foreign language as an instrument of communication' (van Ek, 1977), and finally 'to enable students at a later stage in their lives to obtain greater job satisfaction and to be presented with a wider range of job opportunites' (LEA).

EXPLICITNESS

In the more traditional, structural syllabuses it has always been easy for pupils to know what they must learn but rarely why. Teaching the conditional tense in French historically follows that of the simple future, just as the present tense is followed by the perfect and immediate future. The emphasis in such courses was, and still is, on form: little indication is given of the communicative uses to which these forms could be put but nevertheless, the somewhat arbitrary sequencing of grammatical points is clear, if incomprehensible, to both teacher and pupil.

In the functional-notional syllabuses currently being developed and based on the European Unit/Credit System in the Council of Europe, the emphasis has shifted from form and structure to the use of language in realistic situations. Here, the task and its relevance and usefulness to the learner are very explicit.

164

NEGOTIATION OF SYLLABUS

Given the constraints of the present examination system, it is difficult to conceive of a situation in which school children below 16+ might negotiate their own syllabus. It is also worthy of note that when the admirable Working Paper No. 28 (Schools Council), with its proposals for a far wider reading programmed at 'A' level, offered the possibility of just such negotiation, the profession rejected it.

At adult level, the new 'proficiency levels' might provide an element of choice of sequencing which could respond to the learners' immediate needs.

PROFESSIONAL STANCE

In its appraisal of problems of some key areas of the curriculum (HM Inspectorate, 1977), HM Inspectorate sees Great Britain as being heavily dependent on international trade survival. This opinion has been endorsed by recent, successive governments and by the Duke of Kent in his preface to the British Overseas Trade Board Report: Foreign Languages for Overseas Trade (BOTB Study Group, 1979):

> 'Now that an even higher proportion of Britain's trade is with non-English speaking markets, it has become increasingly clear that the traditional reluctance of the British to learn foreign languages may be seriously affecting our trade prospects.
>
> The Study Group's Report makes it perfectly clear that in many overseas markets British companies cannot expect to compete effectively without a knowledge of the local language.'

Historically the number of girls continuing the study of a foreign language beyond 16+, particularly since the much regretted disappearance of the 'subsidiary' paper at A level, far exceeds the number of boys. Subsequently careers guidance, parental pressure and the introduction of an options system at 14+ have continued to aggravate this situation.

The strong case being made currently by HM Inspectorate for the inclusion of a foreign language in the core curriculum of our secondary schools, together with the analysis of needs in trade and industry, should go a long way towards reversing that trend: by attributing to foreign language learning a practical, as well as a social and educational, value, the professional standing of the subject must be enhanced.

MOTIVATION

It is a fact that after weeks of hard work with the more traditional learning approaches and materials there is little the foreign language learner can do on his own, particularly in his home environment: he can neither express his personal feelings, nor read nor write anything that is of real interest to him.

The intellectual challenge provided by language study and previously considered sufficient motivation for more able pupils, can now however be more easly sustained and perhaps extended across the ability range by the gratification of short-term objectives. Van Ek's justification of the European Threshold level (1977) can equally well embrace the graded tests being developed in Great Britain:

'It will give meaningful direction to modern language teaching and contribute to increased efficiency and motivating power.'

And later:

' ... each successive portion carries its own reward in that successful learners are conscious of having achieved something that is relevant to their own foreign language needs.'

It is this experience of more immediate success which, for the linguistically less-able particularly, provides encouragement and a motivation rarely experienced previously on the long, uncertain road towards the distant goal of a public examination at 16+. The rush to opt out at 14+ is being stemmed by the new motivation and the problem of negative attitudes is being replaced by another which requires more teachers to cope with the flow of successful pupils wanting to 'opt in'.

CREATIVITY AND COMMUNICATION

The particular difficulty experienced in FLT which sets it apart from MTT, EFL and ESL is the limitation of the relevance of the foreign language to within the confines of the classroom: only in lesson time is the necessary model available and the opportunity provided to practise the skills acquired.

Grammar translation courses have been overtaken by the Direct Method and, at a later date, audio-visual then audio-lingual 'methods': learning about the language and the formulation of rules were superseded by the perception of pattern, or so it has seemed. In practice, never has the traditional, grammar translation approach disappeared from view: Whitmarsh has never gone out of print. It is the isolation of experience of the foreign language in the three to five times weekly contact time that has ensured this: grammar must be formalised and noted, pupils must have 'something to hang on to' between lessons - an amalgam of all the 'approaches' or 'methods' emerges as the panacea.

CLASSROOM TALK

'To teach a language effectively it is necessary to get all pupils to speak it out loud' (Ree, 1980).

The language laboratory, that sometime substitute for the one-to-one pupil-teacher communication precluded by over-large classes, has lost credibility. It can be argued that this fall from grace is more attributable to inadequate (initial) teacher training than to the shortcomings of the hardware itself.

In foreign language teaching, pair work rather than group work is taking precedence over the laboratory, though never replacing the tape recorder which supplements the teacher as model.

Role-playing, already endorsed by CSE boards, is further encouraged by the syllabuses of regionally developed proficiency tests.

TESTING AND MEASURING PROGRESS

If pupils in roughly homogeneous groups have been set different learning objectives from the second or third years of the secondary course, it follows that the testing procedures must be appropriate to the objectives. This implies the setting of tests at 16+ and 18+ (and of course at intermediate stages if a 'graded' system is introduced) of a 'profile' type in which the pupil (carefully counselled) chooses from a 'menu' of test items, a 'profile' which best fits his or her course of study. The certificate awarded would show each pupil's performance in the particular areas tested. It would be, of course, for the 'user' of the test (employer or university selector, etc.) to decide which elements in the 'profile' were essential for his purposes.

The clearly defined syllabuses and limited objectives for schemes such as the South West Modern Languages Credit System bring Hawkins' proposals closer to reality than would ever have seemed possible even five years ago. Similarly, other graded test systems provide clear indications to teacher and pupil alike as to what skills must be mastered and which elements of language learned to express which notions. The business of measuring achievement is thus greatly facilitated.

Campaigns for more specific syllabuses at O and A-level have come and gone but no major change has been effected. Vague instructions about mastery in understanding, speaking, reading and writing the foreign language still go hand in hand with the dogged refusal by Examining Boards to reveal the secrets of their marking schemes.

It is true that greater emphasis on aural-oral work in the classroom has been reflected in the allocation of more marks for success in these skills at O-level but the apparent confusion about what constitutes written or spoken language puts into question the validity of the tests set.

The 'oral examination', that is to say the 'viva' or face-to-face communication test, still carries a very small percentage of the total marks awarded. Whereas the enormous difficulty in administering more meaningful 'orals' cannot be gainsaid, little attempt appears to have been made to find solutions to this problem. The backwash effect of this particular situation is very evident in the classroom: whereas in the first two years of the learning process pupils are exposed to a considerable amount of spoken language, by year five the foreign language, as a means of communication, has virtually disappeared. At sixth form level it is often totally absent, for what, ask the teachers, is the point of discussing Göethe in German when the A-level question papers are in English?

The space between good practice and public examinations remains large. The growing success of limited proficiency tests must have a salutory effect on our more established examination procedures.

TEACHING ENGLISH AS A SECOND LANGUAGE IN ENGLAND

E Reid

DEFINING THE FIELD

Teaching English to speakers of other languages in England covers a great variety of educational activities, with very different kinds of students, in very different settings. The EFL-ESL distinction is a convenient rough and ready way of dividing up the field, and making it less likely that significant developments in these various settings might be neglected. However, it should never be lost sight of that the common underlying principles are more important for this paper's audience than the differences, and that the division is by no means always clear cut. It is, for example, not uncommon in technical colleges to find mixed classes of home and overseas students, none of them having English as a first language.

At least ten years ago, it was becoming increasingly evident that many of the children in schools who needed help in learning ESL were not themselves immigrants, but the children of immigrants. This is even more obvious today, making the continued use of the term 'English for immigrants' almost entirely inappropriate. (The organisation now known as NAME, the National Association for Multi-Racial Education, evolved from one called ATEPO, originally the Association for Teaching English to Pupils from Overseas, later the Association for the Education of Pupils from Overseas. Its journal began as English for Immigrants, became Multi-racial School and is now New Approaches to Multi-racial Education.)

The teaching that goes on under the label of 'Industrial Language Training', where LEA's, sometimes under Adult Education auspices, sometimes under Further Education, provide courses for limited English speakers on working premises and during working time, is also a part of the field where some very exciting recent developments in ESL have taken place. There is also a great deal of interesting work being undertaken by members of NATESLA - National Association for the Teaching of English as a Second Language to Adults.

PUBLICATIONS

There is still probably no better introductory survey of the ESL picture as it has developed and as it is currently that June Derrick's 1977 NFER booklet Language Needs of Minority Group Children. (cf. the title of her 1966 book Teaching English to Immigrants.)

As far as journals are concerned, virtually the only one to give sustained attention has been that of NAME, already mentioned. The English Language Teaching Journal, although it has recently appealed for more contributions in this field, has until now published very little, except for a usefully critical account of public policies by Michael Fitzgerald in vol 33 no. 1, 1978, Factors influencing ELT policies in schools in England with particular reference to children from Pakistan, India and Bangladesh. NATE's English in Education has also neglected ESL except for its special issue in 1977, and even that was largely concerned with questions related to the use of literature from sources other than the traditional metropolitan ones. Finally, on a topic which is in danger of falling between the terms of reference of the various working parties, Vivienne Edwards' 1979 book The West Indian language issue in British schools, promises to be the definitive work for some time to come.

ORGANISATIONAL FRAMEWORK FOR ESL

Although there is very considerable variation from one LEA to another in the details of their arrangements for ESL learners, many of these with sizeable numbers of minority group children still make use of the following:

(1) 'Language' or 'Immigrant' or 'Induction' Centres, physically separate from ordinary school, where the most obviously non-English-speaking children attend full-time for a period of time, typically three terms, studying basic English and probably eventually the full range of school subjects, before going to the ordinary schools; staff usually see themselves as ESL specialists, and such centres are now almost always for secondary age children, although in Bradford for example, they are used even with infants.

(2) 'Language Units' actually on ordinary school premises, where children may attend full-time as in the Centres, but more commonly spend part of each day in 'withdrawal classes', taught English either by peripatetic teachers belonging to the LEA language service, or by full-time teachers at the school who may or may not be ESL specialists with appropriate training. Such units are most common in junior schools.

(3) 'Streaming' or 'banding' of pupils, very often done on the basis of reading age, or some pretty informal estimate of language ability with limited English speakers finding themselves disproportionately in classes of 'low ability' children with very heterogeneous linguistic backgrounds, Caribbean, Asian and indigenous. The specialist training of teachers of such classes is quite often in 'remedial' education, and this is evident in the materials used. Sometimes there is follow-up by peripatetic staff of children transferred to 'ordinary' classes, but it is extremely difficult to do this in any very systematic way.

EXPLICITNESS/TYPES OF SYLLABUS/THE FOUR SKILLS

In the schools themselves it is rare to find ESL syllabuses separate from those implied in any textbooks used, but the language services of several LEAs issue guidelines to their teachers, for example in the form of lists of vocabulary and 'structures' which children should have control of. The basis of the selection of language is not always clear, but the type of syllabus implied by such lists is of course structural with perhaps a situational/social orientation. Discussion of syllabus-types in the schools themselves seems to be unusual, but there is evidence of expertise among staff of some language services. For example, NAME published in 1978 a very useful booklet from Nottingham surveying and exemplifying syllabus-types, Gordon Ward's Deciding what to teach in E2L lessons. This is the kind of publication most likely to spread ideas on functional and notional syllabuses into the maintained schools, where the heterogeneous situation referred to earlier is likely to ensure a particularly lively interest.

NEGOTIATION

This concept is, for obvious reasons, rarely applicable in situations where typically there is a mono-lingual English-speaking teacher faced with a mixed class of limited-English-speakers, but there is perhaps some element of negotiation present with older, more advanced pupils who may pull their teachers towards concentration on the linguistic skills necessary to pass public exams, for example more emphasis on writing and reading than on oral work. (In Industrial Language Training there is certainly quite extensive negotiation between tutors, management and in some cases unions, about the communication needs of potential students; interestingly, functional and notional approaches appear to be gaining ground fast here.)

TESTING

This is not an obvious constraint on ESL teaching, either in the form of public exams (there are several CSE 'English for Immigrants' papers, but they are taken by rather small number of pupils), or of school level tests. But most, if not all GCE Boards, continue not to distinguish between native speakers of English and those for whom it is a second language, in the ways in which deviations from some unstated norm of standard English are treated in O-level candidates' papers. This is surely likely to lead to increasing frustration among ESL students with academic potential.

NEEDS AND GROUP WORK

Possibly the greatest difficulty for ESL teachers is their realisation of the very varying needs of pupils even within the comparatively small classes they often teach, and group work is therefore very widespread indeed.

DEGREE OF IMMERSION

The ESL learner in the maintained school is for virtually all official activities totally 'immersed' in English, as he is in the public sphere outside school. However, even within school the amount of individual interpersonal contact with native speakers of English may be quite limited, and many of the children concerned still live in fairly self-contained families and communities which communicate largely in a language other than English. (The degree of support given to mother tongue maintenance by the maintained schools themselves is minimal, but informal socialisation and voluntary educational agencies ensure that English by no means takes over completely as the sole communication means for many minority group children.)

INDIVIDUAL RELATIONSHIP OF STUDENT TO HIS COURSE

(i) 'Ability'/mixed ability/setting

This is clearly not an issue in ESL in the sense it is in MLT. Interestingly for our FLT colleagues, it is simply assumed by teachers that virtually all children will achieve at least a basic ability to communicate in English, and indeed that if they do not, they are probably abnormal in some way. As previously indicated, classes are extremely mixed, and groupings of children tend to be based much more on age and length of exposure to English than on any notions of 'ability'.

(ii) Needs and motivation

It might be possible to work out a detailed specification of communication needs for the child in school, adapting perhaps for lower age-groups the 'English for Academic Purposes' approach developing in HE. At the moment, however, few schools seem to have gone beyond the use of general 'all-purpose' EFL courses.

Motivation in the early stages is universally recognised as high, but it is also a widespread experience now to find pupils in the secondary schools who have gained a basic communicative ability and then ceased to make progress. They sometimes cannot be persuaded to focus on their remaining problems with the language. The educational and social circumstances they find themselves in may not indeed genuinely encourage more progress.

(iii) Creativity

This is not a concept much discussed in the ESL context, certainly in the sense it has in EMT. Sometimes the assumed absence of concern with 'creativity' when dealing with ESL learners seems to convince the EMT teacher that ESL is an entirely sterile and unrewarding activity. A more extensive treatment of the nature of language and of language learning in initial training courses for English teachers in particular might go some way to clarifying the concept.

PROFESSIONAL STANCE OF TEACHER TOWARDS HIS JOB

(i)   'Broad-' or 'narrow-based' language teaching

There is a wide range of opinion and practice among ESL teachers here, ranging from the narrowest, most mechanistically-conceived drill-bashing associated with the still dominant behaviourist views of language and of learning, to a deeply humanistic concern to equip children with the linguistic skills necessary for what Alan James has called:

> '... classifying and reclassifying experience, drawing conclusions, forming hypotheses, presenting a case, modifying it in the light of evidence, of experience, and of other people's hypotheses.'
> ('Why Language Matters' in Multi-Racial School, vol 5 no.3, 1977.)

It is at this end of the spectrum that ESL practice comes closest to the best EMT, and indeed to the heart of the whole educational enterprise.

(ii) Teacher's role/status:

The present organisational basis of much ESL work in Britain described earlier may make it evident why ESL teachers are often seen as marginal in the maintained schools. They are, to take the most obvious point, often physically marginal, either functioning in special centres, as peripatetic teachers, or taking classes in staff-rooms, medical rooms, cloakrooms, even. Where they are permanent full-time members of staff in schools, their departmental affiliations are frequently to the less prestigious parts of the school. And if, as a result of natural predisposition or inadequate professional preparation they adopt the narrow view of their function referred to earlier, they may quite rightly carry little weight when discussions affecting the interests of the pupils they deal with are concerned.

(iii) Literature

This rarely appears in the ESL class, except in the form of simplified and/or abridged texts, and these are seen as essentially means to such ends as 'increasing vocabulary'.

(iv) Model of language

The ESL teacher's training will usually have focused on what are seen to be 'practical' matters, with much less attention to, for example consideration of models of language.

USE OF TEXTBOOK AND ADDITIONAL RESOURCES

Apart from the SCOPE materials and some ILEA publications, there is very little professionally-finished teaching material produced specifically for ESL learners in Britain. There is an abundance of duplicated material produced at teacher centre level, some of which is used outside its 'native' area; there is also considerable use of EFL and ESL materials produced for overseas use. Additional resources in the form of readers and audio-visual materials and hardware are in quite widespread use.

ENGLISH MOTHER TONGUE TEACHING

G Taylor

INTRODUCTION

The following paper is an attempt to characterise English Mother Tongue Teaching as it is practised in the United Kingdom. The task is an onerous and daunting one since principles and practice vary so much that it is often difficult to pull the various threads together to form a coherent picture, except at the level of broad generalisations perhaps. In the process one is inevitably involved in over-simplification. I am also aware of the considerable overlap that exists between the various sections but again this is inevitable given the interrelation that exists between them. Wherever possible, I have attempted to be objective in order to present an accurate account. However, balancing the actual with the ideal has been particularly difficult and it has been impossible to exclude some personal evaluation of the situation.

AIMS: MODELS OF ENGLISH MOTHER TONGUE TEACHING

The picture of EMT teaching that emerges from its current practice is a complex one. There exist conflicting theories about the nature of the task and the aims that practitioners should concentrate on. The classroom itself reveals a diversity of practices that seem to defy attempts to draw out of it a coherent theory that can account for all that goes on under the label English. A visitor to a school might well be faced with classes engaged in activities as diverse as film-making, improvised drama, comprehension writing arising out of any number of different stimuli, both verbal and non-verbal. However, the existence of conflicting theories and diverse practices is not sufficient in itself to lead to the conclusion that all is disunified and incoherent. There may well exist a consensus of opinion about aims: diversity of practice may simply reflect individual teachers' preferences for particular methods of achieving those aims in response to the needs of individual students.

In part this would seem to be true. Few EMT specialists would deny, for instance, that a central aim of their teaching is to enable the pupils to master their mother tongue, 'to create capable users and receivers of spoken and written English'. Similarly, few would deny that this mastery is not in some way linked with developing the pupil's ability to function successfully as an individual and as a member of his society. At this level of abstraction aims are clear and unified. However, it is in moving from these aims to classroom practice, in the precise interpretation that individual teachers give to these aims and the way they may be realised, that significant differences occur. These differences lead to the sometimes bewildering state referred to above and to argue against unity and consensus.

Understanding the nature of the task which gives rise to this situation seems to divide into two main views, each resting on different assumptions about language, the way language mastery is achieved, and the purpose for which it is achieved. One view would seem to be that language in its various manifestations is passive, a static system that, if irregular, can be reduced to manageable areas 'of knowledge which can be learned. From this point of view the purpose of this learning is to comply with certain prescriptive rules, to perform and respond to it correctly. The other view sees language as active, a process through which personal and social development may be achieved, the imagination nourished, understanding of self and the world formed. Language is not seen as separate from the individual but as an integral part of existence, of what he makes of himself and the world. Mastery of language, therefore, is achieved by engaging with it, not as a body of knowledge, but as a variable tool intimately bound up with the central concerns and needs of the individual, and through which they can be understood and fostered. Prescriptive rules to be followed give way to the creation of personal meaning and high levels of commitment in personal expression and response.

Those two poles of thought form the basis of several models of English Mother Tongue teaching which have developed over the past century and currently influence practice, producing the amalgam of activities previously referred to. The more traditional models assume the former of these two views: the skills model and the Cultural Heritage model. These can be seen as complementary, both in aims and practice. Both see their central aim as the transmission of a body of knowledge. The skills model emphasises basic competence in writing and reading. It abstracts language from context, divides it into discrete areas and teaches the contents of these areas as factual knowledge through carefully graded sequential exercises. The pupils perform grammatical exercises, comprehension tests, punctuation and spelling tests, and exercises designed to master the structure of formal essays of the ornate style of certain kinds of descriptive writing. The Cultural-Heritage model focuses attention on knowledge of language as classical literature, defining its aims as transmitting factual information about authors' works and literary technique. Literary works are dissected for examples of metaphor, simile, onomatopoeia, etc. Even what a work is about may be reduced to a pre-packed knowledge. Both these models see the pupil's language as confined to a formal writing and as a means of testing his ability to master the knowledge transmitted. Apart from seeing such knowledge as intrinsically valuable, exponents of this model aim to refine the sensibility of the pupils, to humanise them through exposing pupils to the 'excellence of thought, feeling and moral values that these high points of literary culture contain'.

The more progressive models embrace the second division referred to above: the Personal Growth model and Social Growth model. Again, these are closely connected. The Personal Growth model aims to develop the individual pupil's affective, cognitive and moral growth. Though true of all good teachers, because of the connections they see between language and self, EMT specialists who claim this as their overriding aim see themselves as having a particular care for this area. They see their focus as human experience, both as exemplified in the pupil's personal experience, and in literary works across a wide spectrum. Areas of experience, or themes, are explored through various interrelated language activities: discussion, drama, free verse, play writing, discursive writing, etc, through which the pupil is encouraged to shape his understanding of self and the world, to examine personal relationships, and to form personal values. The Social Growth model, though similar in orientation, focuses on local, cultural and national and international issues. Both these models emphasise language as a personal structuring of meaning and the direction a pupil's work takes may depend on the interests of the individual pupil. Literature in these models is given a particularly wide definition. It is valued for its particular insights into an area of experience and as such it may include modern media productions of film and television as well as writing, from the classics to modern literature, newspapers and children's writing.

These models represent the established theoretical positions taken by EMT specialists. From these it is perhaps easy to see EMT as composed of warring factions entrenched behind diametrically opposed positions. However, such a view would not be an accurate representation of the case. As models these outlines represent extreme theoretical positions which exist, if at all, only in rare cases. In their pure forms they exert influences on the practitioners, but in the reality of the classroom they are not mutually exclusive. It is much more likely that EMT specialists occupy a middle ground between them inclining towards one but drawing to a lesser or greater extent on the other. Thus, though some teachers express adherence to a personal growth model they do not neglect basic literacy or knowledge of literature. Similarly, though basic literacy and knowledge of literature may be extolled by some teachers it is unlikely to exclude work of a personal nature where the creation of meaning by the individual is developed. Indeed, it is possible to identify a Compromise model which draws on some of the elements of the models outlined. Adherents of this model would recognise the need for basic literacy to be extended through absorbing knowledge and practice but would see the need to put this in the context of the exploration for themes based on personal experience or contemporary issues. This model would allow some room for exploration by individuals of personal interests but would contain this within carefully defined limits.

There is one further model which has yet to be defined: the Language/Communication model. I have kept this until last because unlike the others it is still emerging. It arises out of recent developments in linguistics, the application of these developments to education and the dissemination of this information among practitioners. It is essentially concerned with the appropriateness of language as it is used in specific contexts. It sets out to examine the different features of spoken and written language and the way these vary according to certain variables such as context, purpose and audience. It is clearly a very new approach and has only just begun to make its influence felt in the classroom, and it is difficult to see how it may develop or how it may fit in with the others. In some respects it has features of the Personal and Social Growth models in that it sets out to allow the individual to explore experience in linguistic contexts. In other respects it has features of the Skills model in that it has identified certain knowledge to be transmitted. It also, of course, has little to do with literature which is why perhaps it has had so little accpetance amongst EMT specialists. This fact alone testifies clearly to the place literature has in their view of the task.

These models define the breadth of the aims held by EMT specialists. If, as I believe, and the Bullock Report survey would seem to support this belief, the compromise approach rather than any of the extremes represents the majority of EMT specialists' approach, then most teachers would subscribe to them all. In itself this breadth is not a reason for anxiety. What is important is the order of priority given to these by practitioners. If any system of priorities exists, it is defined by the model to which any given teacher inclines: again the Bullock survey would suggest that this in general is in favour of the more traditional models.

This in itself would seem a matter for concern since any EMT specialist who emphasises mechanical skills and bodies of knowledge does so at the expense of the more dynamic theory of language development and individual growth represented by aspects of the progressive models. Furthermore, the fact that several models of EMT exist which make conflicting claims on the practitioner would seem to raise several central questions. Does the compromise position have any unifying theory or is it mere eclecticism; that is, a pragmatic answer of a profession to a situation which it feels incapable of resolving, except by including bits of everything, with an emphasis on a return to the comparative safety of traditional approaches whose effectiveness has long been questioned.

In order to clarify the situation and if necessary resolve the dilemma, there would seem to be an urgent need for EMT practitioners to re-examine their aims and the various conflicting theories that give rise to them. It would seem particularly fruitful to do this in the light of the recent developments in our understanding of language as these would seem to offer a firm, integrated theoretical base to which other major concerns (literature, personal growth, etc) can be related and their conflicts resolved. Out of this could emerge an EMT curriculum that is more clearly unified in theory and coherent in practice, though maintaining something of the diversity that is necessary if individual and local needs are to be satisfied.

EXPLICITNESS

The extent to which EMT specialists have attempted to make the thinking behind their practice explicit to those in and outside the profession in syllabuses and to the pupils in their classes has been very limited. Indeed, the very notion of syllabus as a scheme of work as Bullock indicated (paras. 15, 28), seems to have fallen out of favour with practitioners in recent years.

The reason, in part, would seem to be a reaction against the type of syllabus designed by teachers at the traditional end of the spectrum who see their task as the transmission of knowledge. These syllabuses defined EMT in terms of knowledge divided into rigid compartments, it prescribed sequences in which it was to be taught and the method, often the textbook, to be used. Even here, though such syllabuses would represent an explicitness to the public and other members of the profession, it is unlikely that explicitness to pupils as regards explanations of why activities were chosen was a systematic feature of the methodology, except for matters concerning basic skills and examination requirements. Such syllabuses no doubt continue to exist but under the influence of more progressive approaches to EMT. Some practitioners have felt them to be too rigidly constraining and not to reflect their own beliefs about the nature of the task and the methods necessary to achieve their aims. They have not felt able to define their teaching in terms of a body of knowledge and simple incremental sequences. Their focus on language as a process, on the individual's structuring of experience for himself, on literature and the imagination, leads them to more pupil-orientated approaches requiring greater flexibility for teachers to respond to the needs and interests of their pupils that syllabuses as prescriptive schemes of work could not predict or satisfy. Neither have they felt explicitness to pupils to be an appropriate concept except in defining an area of experience to be studied, for fear of inhibiting the personal response of the pupil. What 'syllabuses' have been produced tended to set out philosophy and long-term aims, to emphasise the need to integrate activities and provide lists of areas of experience likely to be appropriate to particular year groups. Thus it is seen as a definition of position, a discussion document. How teachers approach classroom practice and devise short-term aims was a matter for the individual.

In general, however, the absence of precise syllabuses, as I have suggested, is only explained in part by this influence. It is also, I suspect, a reflection of the lack of certainty felt by some parts of the profession about its priorities and methods, except in the area of basic skills. More recent demands for public accountability have begun to apply more pressure for explicitness in long and short term aims, and methods of achieving them, and it would seem probable that some more precise form of 'syllabus' will again emerge, though it would be more fruitful if it were a document which defined aims and purposes but drew on recent developments in understanding language for its more specific objectives (range of writing tasks, audience function, purpose, etc) while maintaining something of the flexibility of the progressive model by rooting these firmly in an exploration of experience and literature. Thus it would be a focal point for discussion within a department, 'an instrument of policy', but it would also be explicit about classroom practice - a record of successful activities. There also seems to be a clear need for greater explicitness to pupils about aims and objectives, though the level at which this is approached will depend on maturity and its effect will need careful monitoring.

NEGOTIATION OF SYLLABUS

Negotiation involves a shift of emphasis from teacher to pupil as regards the nature and form of the learning that takes place in the classroom. As such it finds little favour amongst traditional EMT practitioners. Their emphasis on prior analysis of pupils' needs, their reduction of language and response to a body of knowledge to be taught in a prescribed sequence and tested, clearly leaves no place for negotiating approaches. In contrast, the more progressive practitioner, recognising the essential relationship between a pupil and his language, maintains that if meaningful language is to occur it must place the individual's needs and interests at the centre of the EMT curriculum. With the Bullock Report he sees 'English ... rooted in the process of experience through language' which involves making the pupil's experience and language an essential base on which development of language and personal growth is built. The pupils becomes involved; teaching, as transmission, gives way to learning, a situation in which the pupil is given some freedom to choose the direction his work will take and its form. The teacher becomes a guide, delineating areas of experience to be focused on, and suggesting approaches, developing language as a response through identifying needs and stimulating involvement. Under this influence workshop approaches flourish; the classroom becomes a place where small group and individual work predominate, where a variety of activities are simultaneously taking place (discussion, drama, tape recording, reading, writing, etc).

Clearly there are degrees of negotiation depending on whether the teacher wants to impose some form of direction on the routes language and response are to develop, or whether he feels that this would be too narrowing and feel it necessary to allow pupils to negotiated entirely the direction they want to take without reference to prior ideas of development. He may wish to ensure that pupils develop in all four language modes, that they develop a range of language styles for different purposes and audiences. Negotiation is also possible in the short term and long term; in that it can be restricted to a choice of activities for a particular lesson, or a choice of direction for longer periods of time.

Though in its extreme form negotiation would not find favour, it would seem to be generally agreed by theorists that some form of negotiation is an essential part of EMT. This, and the popularity of moderate consensus, would imply that at classroom level the practice is reasonably well established. However, the traditional bent of the compromise position would suggest that there is still a tendency to impose rather than negotiate. This is particularly true in a 'back-to-basics' climate. Even when the practice is fairly well established in primary and secondary levels, it withers as pupils near the final year of compulsory secondary education and external examinations exert their influence. Surveys like Bullock and those undertaken by the Schools' Council Writing Project Team paint a bleak picture of the rigid imposing of formal requirements as pupils get older. Variety of language, the centrality of pupil involvement, give way to rote learning of conventional forms and responses.

PROFESSIONAL STANCE

The fact that EMT teaching has a relatively undisputed claim to a part of the core curriculum testifies to its importance in the eyes of teachers and curriculum designers. Even where integrated studies has led to the disappearance of EMT from the timetable of younger secondary school pupils as a separate subject, this is usually accompanied by efforts to ensure that it maintains its identity and influence.

The reason for this high standing is generally related to the development of skills. Not only does society in general exert pressure on schools to produce pupils who can read and write accurately, but since the mother tongue is the medium of communication in other subjects, teachers of these subjects have looked to the EMT specialist to act as a servicing agent to facilitate their work by providing students with a grounding in basic language skills. This has generally meant pressure has been exerted to concentrate on correctness of punctuation, spelling, grammatical conventions, and formal essay writing techniques.

Such an emphasis fitted well with a traditional approach to EMT where a narrow range of basic skills was anyway the focal point. However, the subservience of such a position has never fitted well with the concept of EMT as being important in its own right, and the development of approaches which emphasised the importance of literature and the imagination, the development of language through the personal needs of the pupil, fluency before basic skills, oracy as well as literacy, conflicted strongly with the service role which was firmly rejected.

Indeed, recently the responsibility for the development of language skills required by other curriculum areas has been seen as a whole school reponsibility as well as the responsibility of those in particular subject areas. The Language Across the Curriculum movement focused attention on whole staff awareness of the place language has in facilitating or inhibiting the learning process. They argued that all subject teachers were involved in developing an awareness of the communicative needs of pupils in their particular subject area since subject matter and the language used to embody it were so closely interrelated. This had two facets. Firstly, subject teachers needed to recognise that students need to handle new concepts thoroughly in their own 'expressive' language if they are to get to grips with them. Secondly, subject teachers needed to identify and foster the language skills or communicative needs of students in their area that were necessary for access to the knowledge in the subject, rather than the EMT specialists attempting to develop them in isolation from context and purpose. Thus the EMT specialist rejected responsibility for language in other areas of the curriculum except in so far as he was given the responsibility of developing a language policy for his school. Behind his subject barrier he has generally concentrated on responses to literature and on what Britton has called 'language in the spectator role', the Expressive and Poetic end of the Continuum.

In part this could be seen as too narrow an emphasis. There is a need to recognise that in studying experience we are studying the many ways in which we shape it and are shaped through language. We need to examine as part of this the many purposes for which we use language and the way it is influenced by audience and function. Thus EMT could profitably include a wider range of reading skills than literary appreciation. This would overlap with the demands made on students by their subjects and would reinforce the subject teacher's attempt to foster particular communication skills in other areas. In this sense EMT could make language study its focus, though it would still need to keep its roots firmly in the student's 'needs'. None of this need conflict with the emphasis on personal growth.

MOTIVATION

Motivation is clearly related to needs. Traditional approaches to EMT emphasise the utilitarian aspect of the subject, that mastery of basic skills allows access to jobs or higher educational courses through examination success. It also emphasises the aesthetic pleasure derived from knowledge of the literary heritage. In some respects, of course, motivation is not an important consideration as regards syllabus planning in traditional approaches: what is presented is to be learned.

More recent theories make motivation the cornerstone of their theory and high levels of commitment are considered essential to the development of language. Thus the progressive EMT specialist looks towards the purposes for which language is used and the way these purposes relate to the needs of the individual. It recognises the central importance of language in creating the individual's sense of self, his world view, whether first hand or imagined. It recognises its importance in defining his relationship with others and understanding the way he can influence them and they him. It recognises the place of imaginative literature in extending and shaping that experience for him. This awareness allows the practitioner to draw on the 'natural' drive within pupils to use language for these purposes and to extend and differentiate it through them. It, therefore, rejects the emphasis on skills in isolation, the analysis of grammatical structure, knowledge of the literary heritage of traditional EMT. Skills and grammatical structures, it is argued, do not exist apart from the meaning the individual wishes to communicate, and this will be developed as part of the communicative process. Neither can the literary heritage exist apart from the individual's response to it, his recognition of the writer as employed in the same task as himself, making sense of the world, and engaging with it on this common ground rather than as a voice from the gods.

How far the latter ideas have actually percolated into the practice of the majority of EMT specialists is not certain, though surveys would suggest that traditional practices are still seen as important and this would imply that the motivation possible, though getting close to using language for 'real' purposes, does not hold the sway it should. Again, pressures exerted by examinations limit the extent to which the ideal exists at all in the final years of secondary education. It takes a skilful teacher to maintain one in the face of the other.

CREATIVITY AND COMMUNICATION

'Creativity' has long been considered a major part of EMT, though to what extent this is an accurate picture is questionable. The Bullock survey, for instance, finds little evidence that 'a climate of unchecked creativity' predominates. However, it would certainly seem true to suggest that to a lesser or greater degree some form of 'creativity' has become a part of EMT practice though it has not been held in high esteem by some sections within the EMT world or interested parties outside it.

In essence, 'creativity' in EMT is essentially the progressive EMT position which emphasises the individual's need to engage with language and experience as a means of structuring personal meaning (as elaborated in the previous section and section 1 above). It is not as a theoretical position that the problem (in the sense that it has been condemned) lies since it clearly holds the key to meaningful language development. The problem seems to lie in the way it has been interpreted by some practitioners and realised by them in classroom practice. Any movement away from total focus on basic skills will inevitably bring cries of anguish from those totally dedicated to the traditional model, but the problem of interpretation and practice in one that the profession must grasp.

In certain cases, particularly perhaps in the early years of the progressive movement, practitioners had fostered fluency but did little to direct that fluency. They extolled the virtue of self-expression and personal involvement and rejected an emphasis on structural features of language and formal, surface correctness. This had the effect of freeing language but not necessarily of ensuring its development. It was quite easy in such situations to lose sight of language as a medium and to reject too firmly considerations of form.

However, there is (and may always have been) a movement to recognise that the medium of language cannot be ignored in the creative process; that good EMT takes into account the need to examine the possibilities inherent in the language to shape and structure experience or communication and that this examination, this making aware of the nature and power of language, is an essential part of the process. It is seen that such an emphasis is not a 'barrier to the release of creativity' but an essential part of it. Britton's 'poetic' category focuses on the language as much as the experience, though in a wider and deeper sense than in the traditional model: it emphasises the appropriateness of language, its nuances, its rhythms, its sounds, its overall structure, its shape in relation to its purpose and audience. Similarly, the transactional category identifies levels of abstraction and their inter-relation that need to be developed. Good EMT keeps a fine balance between the communication and the medium, knowing when to emphasise one, and not allowing one to swamp the other.

There is much that still needs to be done in bringing together in practice the two facets of creativity, but the linguistic view of the task as exemplified in Britton's work would seem to offer practitioners a basis on which to achieve it.

CLASSROOM TALK

Talk as a feature of EMT has received considerable attention in recent years. Traditional models tended to neglect the development of spoken language in favour of writing. More recent approaches have questioned this neglect and have affirmed the importance of the equal development of spoken language and some its centrality.

The arguments in favour of spoken language have been well rehearsed. Spoken language is closest to self; it is the form of language which is most familiar to us. Through it we can most readily engage with our experience, explore it, shape it, and speculate about it. It is a central means whereby we interact with others, clarifying our ideas, taking into account the ideas of others and modifying our own, and attempting to influence theirs. Its value, therefore, in the classroom, particularly when experience is the focal point, cannot be overstressed. Moreover, it is argued that for perhaps the majority of pupils it is the central language mode outside and beyond school. It is pointed out that they may write and read rarely but speaking and listening will continue to be of great importance.

Together with these insights into the nature of talk have come research projects and surveys (Barnes, Stubbs, Sinclair, Bullock, etc) that have revealed the limitations of traditional approaches to talk in the classroom. Class discussion with its question and answer format was revealed to be dominated by the teacher who spoke for 75% of the time ensuring that he developed his language while pupils were either silent or at best were cast in the role of guessing what was in the teacher's mind. Such 'discussion' encouraged conformity rather than meaningful com-munication, performance rather than exploration. Nor did it develop a wide range of verbal strategies or kinds of language that casting pupils in other roles would encourage: initiation, speculation, questioning, co-operation, etc.

In answer to this, small group work, pair work, simulation games, drama, role play have all been developed as a means of encouraging meaningful talk and development of spoken language. In these situations the pupil may assume many roles and hence develop many forms of language. He will also be more directly involved.

However, despite the importance that such arguments give to talk it would seem EMT, in general, as with other subjects in secondary schools, has not encouraged talk in its classroom activities to the degree that it has been exhorted to. There exists, no doubt, excellent work of the kind outlined briefly here but not, it seems, as a general rule. Again it would seem that EMT teachers find it difficult to break with traditional forms, perhaps because they prefer domesticated pupils or perhaps because they genuinely do not understand the purpose of talk and the benefits it can bring. They may not see how it is possible to make these practices part of their teaching. If this is the case the implications for initial and in-service training are obvious.

TESTING AND MEASURING PROGRESS

Unfortunately the legitimacy of such questions does not resolve the problem that faces practitioners when attempting to answer them. Language production and response is a complex process drawing on general aspects of cognitive and affective abilities, as well as the more obvious linguistic skills. Even the latter can be divided into various sub-skills which interrelate in involved ways, and moreover variables outside the individual's control may influence his performance. The practitioner, therefore, is faced with having to decide what features of language are to be measured, what criteria he is to use to judge them by and how such judgements are to be made reliable so that other practitioners faced with the same language would produce similar results.

At the moment there exist no simple answers. In writing, for instance, it is not sufficient to concentrate on the surface features of the writing, the handwriting, spelling, punctuation and grammatical correctness. It is recognised that judgements of these have their place, but concentration on them alone would be to neglect other essential features of any written production. Writing is an expression of meaning and assessment must take into account cognitive and affective features of the language. These involve judgements about the ability shown by the writer to organise his thoughts, the level of abstraction at which he operates and the way in which he interrelates various levels; the control and the responses to the world he reveals in his expression. There are also factors relating to the communicative situation of the writing: how well it fulfils the purpose for which the writing was produced and what awareness and sensitivity to audience it shows in choosing appropriate language. Any assessment of writing must somehow take all such factors into account if meaningful results are to be achieved.

In reading, a similarly complex situation exists. In addition to the mechanical skills of decoding, there are comprehension, interpretation and evaluation skills. These latter involve assessing the pupil's ability to actively interact with the text to bring his own knowledge and experience into relation with it to make sense of it and judge its quality. Indeed the purposes for which one reads vary and and it is necessary to assess how flexible the pupil's reading strategies are. Can he skim read as well as respond deeply? Can he extract relevant information? Does he enjoy reading?

Oral abilities, speaking and listening, are even more complex. Here we are not concerned with the performance of one individual and the language he produces and responds to, but with the simultaneous performance of several individuals in a constantly changing interactive situation. The language is more ephemeral, less formally structured, and is most sensitive to context variables such as situation, number of people involved, and the level of formality. Meaning is also communicated through paralinguistic features such as intonation, pace, facial expression, stance, etc.

Clearly, the teacher is confronted with an enormous task if justice is to be done in accurately assessing the language abilities of pupils. Simple results, such as those of standardised tests of reading, are insufficient. So too are the majority of external examinations set by 'O' level Boards which still reduce language ability to essay writing, comprehension tests and factual knowledge of literature. It is necessary to devise a much more flexible tool that takes into account the various features of language and judges these on well established criteria. Some assistance is being given in the search for such criteria by research projects (Harpin, Wilkinson) and the work of the APU. However, it is unlikely that these will provide simple objective tests available to the teacher. The most valuable means of assessment is likely to be the subjective impression of teachers who are constantly in contact with the pupil. If so, they need to be well informed about the nature of language.

CLASSROOM ORGANISATION/MIXED ABILITY

As with so many features of EMT, classroom organisation depends on the approach adopted. Where transmission styles predominate, classroom organisation focuses on the teacher as giver of information. Desks are so placed that all pupils face the teacher and not each other which informs them that exchange between each other is not encouraged. In progressive styles desks are so arranged, perhaps in small groups or in a circle to indicate the corporate nature of the activities or the importance of pupil to pupil contact as well as pupil to teacher. In the latter case it is as a workshop that the classroom tends to function; in the former as a lecture theatre or examination room.

The principle under which the pupils are grouped in EMT is a matter that has led to some controversy and continues to do so. Some traditional teachers would argue that pupils should be rigidly streamed according to ability. More moderate groups might favour less rigidity but would argue that those of highest and lowest ability should be taught separately. Those nearest to the progressive end of the continuum would favour completely mixed ability groupings.

Those who favour streaming argue that the language and personal needs of pupils differ in kind rather than degree and that whole groups of children can be identified with similar needs. In particular, they argue that the most able need the challenge of certain kinds of language and literature which they can only get amongst pupils of equal ability, and that the least able need the remedial help of small intimate groups where they can receive individual attention and be protected from unreasonable language demands.

Those who favour mixed ability teaching are those who emphasise more child-centred teaching. They argue that no group of pupils is ever entirely homogeneous and rigid streaming simply ignores the strengths and weaknesses of pupils, treating them all as having equal needs. Mixed ability teachers argue that they wish to cater for the needs of individuals not in a competitive atmosphere but in one of mutual co-operation where individuals or groups of individuals pursue work that is appropriate and relevant to them, whatever this may be. They also point to the depressing effect on pupils of being in low ability groups and the raising or lowering of expectations that accompanies teachers' attitudes to difference in the stream. Thus, it is argued that the language demands on low streams are uniformly low, depriving them of the stimulus they need and the consequent suppression of achievement, whereas the mixed ability group provides a rich language environment for all pupils which will encourage language development throughout the ability range.

The question of mixed ability will no doubt continue to be controversial, though the Bullock report saw it as 'the form of grouping which offers the most hope for English teaching' (15-12). A recent HM report found the practice of mixed ability teaching to be unsatisfactory, which would suggest that though the process is sound and fits well with informed views of language development, there is a need for a development and dissemination of good practice if it is to be successful with the generality of EMT teachers.

CONCLUSION

In 1967 John Dixon wrote that English Mother Tongue's 'conflicting emphases challenge us today to look for a new coherent definition'. In looking at the present EMT scene, one feels that the challenge is still with us. No doubt there are some who have achieved this and whose practice is a logical and exciting development from it, but surveys would seem to suggest that this is too infrequently the case. There certainly exists the knowledge to answer Dixon's challenge. The 1970's have brought very significant developments, particularly in the field of language and communication, which could underpin a coherent curriculum. This is not to suggest that diversity will cease to exist since it is essential to maintain the flexibility that allows practitioners to respond to the needs of individual students whatever their local circumstances. The answer would certainly not seem to lie in centralised curriculum but in the examination theory and practice at local level. In a subject that involves the deepest feelings of its practitioners, it is perhaps unlikely that even at local level unity will be easy to achieve, but the constant drive towards it through the increased knowledge and the development of materials that reflect this seems imperative.